$\mathcal{L}$ove Smarts

To my good friend, Don.
I hope you enjoy it.
Cheers,
Kathy

$\mathcal{L}$ove Smarts

A singles guide to finding that special someone

Kathy Tait

Self-Counsel Press
a division of
International Self-Counsel Press Ltd.
Canada   U.S.A.

Printed in Canada

First edition: September, 1994

Tait, Kathy, 1944-
    Love smarts
    (Self-counsel personal self-help series)

    ISBN 0-88908-797-0

      1. Dating (Social customs) 2. Man-woman relationships.
3. Interpersonal relations. I. Title. II. Series.
HQ801.T34 1994   306.73   C94-910627-5

Cover Photography by Terry Guscott, ATN Visuals, Vancouver, B.C.
Illustrations by Dianne Pollock

Self-Counsel Press
a division of
International Self-Counsel Press Ltd.

1481 Charlotte Road	1704 N. State Street
North Vancouver, British Columbia	Bellingham,Washington
Canada V7J 1H1	98225

C *ontents*

Preface

My dearest hope is this book will provide practical help for men and women seeking to find the right person to share their life.

It is designed to be useful to all single people, male or female, from 19 to 90, never married, or divorced or widowed.

I wish I had a book like this in 1980 when my ex-husband and I split up. I had been a stay-at-home mom for the first seven years of my daughter's life, aside from working one day a week as a reporter at *The Province* newspaper.

When we separated, I returned to full-time work. My daughter and I moved to a tiny house closer to my work and her new school.

Those first years were tough, but we survived. We built a new and different life. I think we did extremely well, but it would have been nice to have had a book then to help me understand the singles world I was entering and to realize there were thousands going through similar struggles. In the early eighties there was very little for newly single people in terms of support and comfortable ways to meet.

I spent the next eight years establishing a stable and solid home life for my daughter, developing my career, and dating. I was learning about relationships and what I wanted in a mate. More important, I learned about myself — my talents, needs, and my enormous strength. It was a time of incredible personal growth.

As a journalist, I began to see what was missing from our newspaper, and just about every other newspaper in North America — information to help couples stay together and avoid becoming a divorce statistic. So I approached my paper and suggested the love column. Much to my surprise, they said, "Go for it!"

That was May, 1987. I offered to help readers with their love problems. I asked them to write in with relationship problems and then I would take it to a marriage expert — usually a psychologist or a social worker, or a family systems therapist specializing in marital counseling. These wonderful men and women showed me there are answers to even the most difficult relationship problems. All it takes is a desire to learn.

And readers of the love column have learned along with me. They have trusted that I will give them some useful direction with their relationship problems. So the number of letters has risen steadily and today on average I receive 25 to 50 letters a week. As well as answering love problems, I explore, in depth, various relationship issues, like extra-marital affairs, spousal assault, differing communication styles between the sexes, and what to do about lack of sexual desire.

Today, more than 1,100 columns later, I'm still learning from readers and experts about being single, about dating, about relationships, and about being in a committed partnership again.

I think my column, which appears three times a week in *The Province,* has been useful in reflecting the issues and concerns about meeting people and sustaining relationships. This book is designed as an extension of the love column — a comprehensive, step-by-step guide to finding that special someone. And it is also designed to put being single in some context and help you feel confident in making new friends and romantic connections.

Each chapter deals with an aspect that never married and single-again people have told me is important to them. The Appendix at the back of this book contains specific names, addresses, and phone numbers of clubs, organizations, and services throughout North America that I hope you'll find useful.

One final note: *Love Smarts* is written primarily for heterosexual relationships. While I think the book may still be of use to those seeking homosexual relationships, I have not felt qualified to address the special dynamics of being a gay or lesbian person in our society.

$\mathcal{A}$cknowledgments

I could not have written this book without help. First, I thank the readers who have let me know over the years what issues concern them.

I thank my sweetie, Pat Morgan, for talking me into buying a home computer a few years ago and then never saying a negative word on the evenings I retreated to my study to write.

I thank my ex-husband, John Griffiths, who took my completed manuscript, carefully edited it for me, and made thoughtful suggestions for improvements, most of which I used.

I thank my daughter, Melanie Griffiths, for bearing up, remarkably well, under the embarrassment of having a love columnist for a mother and for being the wonderful young woman she is.

I thank my newspaper, *The Province,* for publishing the love column and especially managing editor Neil Graham, for providing moral support. As well, thanks go to Greg Nutchey, computer systems assistant, and Steve Proulx, manager of Pacific Press editorial services, who each saw me through all my computer needs and who somehow managed to smile through one dumb request after another.

Finally, I want to thank Ruth Wilson, managing editor at Self-Counsel Press, for her kindness and encouragement throughout the writing of this book.

$\mathcal{I}$ntroduction

I'm among those who have seen life from both sides — single and married. When I finished university, I moved into my own apartment. Several years later I married. Then, 13 years later, like so many others, my husband and I split up. My daughter and I lived together. I dated for about eight years, then met my sweetie about six years ago. About four years ago we built our house together. Like many divorcees, we haven't legally married, but we're still together, happy, and consider it a committed relationship.

But I don't regret those single years. Certainly for those who've just come out of a marriage, the first few years can be horrendous. But it's important to realize that even if you have been in a relationship which is now over, gradually you'll find that being on your own is a time to learn more about who you are and what you value. It gives you the chance to try new things without worrying you're neglecting someone else.

Being alone doesn't have to mean being lonely. And being alone is definitely better than being with an unsuitable mate!

I think single people need to get the most out of being single. Too many people rush through singlehood in a mad dash to find somebody. They don't savor the fact that they're free to go out with different kinds of people. They don't realize how much fun they can have or how they may pursue their own goals and their own personal growth. Rather than focus so much on a man, a woman can focus on her career. And a man can become more independent by learning to cook, clean, and schedule on his own.

And there's more. Some things about being single are fantastic.

From a man's point of view:

- You don't have to shave if you're not in the mood...if ever.

- There's no one around to tell you you're selfish, immature, and come from a dysfunctional family.
- You don't have to have a clean fridge, or have any food in it.
- You can go out with the guys as often as you want and no one will complain you're home three days late.
- There is no one to bug you about leaving dirty dishes or power saws on the kitchen counter, or leaving the toilet seat up.
- You can hog the bed without getting an elbow or a knee to tell you, "back off buddy."
- You can watch war movies in the middle of the night.
- Nobody ever says: "When it's your turn to cook, how come it's always spaghetti?"
- You don't have to shower on weekends.
- You don't have to talk about feelings.
- You can scratch where you want to scratch, as long as you want to scratch.
- You can make rude noises.
- Only you get to see your credit card bills.
- You can wear whatever you want and throw away the ties.
- There's no job jar.

Ah, the wonders of privacy and freedom! The happiness without a mate!

(Write to me if you have additions to the list. My address is on the next page.)

From a woman's point of view:

- You can have as many blankets on as you want. There is no one trying, all winter, to take your half, or all summer to suffocate you with theirs.
- If you want to pig out on candy after a big meal, no one gives dirty looks or makes comments.
- You don't have to cook.
- You can slurp tea in bed in the middle of the night if you choose, or read.

- The bed just needs to be tucked in the morning, not totally remade.
- You can watch any movie you want — no matter how romantic, how long, how old, how stupid, or how intellectual.
- You can look as ugly as you want for as long as you want, without worrying he might have noticed.
- You don't have to listen to car engines or stories about car engines.
- There's no one changing your radio station.
- You can make rude noises.
- You can go out with your girlfriends as often as you want.
- There's no one to spy on you to see if you've turned out the lights and turned off the heat.
- You can have all the closets to yourself.
- You can go to bed in your oldest, most torn, and most comfortable nightie. You don't have to worry he's going to say he likes skin, not cloth.
- There's no one to leave the sinks and soaps dirty. And no one to fold the towels the wrong way.
- The toilet seat is always down, and there are no sprinkles on the floor.

Hah! The relief of it.

(Write to me if you have additions to the list. My address is Kathy Tait, "Love Smarts," The Province, 2250 Granville Street, Vancouver, B.C., Canada V6H 3G2.)

I know one woman in her mid-eighties whose husband recently passed away. Betty is wasting no time enjoying the single life. After the funeral, Betty was given her late husband's ashes in an urn. Returning home she placed the urn in his favorite chair and proceeded to turn on every light in their elegant condominium. Betty's husband, a survivor of the Depression, had always been a penny-pincher.

"Well, how do you like that?!" she challenged his ashes. That, she says, was the first moment of personal freedom in her entire life.

"When he died, I gained my strength," Betty says. "I just felt at long last I could be my own self. I can say, spend, see, and cook what

I want when I want. I can put myself first for the first time in my life. I finally have my own identity."

Certainly not all widows and widowers are as positive about being single as Betty is. When I wrote a column saying my life would probably still be pretty good if I outlive my sweetie, some readers told me I didn't know what I was talking about. First, here's what I said:

> *After several years of feeling alone and empty, I will gather unto me all my female friends. We will plan trips and adventures. If I haven't already done so, I will write a book.*
>
> *I will also savor the company of my friends as we share tea and crumpets and terrific conversation. Hopefully, my daughter and I will remain good friends and I'll be the best granny ever. I'll garden and go for walks. Maybe I'll take some university courses. It doesn't sound bad to me.*

I asked readers, "Is it not possible to live quite happily without a man in your life?"

Some readers told me finding happiness is more difficult when you're an older woman, while others told me it's the older gent who finds happiness most elusive. Most of the letters underlined how painful grieving is and how some people get stuck. Here's a sampling:

- *I suppose it is possible to live happily without a man but I would prefer not to. In my age group (I'm 62), I am having difficulty finding single companions, either male or female! I have joined a few singles groups but so far no luck. I answer companion ads, join singles groups, and yes, I guess I can live without a male. But it sure would be great to have a partner for dinner, movies, walks on the spur of the moment. And that's to say nothing of the physical and intimate side of a relationship. NOTHING can replace that — and I am left with a great gaping hole in my soul.*

- *Can't you live without a man? The answer is simply "we have to." But you, Kathy, know nothing. Just take one day and notice all the little things that would never be again. Never feel a man's hand at your waist. Never know his hand in yours again. There are countless little things you take for granted that you miss so much after living 40 years with a man. Who do you tell the silly things to? Who rejoices at my grandson's first steps and my granddaughter's As in the report card? I'd like to find someone to spend the rest of my life with but am wise enough to know it's not going to happen. Loneliness is a fact I'll have to live with.*

Still, I know lots of women who are happy enough in their later years, despite losing their husbands. The fact is, women have to face this reality. Women still live longer, statistically, than men. Yet those last years can be very fulfilling if women accept and embrace their new status. Here's what one man had to say.

I believe it's easier for a woman to live without a man than a man to live without a woman. My wife passed away three years ago. There are so many things I wish I had done and said to her. I loved her but rarely told her so. I feel so guilty. I'm so lonely.

It took me years to get my life fully back on track after my ex-husband and I separated. I had to learn to be alone, but not lonely. I got to know and value myself. I now cherish happiness on a day-to-day basis, never assuming it will last forever, and I see sharing life with others as a bonus.

Maybe that's one reason I've thought about my later years and the possibility of being alone again. I realize that, in the cosiness of a relationship, there's a tendency to have less time for friends and other interests. That's dangerous. Making your mate your whole life isn't healthy. Being able to maintain independent activities is a plus, now and later on.

The following letter illustrates what I'm talking about.

Yes, I can live without a man. It has taken a long time, as I had to learn to live with myself. My three have flown the coop now, and I find gentle breezes in my heart. I truly am looking forward to the days to come.

And look at it another way. While older singles who have been married and lost a spouse through death or divorce often struggle with living alone, I think many younger singles actually treasure it.

These young singles who stay that way through choice and who don't live with family or relatives, may actually be forging new lifestyles. They appear to be forming associations of friends they value as much as family.

They get together regularly, talk on the phone, look after each other in sickness, travel together, and develop a rich life. Many women speak of female friends as permanent parts of their lives, the men as transient.

So it's clear, happiness has a lot to do with getting over past hurts and losses, establishing meaningful friendships, and developing a positive attitude.

As one single woman put it: "The difference between being unhappily single and unhappily married is that, in the first case, one phone call can turn it around; the other takes a lot more work."

First, some figures

Today in North America, if you're single or single again, you're in one of the fastest growing segments of our society. The single population is bigger than it has ever been.

In the United States, the percentage of single adults over age 18 — those who have never married or are divorced or widowed — reached 39% in 1991. This represents a jump of 13% in two decades. In Canada the percentage of singles in these categories was 36% in 1991.

Some experts believe singles will be the majority group one day, so while this book focuses on how to find that special someone, realize that if you're single, you're not alone.

You may be wondering why your numbers are growing. Well, for one thing, more people are choosing never to marry. About 14% of women and 17% of men will never marry, a rise of about seven percentage points since the early seventies.

And those who do marry are marrying later. In the United States, the median age for first marriages has risen to 26 for men and 24 for women. In Canada, it's a year later for each sex.

Nowadays it takes longer to get an education and a career going, so that is one explanation for the higher age of first marriages. And by putting off marriage until they're older and established, some people become less marriageable — more set in their ways and less willing to compromise in a relationship.

As well, more women have joined the full-time work force, allowing them to have status and income stability without being married. Single women are no longer characterized as spinsters or old maids. And single men may not necessarily be viewed as pathologically independent or mommy's boys.

As well, the divorce rate has been climbing. Divorces are now easier to get and involve less stigma. The average Canadian marriage now lasts just 31 years; the average American one a mere 24 years.

And the rate of remarriage is dropping. Statistics Canada says the number of marriages, including remarriages, dropped by 8% from 1990 to 1991 — a bigger drop in one year than ever before seen in Canada.

Being single is not only okay, it is a viable option. For many, it is the status of choice. It means fewer compromises and more time and energy to pursue careers. It allows greater freedom to travel and change jobs.

Do you remember that Harvard-Yale study that hit North American women like a bombshell in 1986? You know, the one that said college-educated women who are still single at age 35 have only a 5% chance of ever getting married and that at 40 they have a minuscule 2.6% probability of marrying.

Newsweek reported they were more likely to be killed by a terrorist! The magazine claimed the study touched off a profound crisis of confidence among America's growing ranks of single women. It infuriated the contentedly single, who thought they were being told their lives were worthless without a man.

More people today are choosing never to marry.

Well, that man shortage scare was subsequently debunked by a U.S. Census Bureau demographer. Indeed, a 1993 poll found that more men than women want to marry — a reversal of everything we've always believed! This poll, conducted by the E.W. Scripps School of Journalism at Ohio University and the Scripps Howard News Service, found that 49% of single women in the United States do not want to get married. But 66% of the single men do. Many women are deciding to commit themselves to careers and there's increasing pessimism over the possibility of a successful and happy marriage.

However, the poll found the desire for marriage varies according to age. Eligible women between ages 18 and 24 overwhelmingly want to get married — 93% — compared to 88% of men in that age category.

Yet unlike men, women's desire to marry drops quickly with age. The survey found that 70% of the single women between 25 and 34 want to marry, compared to 87% of the men. Only 53% of the single women between 35 and 44 said they wish to wed, compared to 56% of the men.

The desire to marry drops to very low levels for both sexes among unmarrieds above age 45. Perhaps these women have given up, believing there is no one suitable for them. Perhaps it is because a job and a rich social life with friends make it less urgent for women to want a man. Still, 10% of the single people of retirement age said they would like to marry.

Enough of figures; let's look at life!

1
The urge to merge

Single is becoming the status of choice for more and more North Americans, but most men and women still want to connect with someone special.

There is nothing wrong with that. The need for intimacy and belonging has been around as long as humans have. Throughout the world many more people marry than stay single. In North America, more than 90% of men and women marry at some time during their lives. And more than 75% of those who divorce marry again.

It seems most people are drawn to the idea of having someone to go home to and with whom to share their feelings and experiences.

A relationship is good for your health

Scientists are discovering that being married or in a relationship is good for your health! Numerous studies conducted over the last 20 years have established that married people generally are healthier than single, widowed, or divorced people, regardless of age. However, some other studies have found that married men enjoy better health than married women.

Singles are sicker, more accident-prone, respond less well to treatment, and have a higher risk of dying.

Married people have lower mortality rates for a wide range of conditions: stroke, accidents, influenza, tuberculosis, and almost all forms of cancer, including the big ones such as lung, breast, and colon cancer.

Researchers do not know why being married or living together is generally healthier. They suspect co-habitation may foster a healthier lifestyle, provide key psychological and social supports, and reduce stress.

Dr. David Spiegel, a pioneer in the field of psychoneuro-immunology, says our physical and emotional well-being and longevity has much to do with our relationships with other people — good friends, other relatives, even support groups and social clubs — as well as spouses.

Finding that special someone takes love smarts

But finding a suitable partner to create that stable supportive home life is not as easy as it used to be. The changes in North American society over the last 30 years have made connecting more and more troublesome. The rules and forms of the past do not exist. People don't meet as easily. They have more pressures to distract them and are not as sure of what to say or do when the chance for a connection does arise. Often they don't want to go out and find someone; they want to find someone so they don't have to go out! Grrr!!

That is the point of this book. It's designed to put being single in some context and help you find the person you're looking for with some confidence. More detail is in subsequent chapters. But right off the bat, here are some things you can do now.

The basic law of the universe

First, stop feeling awkward about being single and wanting to find a mate. It's natural. You need to tell everybody you're looking!

Second, stop saying, "I want a relationship, but I just don't like the dating scene." I've heard that from singles so many times. Groan. Sure, it's harder when you're older and perhaps divorced than it was in college when almost everybody there was single. But even college students have difficulty finding dates; believe it.

Remember, everything worthwhile in life requires some effort. It seems to be the basic law of the universe: When you put out, things come back to you. If you want a career, you have to get the necessary skills and use them. If you want a job, you have to go for job interviews. If you want a baby, you have to go through nine months of being pregnant (unless you're a man). If you want a yacht, you usually have to work and save hard. No pain, no gain. You snooze, you lose.

So, decide what you want and believe you can get it. There will be a lot of setbacks — but once you take control of your life, have a clear goal, and persist, it will start to work for you.

Third, stop saying "no one wants a woman with kids" or "all the single guys are gay" or "women want Mr. Perfect" or "women are only interested in a hunk who owns General Motors."

Women complain men are rats. Men complain women are bossy. Men and women complain they never meet anybody. Negative thinking and behavior that has become rooted — tales about the awfulness of the opposite sex turn off potential partners.

Instead, look at your excuses. Maybe they're really telling you something else. Many people think they want a mate, and say they do, but actions speak louder than words. They're not doing anything to make it happen. They make absolutely no efforts to find a partner. Or they give out mixed vibes. Perhaps these people have not resolved the pain of losing a past relationship so, perhaps subconsciously, they do nothing effective to get a new one.

If you're reading this book right after the breakup of your marriage or a relationship, you may need some time before you're ready to get involved again. That doesn't mean you shouldn't read the book, but now may not be the time to start acting on it. Read it again a few months or a year from now, when you'll have more energy to pursue the many suggestions that are coming up in subsequent chapters for finding that special someone.

If you're still raw from the grief of losing your spouse through death or divorce, do yourself a favor. Join a support or therapy group. In Vancouver, where I live, the Living Through Loss Counselling Society offers low-cost individual counselling as well as support groups for divorced or widowed people. Ask around your community. Perhaps your family doctor knows of something.

Realize that when any major thing in your life is ending, such as a marriage or a job, there will be a period when your major task is letting go. Then there's a period of almost nothingness when your energy is low, you don't feel too optimistic, and you don't know what you want or where you're going next. Give yourself this time — you need it, even if you don't know it — and don't push yourself too hard.

Realize that stress and grief may actually change your brain chemistry and create depression. If it doesn't lift — if you have no energy, no motivation, you feel hopeless, and you've been feeling this way for months — please see your doctor. Too many people don't realize they're actually clinically depressed and suffer unnecessarily. It is nothing to be ashamed of; it's normal. Science has made amazing advances in the safe and effective treatment of depression in the last ten years. You can get out there and live again!

The key is not to get stuck here forever. There should come a time for new beginnings and establishing a new life. That's when this book can be bedside reading as you plan for a new life — one that may eventually include a new partner.

Virtually everyone can find a suitable mate if they really want one

I've seen it time and time again. When a person has really decided that he or she is fed up being single and wants to find a lifetime partner, things start happening.

First, these people turn the half-empty glass into a half-full one. They start to think of why a relationship *will* work, instead of why it will fail. They make a list of their own good qualities and try to build on them, rather than looking at all the minuses, and wallowing in them.

Second, they stop setting impossible standards for their prospective dates to meet. They start to look at the good qualities. Instead of impulsively (or compulsively) scratching possible names off their lists, they're thinking of good reasons to put people onto their lists and into their calendars and lives.

Third, they get out more. They take responsibility for making a new life, and they take up new interests. They join a club or organization. They go to the weddings, the funerals, the barbecues, the birthday parties, and the office parties. They keep themselves open to meeting new people. They accept invitations to meetings, to their child's soccer banquet, to work on some extra community or job-related project. They get involved.

Fourth, they "let go and let know." They let go of their fear of embarrassment, and they let their friends, relatives, and co-workers know they're looking for a relationship. "Seriously, I don't want to impose on you by casting you as a match-maker, but if you happen to know a single chess-player who likes antique furniture and Billy Joel, don't keep it secret!"

Fifth, these people who are successfully joining the search for a partner set some ground rules — and stick to them. They're interested only in available men or women. No more affairs with married folk, no more dates with practicing alcoholics or drug abusers, and no more setting sights on those they can't attract.

Sixth, they let go of the hangovers and the garbage generated by previous relationships. They never utter critical sentences such as "All men are..." or "The trouble with women is they want to...." They treat everyone as an individual, fairly and honestly, and accept that most people are doing their best to get along in the world.

These are people who've finally dealt with their hurts and their grief. And because they have direction, they are more attractive to others.

Dump your baggage

So deal with your emotional baggage — from childhood, from your parents' miserable marriage, from your own marriage and divorce, or from past failed relationships. Find counselling or support groups. They work. Give them a chance. Often, the person who says "I don't need it" is the one who will benefit most.

Don't be bitter or blame other people for past problems. People who try to start new love affairs filled with old angers and resentments are a turn-off. Take control. Accept responsibility for how your life has been and how you want it to change and improve.

If flying off the handle is a problem you have, or if you're too passive, sign up for an assertiveness training course. These courses can be extremely beneficial to many people, not only for relationships but also in the workplace.

You might also look into taking a communication skills course or a course on conflict resolution. You can find out about these courses through your local community center, adult education center, family service agency, or YW or YMCA.

I talked with author Susan Jeffers. Jeffers, the author of *Feel the Fear and Do It Anyway* and *Opening Our Hearts to Men*, recalled spending a lot of energy putting men down for years after she and her first husband split up in 1972. "I was a male basher; I was angry at men," she told me.

"A lot of women are angry at men because it's very hard to take full responsibility for your life. It's much easier to blame than to see our own poor choices."

While Jeffers is still an ardent feminist who feels the future for relationships between men and women looks bleak, she believes we are in a transition period and are going in the right direction. We're going from traditional marriages, where two people join to complete each other, to equality, where two complete people marry to support each other's growth.

"When I was angry, self-righteous, and judgmental, I said I was looking for a kind, loving man and couldn't find any. Of course not. It doesn't work that way. Now I say we need to put up a mirror rather than a magnifying glass. We need to make a list of the qualities we want in a man and then create those qualities in ourselves because like attracts like."

Jeffers says that healthy people pop into our lives when we are healthy ourselves, when we use our power and take charge of our lives, and when we understand that a relationship is only a part of life.

One of the most meaningful things Jeffers discovered in researching her books was the intensity of pain men feel when they lose a relationship. "I think a breakup hurts men and women both just as much. But women are able to express it, whereas you rarely see men express it. Having sat in some men's groups, I've witnessed the extreme pain, the sense of powerlessness they feel. I think some of the violence we see when breakups occur is a clue to this pain. I'm not condoning violence, of course, but I think it shows there's a lot of people feeling very helpless."

Letters to my love column from men are among the most painful ones I receive.

It used to be the very last thing most men did was read books about relationships or join a support group. But I see this changing. Indeed, as many men as women write to me for advice at the newspaper. More men are now initiating a visit to a marriage counselor when things get bad at home. Some now look for male support groups equivalent to the very popular groups available to women such as Women Who Love Too Much. Some find support groups within the men's movement. Some find groups such as Alcoholics Anonymous, Al-Anon, Adult

> Men have just as many problems as women when their relationships end. But their ways of coping are often ineffective.
>
> Typically, they try to ignore their feelings and problems or they:
>
> - Talk about them incessantly, especially to dates.
> - Get so tough and defensive they're cut off from living.
> - Pretend they're okay, while they're actually bursting with anger and bitterness.
> - Drink themselves to death.
> - Work themselves to death.
> - All of the above.

Children of Alcoholics, Sexaholics Anonymous, and Emotions Anonymous. Many find these groups help them not just to deal with the immediate problem, but also to develop fruitful, positive, balanced new lives. As well, I see more men trying to figure out what's behind the male and female communication gap, questioning their role in the aftermath of feminism.

This soul searching and growth is good. Not only can baggage make it impossible to make a connection with another person, it can be carried into new relationships.

One man in his late thirties I interviewed admitted he has a pattern of going for women who won't give him the time of day. He's average looking but he always goes after knock-out women in their twenties. Going for unavailable women may be this man's defense for preventing marriage and the emotional suicide he thinks such a relationship would bring.

"My closest friend, who is a psychologist, thinks I'm attracted to women I can't have," he said. "He thinks my view of marriage is a way of distancing myself from real intimacy, which I fear. It's true I don't have a high opinion of marriage. My parents were divorced and over 90% of the stories I hear are about miserable marriages."

Notice how not dealing with emotional baggage has affected this young woman who wrote to me:

Dear Kathy:

For the longest time now, I've wanted a relationship to lead into marriage. And it almost happened. But after being engaged for four months, I discovered he was not only lying, but cheating on me. I called everything off. Ever since then I haven't had any desire to see other gentlemen.

I'm 20 years old. I have a fantastic day job, two night jobs that collide with one another, and I'm also attending college part-time. I received all these positions after breaking up with him.

I've had enough of being hurt by the male species. I find men annoying. The majority of them always complain and bicker and I cannot stand whiners.

People tell me I'm too independent to be involved in a serious relationship. And I somewhat agree. Is it wrong to feel this way?

Also, I've always wanted a child. Is it wrong to want a baby excluding the father-husband?

Independent but confused

Clearly this woman needed grief counselling. Either that or some time to get over her hurt and anger. She was not ready for another relationship, even if she had wanted one.

And she needed to see that just because one guy is a cheater, that doesn't mean all of them are. She needed to work through this and learn to trust again — not blindly, but willingly, with her boundaries intact.

This woman was also doing what so many men and women do after a relationship breakup — she took on more and more work, perhaps to avoid or escape her hurt, sad, and angry feelings. It's better to deal with them directly.

And she was also jumping to the conclusion that a baby, without the bother of a husband, might be the answer. Many women tell me they're going to do this after the breakup of a relationship. I feel it is a serious mistake. The importance of *good* fathering has been far too neglected in our culture. Children need the modelling and nurturing of two good parents (even when they're divorced).

As well, what kind of attitudes about men and women might this woman project on to a child if she has not dealt with her own hurts? Furthermore, like so many people, she was confused about independence and marriage. There's nothing contradictory here. The truly independent person has a lot of room in his or her life for an intimate partner. Independence is good for a relationship. It prevents a couple from becoming too enmeshed and gives the relationship its vitality.

Perhaps this young woman's friends really were saying she was too uncompromising or competitive. With good conflict resolution skills and a desire for maintaining a relationship, people can be independent, yet intimately involved.

It's common for people who are hurt to generalize about bad experiences. Far too often we see people who judge all men or all women by one or two bad happenings. Stuck in this frame of mind, can you imagine how this person appears and feels to others?

Sometimes unresolved issues show up in the form of extreme neediness. One man described a woman he dated for a while as a lamprey eel, sucking his very life away with her dependence upon him. It is a sad thing when a person will bend and scrape and abandon his or her identity and integrity to have a relationship. Aloofness is a turn-off, but so is compromising yourself as if the person you want is the last guy or gal on earth. Be yourself. Don't be a chameleon, changing personalities for every date who comes along.

If your marriage has ended and you see others who've jumped from one marriage into another, don't look at them enviously, thinking how lucky they were to avoid the single stage. From what I've seen, those rebound marriages are very often disasters. People need time to recover from the loss of a relationship and start fresh to connect again from a position of health and strength and balance.

Maybe you're ambivalent. I see this a lot in single men and women. It sometimes looks like aloofness or arrogance. Sometimes it masquerades as independence. Sometimes it takes the form of radical feminism or male chauvinism. Sometimes it's not obvious, but it shows up later in a relationship as fear of commitment. (More about commitment later in chapter 21.)

Other men who are unable to form intimate relationships may actually be suffering a personality disorder, perhaps resulting from not bonding normally with their mothers in very early childhood.

Some men, and perhaps some women, seem to be almost asexual. They don't emit any sexual vibes. There's no spark, no tension that attracts the opposite sex to them, initially at least. It's really hard to know why this is. Sometimes the person might be homosexual but denying it. Or perhaps, long ago, one rejection was such an assault on an already low self-esteem that he or she lost any ability to connect with another.

The hurt may be recent or it may go way back. To not allow a relationship develop is a way to protect against being hurt again.

To all of you, this message. Examine your particular baggage. Get to understand it. Remind yourself you are normal. Then dump the baggage.

Sometimes what looks like aloofness, arrogance, or ambivalence comes not so much from deep emotional damage but merely a lack of social skills. And the solution is as simple as learning these skills, including how to make conversation, how to pay attention to the other person, and what's expected in certain situations. (For more information, see chapters 8, 9, and 10.)

2
Preparing to connect

It's quite normal to feel lost, alone, and very insecure after a marriage breakup or the death of a spouse. You'll need to give yourself time to grieve, without rushing it.

Later you'll start to rebuild your life. It's important to see that you've been given a tremendous opportunity to grow as a person. It's an opportunity you may not have had when you moved from your family of origin into your first marriage.

Rather than seek immediate yet artificial security in the arms of another, try to make independence a priority. You won't be alone for the rest of your life. That's just your mind painting a disaster scenario, something you're apt to do right now.

Len Macht, who runs a singles social club with about 250 members, says the biggest mistake men and women make is trying to get connected too soon. "They're still in shock, anger, denial, depression, and all that emotional turmoil and they don't think they can survive alone. They connect with somebody, anybody. They don't sit still long enough to work on themselves. They need to figure out what went wrong, what to do differently. They don't analyze their strengths and realize the people they can turn to for support. They beat themselves up. They get involved with someone, get into sex quickly and then they wake up three months later knowing it's a mistake."

If you work at becoming emotionally and financially independent, you'll go into a future relationship as an equal and have a much greater chance of making marriage a success.

Look at it this way. Everyone should marry one wrong person, so that next time you have greater appreciation of the right person! Just kidding. Perhaps your relationship failed because you were the wrong person or maybe you did marry the right person, but didn't know how to sustain the relationship. You need to learn that now, before you get involved again.

Low self-esteem is the biggest stumbling block to finding a new relationship. And it's fairly typical for self-esteem to drop enormously upon separation and divorce.

High self-esteem is the ultimate aphrodisiac. Even across a crowded room, it's easy to recognize who's got it — by their facial expression and stance — and who doesn't.

I know many people who think that if they had a partner everything in their lives would be so much better. That is faulty thinking. Yes, in the short-term, while the relationship is in the infatuation and romance stage, their bodies pumped with the brain chemical phenylethylamine (PEA) (see chapter 4), everything seems so much better.

But that only lasts for a while. When they come down to earth, these people face the same inner problems they had before and which they thought would be answered by this special other.

Sure, having a partner can be wonderful and it can be that way forever. But it doesn't make you happy unless you're happy anyway. A mate will not be the answer to all, or even most, of your problems or needs. And when you do find a suitable partner, you'll need to have something to offer. Not vice versa. We must have a strong enough sense of self if we are to be able to love another person successfully and genuinely.

Things you can do immediately

So you've begun the process of resolving your past hurts, perhaps through individual counselling and a support group. Your self-esteem is improving.

Here are a few more things you can change immediately about your life. The first sounds corny but it is important.

Start smiling at people, even if you don't feel like it at first, even if you think it's a bit phony. You will find as people smile back at you, you will feel happier. People are attracted to happy people. They become friendlier, feeling that you are more open. They may even initiate conversations. Make this the new you. Make smiling a part of your manner and make a point of making life a little nicer for others.

Start looking at what you need out of life and start doing things for yourself that give you pleasure, like taking up a new hobby or a new career. Or treating yourself to a trip — even a small one — once a year. Maybe it means a weekly visit to the beauty salon, getting a dog, or buying a boat.

Become aware of what you're good at. List your strengths and skills and be grateful for what you have. Stop listening to anyone who puts you down. Surround yourself with people who believe in you. Give yourself credit for your accomplishments. Let go of perfectionism. After all, nobody is perfect. Why should you be? Perfectionism just takes away from your happiness. Instead, forgive yourself when you make mistakes — now and for those you've made in the past. Learn from them.

Make a conscious effort to be optimistic and positive. You can actually train yourself away from pessimism and negativity.

Gain a feeling of control in your life. Make your own decisions, take responsibility for your life, set the directions you want. You can take courses or read books to help yourself. Don't wait for other people to direct you or to take the responsibility that is rightfully yours. Personal control helps you feel good about yourself. It's essential for emotional health.

Think about the routines, the rituals, and the traditions you value. Hang on to the ones that give your life meaning and throw away those that don't. I found, for example, that when my marriage broke up some 14 years ago, I hung on to some traditions especially at Christmas time. It helped my daughter and I immensely in getting through that difficult time. My routine of being a good housekeeper and keen gardener gave me a sense of control and continuity in my life. And I helped my daughter to continue the things she enjoyed. We always had a cuddle at bedtime and talked, as we did before the breakup. We also developed some new routines and traditions which gave our lives love and meaning.

Be self-caring. Learn to say no. Learn to set your boundaries so that others can't hurt you. But don't create walls. Meaningful contact with other people is very important to your happiness.

Become a desirable person by attending to your appearance. Do you need to improve your cleanliness perhaps, your fitness, your grooming, or your style?

Improving yourself in those areas will boost your self-esteem and make you more attractive. Analyze your everyday appearance, even at work, and how you appear to those around you. Don't wait until your first date to spiff up. You may never have a first date with that attitude.

Ask yourself if your outer appearance matches your new inner self. You've likely changed a lot since you were married. And now that you're on your own, you may find the world has changed a great deal too. You may need to bone up on what's going on out there. Start reading magazines and keeping up on the latest changes. Go to restaurants and observe people. See what's in and what isn't. Don't become some trendoid or try to look like you're 16 again. You don't have to have a ring in your nose or purple hair. Just figure out whether your style is in keeping with the new you and the new world.

Okay men, say you work at a dirty job all day. No one expects you to be Mr. Clean while working with diesel or paint or whatever. But go home and have a bath *every night,* clean your fingernails, and for goodness' sake wear deodorant. You may *think* you don't produce B.O. because you're used to it. But you likely do. And it's a turn off. Moreover, it's a scientific fact that women perceive odors better than men do. So bathe or shower every day and wear clean clothes.

Make sure, whatever your length of hair, that it looks good. Visit the stylist once a month. If you're over 40, get your nose and ear hairs clipped if they need it!

Get your shoes re-heeled and polished. People pick up on little details like this — in the first few seconds of seeing you. They may decide instantly that if your heels are worn down and scruffy, you're worn down and scruffy too. Make sure your pants aren't dragging on the ground. Most cleaners do small alterations and repairs.

Get your beard trimmed. If you're balding, for heaven's sake, don't grow your hair long on one side to cover this bald spot. It looks ridiculous and is a sure sign of being out of touch with style and being unaccepting of yourself. Every time I see a man like this I giggle to myself imagining him in the shower with flowing locks on one side and a short fringe on the other.

And whether you're a man or a woman, get your teeth fixed. Have them cleaned regularly by a hygienist. You may not be able to detect bad breath yourself but you may have it. Floss your teeth and brush them (and your tongue!) at least twice a day. Change your underwear daily. I don't mean to sound like your mother, but these things *are* important.

Analyze your clothes. Are they out of date? Do you figure "they've still got good wear in them" like my sweetie does, even though they're all ten years old or more? Package them up for the charities. Get some new outfits. Go to a good haberdashery for suggestions on a basic wardrobe. Maybe you can only afford one thing from that establishment, but take note of the advice and build a wardrobe over time.

This advice also goes for women, but women tend to be already more conscious of their cleanliness, grooming, and style.

If you smoke, realize that in North America you're in the minority and a lot of people will find your habit repulsive. You'll likely only get another smoker to date you. The rest unfortunately will be turned off by your breath and the smell of stubs in the ashtray. It's also unhealthy.

Same goes for heavy drinking or the use of drugs. You're severely limiting the numbers of people who'll find you attractive.

Get some exercise on a regular basis. It'll make you feel good and probably improve your posture and your appearance. I don't think everyone has to be super slim. And there's no one quite as boring as the self-absorbed fitness fanatic. But the reality is, most people find extremely overweight people unattractive. And first impressions *do* count.

If you're a woman, don't wear excessive amounts of perfume. Some people are allergic and others just find it sickening. Perfume and makeup should be understated rather than overstated.

Here's a letter from a man who made some changes similar to those above:

> *Dear Kathy:*
>
> *I used to be one of the untouchables. Now I have changed my attitude and am enjoying my life a whole lot more. Here's some advice from a 49-year-old man:*
>
> *Be a friend. You can make friends with women, as well as men. Act your age. Older men tend to think only the women around them have aged over the years. Look in the mirror. Stop chasing younger women.*
>
> *Give up booze.*
>
> *Get fit. The ladies are as repulsed by a 40-inch beer belly as men are repulsed by obesity in women.*
>
> *Listen more and talk less.*

Love. Show others you care about them, not just about yourself. Isolation is partly created by appearing to be self-centered.

Former untouchable

I think that man had good advice. And Len Macht, a singles club chief, has some good tips too. He says that when you are ready to meet other singles, it's important to knock off the intensity. Just enjoy having fun without focusing on finding someone. Lighten up. If you're playing a role, drop it and just act like a human being.

So when you've attended to your appearance and developed good habits, then for heaven's sake, *accept yourself as you are.* Life's too short for obsessing over your looks or comparing yourself to Kevin Costner or Michelle Pfeiffer. Spend time doing that and it'll depress you. It will also waste energy that could be used making your life interesting and productive.

Get a life!

Look at what's missing (other than a mate) in your life. Is your job lousy? Maybe you should be working on changing that by upgrading your skills and knowledge. Are you lacking in friends? Now's the time to start thinking about how you can develop new friendships and maintain and enhance those you already have. Network — join activities and meet friends of friends. If you are invited out, go. Don't look at every member of the opposite sex and ask, "Is he or she *The One?*" Go out with a lot of people, not just the ones with instant chemistry — remember, there are not going to be many of those around and sometimes, chemistry develops.

You will need to start thinking about how you can become the kind of person who brings out the best in people. Try to see the best in everyone you meet. When you meet someone or when you date, find what's good and interesting in that person, instead of sitting back and waiting for that person to give you a performance.

Work on building other people's self-esteem. That way you'll get your focus off yourself and help others to feel good.

As you are building a life, let your friends know when you're ready to start meeting new people and ask them if they can help you broaden your horizons. Too often friends assume they're being intrusive if they know of someone or a group of people they think you might enjoy. People are terribly reserved these days. So it's important to let them know you're open to doing new things and meeting new people.

Men, unless you're disabled, learn to dance. So you don't like dancing, you say. Why? Because you're not good at it? Because you remember having to in high school and being rejected? The fact is, most women love to dance and if you dance you'll be in demand. Besides, dancing can be part of the mating ritual. Don't tell me you really don't like being close to someone, holding her so close you can whisper sweet nothings in her ear....

Men and women need to learn some new things, and become good at the things they're not good at now. For example, if you feel a little weak on financial matters or household budgeting, take an investment course, learn about money, banking, real estate, and the country's economy and its place in the world. I'm not suggesting you get involved in high-stakes schemes. But if you learn as much as you can, over time you'll get a feeling for how you can protect your future.

If you feel socially awkward, perhaps you need a course on etiquette. Books with pictures are available in the libraries. When you know which utensil is the correct one at the dinner table, your confidence grows.

Register with an image-consulting firm for training in social skills, manners, and appearances. At Premier Image Inc. in Toronto, classes range from a $100 session to spruce up grace and style in teenage boys and girls to a $4,000 Well Mannered Weekend to polish company executives.

Learn about wine, beer, and spirits, even if you don't drink them much. Learn about coffees and how to make them. Learn to cook if you don't know how. When you're single, it's not much fun choosing between eating out or microwave dinners.

Learn, learn, learn. The more you learn, the more the world seems interesting. Develop an enthusiasm, a zest for life. There's very little that is as attractive as the person who is hooked on life, mad about Mozart (or mozzarella), truly engaged in the world around him or her, involved, sniffing the sea air or the bouquet of carnations, vital, having fun, seeing what's precious, feeling the sun's warmth, or hearing the breeze through the trees.

Care about other people, about the neighborhood, about current events. Balance self-concern (which is important) with concern for others. Read the papers, watch the news. If you don't understand something, ask people questions, take a course, go to the library. You might become an expert on something.

If you're unhappy with your job, get more skills in your off hours, so you can either change jobs or get promoted or start a business of your own on the side.

Do what you've always wanted to do. Get a life — one that others will enjoy sharing with you. Finding a mate may be something in the near future, perhaps not right away, but romance can happen at any time, any place, at any age. And if it does, go for it!

3

*W*hat do women want?
What do men want?

If you've listened to any golden oldies or movies from the thirties and forties, you'll know just how radically relationships between the sexes have changed since then. Women don't call their boyfriends "Daddy," and men no longer call women "baby doll." Women today who still want men for "diamond bracelets, champagne, and caviar" are about as popular as men who want women as sex toys. But political correctness aside, basic biology and social conditioning still operate in attraction between the sexes, so the issue can be really confusing.

Initial attractions

I recently asked readers to tell me what attracts them to the opposite sex and then what qualities they want in a mate. Men said they are attracted to:

- "Smiling, wide-open, inquisitive, challenging, alive eyes. Warm, inviting smile. Soft yet strong voice, full of clear intonation, determined, independent and strong. Hair — any color, but soft and flowing."

- "Intelligence. Tasteful clothing, following sensually the female form. Perfume — the right one can drive any man up the wall and along the ceiling. Not overpowering. Delicate. Passion and compassion."

- "Not too thin, nicely developed figure, not over five-foot, eight inches."

- "What the eyes see first — does she care how she looks, dresses, carries herself? Then what I hear — is she intelligent, witty, self-confident, easy to talk with?"

- "Overall physical beauty, smile, friendliness."

- "Spontaneity as evidenced by sparkle in the eyes, with smile, confidence, trying new things. Appearance that is tasteful and tidy."

- "Big hair, shapely butt (boobs don't matter), smile, friendly personality, easy to talk to. I usually like short."

Female readers had these preferences:

- "A man with an air of confidence, a warm smile, and sparkling eyes."

- "A quiet, gentle person with a nice smile, neat and tidy, with a great sense of humor."

- "A stimulating conversation, a man who smiles and laughs. I feel this shows he loves life and is not a dark and moody person. A hairy chest has always been a physical trait I'm attracted to."

- "It will be his eyes and his smile that first attracts me to him."

- "A man who is clean cut, dark hair, medium to husky build, extroverted, fun and funny, considerate, witty."

- "I seem to be attracted to men who wear glasses...that coupled with confidence in himself. Very important is if a man shows interests in me. His interest in me first starts the ball rolling."

- "A strong physical build, smiling eyes, gentle friendly smile, strong legs, hairy chest."

- "The very first thing — he's self-confident, but not arrogant."

- "Someone who looks like he just finished work at a construction site and needs a good home-cooked meal and a shower. WOW!"

- "The slightly rough-edged overweight guy with facial and chest hair."

So it seems men and women in this survey were generally attracted in the first moments to physical traits that project energy, warmth, and self-esteem — sparkling eyes, warm smiles, an air of self-confidence, spontaneity, and good looks.

Men tended to favor soft curves; women, strength and confidence.

In a recent, more scientifically structured, cross-cultural study, psychologist David Buss found men are attracted to young, good-looking, spunky women, while women place a premium on status, maturity, and resources. In the old days, women clearly traded beauty and youth while men traded wealth, position, and power. Today, these things are still important to many singles, especially if you add intelligence to both profiles.

Anthropologist Helen Fisher says in her book, *Anatomy of Love,* that there are some physical characteristics that incite romantic passion around the world: "Men and women ... are attracted to those with good complexions. Everywhere people are drawn to partners whom they regard as clean. And men in most places generally prefer plump, wide-hipped women to slim ones."

American tastes in romantic partners show some definite patterns. In the seventies, a university survey said men tended to prefer blondes with blue eyes and lighter skin color, while women liked darker men. But few men liked very large breasts or the slender, boyish female figure, and almost none of the women were attracted to an extremely muscular physique. Both sexes preferred the average. Too short, too tall, too slight, too muscular, too pale or dark, were unpopular. I suspect, however, these preferences might have changed since the seventies.

If you go by the companion ads, men want women who are slender, petite, who have models' bodies. They might use words like fit, athletic, attractive. One man asks for "tall, willowy, drop-dead gorgeous, creative, intelligent, slender, sensuous, and passionate." Another wants "long legs and long hair." Another, "skinny and cute."

Women can be just as superficial. The equivalent of a man's quest for slim is the woman's quest for tall or rich. But women also ask for "mentally stable," "financially stable," "employed," "monogamous," or "educated professional."

Academics who have studied personal ads as a social phenomenon, note that many men think about the woman's body whereas women appear more concerned with the man's character and personality.

Aaron Ahuvia, who teaches marketing at the University of Michigan School of Business Administration, and Mara Adelman, assistant professor of communication studies at Northwestern University, have researched singles dating services and personal ads. They found most women are as eager as men to find attractive mates, but find it unseemly to say so in their ads.

"It's no secret in our society that men are attracted to good-looking women," says Ahuvia. "If you are at a cocktail party, you can screen subtly, without making a big deal about it. But when you put it into writing, you have to be explicit."

The two academics published a review of research on singles ads that included 91 entries, and the following findings:

- Men seek attractiveness and youth from women, and offer financial resources and promises of marriage in exchange.

- Women are more likely than men to seek financial security and marriage.

- People tend to offer personality traits that they think are valued by members of the opposite sex. Women claim to be independent, adventurous, and competent; men advertise themselves as warm and considerate.

- Women with children usually do not mention them in their ads.

- Men receive more replies to their ads if they say they are older and taller; if they mention educational and professional success or "a penchant for expensive cultural activities"; or if they seek a generally attractive woman but avoid sexual references.

- Women receive more replies if they say they are younger, slimmer, or athletic; if they say they are intelligent; or if they mention sex.

Ahuvia says the studies seem to find that traditional gender roles are alive and well in the singles ads.

Both men and women are looking for people with qualities that convey high status, he says. Men are impressed by beautiful women, but women are impressed by successful men.

Women want to marry men at least as professionally successful as themselves, and some men are just as put off by women's requests that they be "financially secure," "professional," or "educated" as women are offended by requests for thinness.

"Men don't like to feel any more like a walking wallet than women like to feel they could be decapitated and no one would notice," said Ahuvia, who gives classes on how to write effective personal ads.

Men tend to marry women who are younger and less professionally successful than themselves, says Ahuvia and Adelman. And single people have noted an oversupply in the market of successful single women in their late thirties and forties, and an undersupply of single male counterparts.

"Men tend to overestimate themselves a little bit," says Ahuvia. "If they got just what they thought was on par, they'd probably get more than they deserve."

In addition, he said, women generally refuse to marry men they consider unsuitable, preferring to stay single instead.

Inner qualities

In my survey of readers, I also asked men and women to tell me what inner qualities they wanted in a partner.

Both men and women said a sense of humor was tops on their wish list. Women next sought men who were honest, kind and caring, intelligent, confident, and positive. They wanted men who appreciated family values and who liked kids. They wanted men who were independent, communicative, and good listeners. Finally, they wanted men to be financially self-sufficient, have goals, be respectful, responsible, and loyal.

That fits with what Robin Dunbar of University College London told the 1994 annual conference of the British Psychological Society. He said that males who are seeking long-term partners through personal ads should promote their abilities as a parent and their sound family values. His analysis of 800 ads placed in two U.S. newspapers showed a shift in what women wanted. "Women are increasingly financially independent and can look after themselves. There is a shift to asking for good parenting abilities. Men haven't caught on to this yet."

In my readers survey, men rated a sense of humor tops, but then wanted women who were fit, intelligent, kind and caring, honest, emotionally stable, confident, good at communication, and open-minded. They also wanted women with good self-esteem and who were loyal.

Men also indicated they are a little confused these days by women. They say women claim to want kind, communicative men. But then women actually choose men who are completely opposite. What's going on here? This question was put quite articulately by a 31-year-old man who wrote to me a few years ago:

> *Dear Kathy:*
>
> *I'm very passionate about women. But I have never had a date and I'm still a virgin.*
>
> *I'm an average guy: average looks, average income, average personality, fairly intelligent, with some interesting hobbies and the odd talent. I have asked out maybe 100 women in my life — sometimes confidently, sometimes not. Through increasing frustration, I make the following observations:*
>
> *Male chauvinists never have trouble getting a date.*
>
> *Nice guys get dumped more often than jerks.*
>
> *Alcoholics, drug addicts, and other men with serious problems can always attract more women than stable guys.*
>
> *Women may say they want sensitive, understanding Alan Alda types, but those aren't the men they go after.*
>
> *In my more cynical moments, I believe the only reason a nice guy ever gets a woman is because there aren't enough jerks to go around. I find myself in groups of men discussing women and I end up defending women's lib. These guys never had trouble getting girlfriends despite their attitudes, while I never dated. Imagine how my arguments looked through their eyes: "Gee, maybe we should treat women like you do. Then we'd be as popular with them as you are. Ha ha."*
>
> *Why are so many women like this? I have a few theories:*
>
> *With alcoholics, for example, a woman's mothering complex asserts itself — the poor dear just needs someone to love him. Or women want to "mold" their men and a guy with no major hangups appears too set to be altered.*
>
> *Deep down women feel liberated men are wimps. No "real man" would let a woman be his equal.*

Do women like to be dominated? There are far more personal ads by women specifying "tall" men than there are ads by men asking for busty women. Why are women so hung up on height? I am 5'10" by the way. Could it be they like to feel protected and dominated by a man and can't get those feelings with a short man?

Perhaps women just have a lot further to go in their quest for liberation. Men clearly have a long way to go.

Food for Thought

I told this man I hoped his frustration in getting dates would not drive him to male chauvinism! Believe it or not, I said, more and more women are turned off by male chauvinists, by men who expect to be served without serving back, and by men who make demeaning remarks or tell disrespectful jokes about women.

Emotionally healthy people attract other emotionally healthy people. Dysfunctional people attract dysfunctional people.

Very often, women who are attracted to alcoholics, drug addicts, or abusive men are women who were brought up in homes where addiction or abuse occurred. They grew up to be rescuers, over-functioners, or victims. They feel comfortable with the dysfunction, although they don't recognize what their attraction is.

Emotionally healthy women do not want to be dominated, abused, or responsible for looking after dependent men. They want to give and receive equality and respect.

As far as women desiring tall men or men with good jobs, I believe something entirely different is happening here. I subscribe to the theory of genetic memory which says we have impulses and skills passed down through the centuries that were more useful to cave dwellers than they are today, but still exist within us.

Women may say they want a sensitive man, and I think they do. But many also want traditional male qualities. At a subconscious level, they still often seek tall, strong, powerful men who will give them strong, healthy babies and be able to protect and provide for them. And many men still seek soft, nurturing women with ample breasts for nursing. This sounds a bit primitive but it may explain a lot of behavior.

I asked the reader to look at his pattern of who he's attracted to. I asked: Are you approaching women who will value your qualities? Or are you setting yourself up for failure? What approach do you use? Does something you do or project scare them off? Do you come on too strong or not interested enough? Are you so self-monitoring that you do not focus enough on them?

This is a tricky business and there's no value in guessing. I suggested he seek personal feedback from objective friends and even past female acquaintances.

But another man had this view:

"Men and women are incredibly superficial. He goes for looks, she goes for bucks. If a guy's unemployed, I guarantee no woman will be interested in him. Women expect men to be like them — articulate, verbal, sharing feelings, vulnerable. In reality most men (75%) don't have those qualities. They have learned long ago to be strong, silent, invulnerable.

"Women should realize they need to get their intimacy needs met with their women friends or hunt for the 25% of men who are capable of being intimate. Women sleep with the cold, macho types. They just want to be platonic friends with the warm and sensitive ones. They are attracted sexually to men with no intimacy skills."

Hmmmm.

A female reader had this view:

Dear Kathy:

I'm a psychology student and have read letters to you from men wondering why they are having difficulty finding women. Through research I've been able to determine several reasons.

Women have higher standards than men do. I found the following reasons given for rejecting members of the opposite sex: Men may reject women because of unattractive facial features, excess weight, and older age. Women may reject men because of unattractive facial features, excess weight, younger age, low paying job, lack of social status or power, short stature, baldness, lack of muscles (skinniness), low quality car, excessive sensitivity or insensitivity, cheapness.

On average, the men in the survey (200 university age men and women) found 50% of women in their age group

(18 to 30) attractive enough to date. The women indicated only 20% of men fit into their range of acceptability.

Certain biological theories hypothesize that this discrepancy is easily explained. The female of most species (including humans) is excessively selective when reproducing to ensure only the most powerful, muscular males mate, thus ensuring the healthiest babies. Although humans possess advanced abilities that separate us from the rest of the animal kingdom, our basic instincts remain the same.

Very few women go into artificial insemination clinics asking for the sperm of a 5'1" man who works at a gas station. They are more likely to ask that the father be over 6' and be a doctor or a lawyer.

Student

California psychologist and UCLA professor Herb Goldberg writes about how gender differences attract us, but how they can also later repel. He says that in the beginning, she likes his strength. He likes her softness. He's tough. She's gentle. He's protective. She's nurturing. It's exactly their oppositeness that makes them so attracted.

Dr. Goldberg calls them traditional couples. But he says traditional gender differences operate in liberated couples as well. Being liberated (he's open and caring; she's strong and independent) only confuses the issue. Neither sex has really shed conditioning.

Modern women may say they want someone sensitive and communicative but still get excited by men with an aura of mastery, strength, and independence.

Modern men may encourage strong, independent behavior in women but fall in love with sweet, compliant women. They can tolerate only a limited amount of aggressive, dominant behavior. To varying degrees, modern men merely cloak their male core in sensitivity and modern women still want a man to take care of them.

In his book, *The Inner Male,* Goldberg says being different also means we are emotionally different, and that's why all the communicating in the world doesn't work sometimes. But he has solutions. (More about that in chapter 22.)

Some psychologists say people are attracted to qualities they lack in themselves. The person you choose reflects a part of yourself you

(subconsciously) wish you had developed but haven't. That's why relationships can be so difficult: the traits you first found so attractive increasingly grate on you. You may then try to change your mate to be more like yourself or increasingly reject him or her because he or she is different.

That route usually spells disaster. Nobody wants rejection or to have his or her personality changed. Better to either choose a partner from a personality type that fits with yours or see the value in your mate's different personality, learn how he or she does it, and expand yourself to include those traits.

But beyond initial physical attraction and beyond the ads, what do men really want? I don't know if we can generalize. Maybe what they really want is what this man said:

WANTED: GOOD WOMAN

Must be able to clean, cook, sew, dig worms and clean fish. Must have boat and motor. Please send picture of boat and motor.

The ad is a joke of course. Yet I know cynics who would say it's right on. It's hard to know what men really want but here's what psychologists Connell Cowan and Melvyn Kinder say:

- Men want to be related to realistically. They want to be seen not as a jerk or a superman but a flawed and struggling limited person.

- They want a woman who is satisfied with him the way he is and has her own life and isn't always trying to make the relationship more intense.

- A man wants a woman who enjoys the moment and the relationship as it is. He doesn't want to be criticized and told he is unloving.

- He wants a woman who can seek her own darker side, a woman who recognizes her own ambition for him and lets him be, and develops her own ambition for herself.

- He wants a woman who doesn't talk incessantly and who doesn't pursue relationship talk and analysis when he's focused elsewhere.

- He wants a woman who values the work he does and doesn't resent his involvement in his career.

- Men often find separateness stimulating. That's why a relationship-obsessed woman can drive men away. The demands of her underlying insecurity become oppressive.

And what do women really want?

- A man who gives her attention, makes her feel special, and who is a companion. A woman wants a man who does things with her — who shares the responsibilities.

- She wants someone who shares fun times. For some that means a man who will watch a TV movie with her some nights. For others it will be a man who likes to go away with her for a weekend. Or a man who enjoys spending family time with her and the children. For another woman it might be a man who's interested in her career and willing to give her support on a special project or two.

- A woman doesn't want to be just seen as the cook, or the cleaner, or the mother. She wants to be treated and respected as an equal. That means a man who will do his fair share of the housework and child care.

- She wants to be seen for the special person she knows she is. She wants him to create some excitement too. Some stimulation.

And especially, perhaps, some romance.

Now might be the time to answer the questionnaire on the following page.

WORKSHEET #1
WHAT DO I REALLY WANT?

Put a check mark against the qualities you seek.

	Men use this column	Women use this one
1. Warm	☐	☐
2. Inquisitive	☐	☐
3. Soft	☐	☐
4. Strong	☐	☐
5. Determined	☐	☐
6. Independent	☐	☐
7. Sexy	☐	☐
8. Intelligent	☐	☐
9. Tasteful	☐	☐
10. Sensuous	☐	☐
11. Good-looking	☐	☐
12. Witty	☐	☐
13. Confident	☐	☐
14. Passionate	☐	☐
15. Compassionate	☐	☐
16. Approachable	☐	☐
17. Good conversationalist	☐	☐
18. Beautiful	☐	☐
19. Friendly	☐	☐
20. Spontaneous	☐	☐
21. Tidy	☐	☐
22. Large breasts	☐	☐
23. Long legs	☐	☐
24. Short	☐	☐

	Men use this column	Women use this one
25. Tall	☐	☐
26. Well-shaped bottom	☐	☐
27. Quiet	☐	☐
28. Gentle	☐	☐
29. Outgoing	☐	☐
30. Sense of humor	☐	☐
31. Has zest for life	☐	☐
32. Hairy	☐	☐
33. Dark hair.	☐	☐
34. Husky	☐	☐
35. Fun	☐	☐
36. Considerate	☐	☐
37. Rough-edged	☐	☐
38. Energetic	☐	☐
39. Has high self-esteem	☐	☐
40. Younger than me	☐	☐
41. Older than me	☐	☐
42. Wealthy	☐	☐
43. Has nice skin	☐	☐
44. Clean	☐	☐
45. Slim	☐	☐
46. Plump	☐	☐
47. Blue eyes	☐	☐
48. Brown eyes	☐	☐
49. Hazel eyes	☐	☐

WORKSHEET #1 — Continued

	Men use this column	Women use this one
50. Fit	☐	☐
51. Muscular	☐	☐
52. Athletic	☐	☐
53. Energetic	☐	☐
54. Dark	☐	☐
55. Powerful	☐	☐
56. Professional	☐	☐
57. Petite	☐	☐
58. Creative	☐	☐
59. Rich	☐	☐
60. Employed	☐	☐
61. Educated	☐	☐
62. Emotionally stable	☐	☐
63. Financially secure	☐	☐
64. Adventurous	☐	☐
65. Competent	☐	☐
66. Considerate	☐	☐
67. Successful	☐	☐
68. Likes children	☐	☐
69. Sensitive	☐	☐
70. Communicative	☐	☐
71. Good listener	☐	☐
72. Sweet	☐	☐
73. Compliant	☐	☐
74. Good parent	☐	☐

	Men use this column	Women use this one
75. Loyal	☐	☐
76. Responsible	☐	☐
77. Goal-directed	☐	☐
78. Open-minded	☐	☐
79. Average	☐	☐
80. Protective	☐	☐
81. Articulate	☐	☐
82. Vulnerable	☐	☐
83. Invulnerable	☐	☐
84. Caring	☐	☐
85. Macho	☐	☐
86. Nice face	☐	☐
87. Bald	☐	☐
88. Overweight	☐	☐
89. Accepting	☐	☐
90. Attentive	☐	☐
91. Companionable	☐	☐
92. Sharing	☐	☐

What did the questionnaire tell you? Are you a man who checked off such things as sexy, slim, petite, and compliant? Are you a woman who checked off strong, tall, wealthy, and professional?

How do you think the other sex feels about your list of check marks? Are you a stereotype? A chauvinist? Is it time for you to think about — and develop — some new values? Work on it. It works!

4

The mystery of attraction

Love is what happens to men and women who don't know each other.

Somerset Maugham.

What I think Maugham was describing wasn't love but infatuation. Call it what you will — infatuation, chemistry, or being in love — it is only the initial driving force in a new relationship. It is not love and it's not a guarantee of an enduring or solid bond.

Nonetheless, after initial attraction, infatuation starts the whole process rolling, and it remains one of life's most baffling mysteries. Why are we uncontrollably and compulsively drawn to one person, while another leaves us cold?

This universal human phenomenon starts in that moment when another person begins to take on a special meaning, something beyond just sex. Some scientists say romantic love exists to prevent the one-night stand. It's nature's way of getting sexual partners to stay together long enough to produce and care for a child, thus promoting survival of the species.

In any case, attraction can happen in a second or it can develop over time. It can be to a complete stranger or to an old friend seen in a new light.

But it must be there if a romantic liaison is going to happen. I'd hate to be in the matchmaking business. Only the people involved can know when there's a spark. Predicting that spark is almost impossible. Let me give you an example.

Some years ago five single women got together and asked me to help them find mates. Through my newspaper column I put out the call for five single men. Here's that column:

WANTED: Five single men. Need not be tall, dark, and handsome. Bald or gray is fine.

Must be well educated, successful, outgoing, have integrity, be in touch with the pulse of the city, and enjoy the arts as well as outdoor sports.

Especially important — must not feel threatened by successful, independent women.

I have five attractive, outgoing, and successful single women who want to meet you, treat you to dinner, and try to solve their dilemma of how to meet suitable single men. One woman is 38, outdoorsy, loves to ski, sail, and cycle, is the mother of two teenagers, and owns and runs four restaurants. She is arranging the dinner.

Another is 49, in the art business, a power walker and cyclist who enjoys travel, the theater, opera, and ballet. She is a mother of three.

A third is a writer, 44, mother of two, a workaholic, and loves gardening. A fourth is in her early fifties, a successful realtor, and loves people, music and the arts.

The fifth is the only one who has never married. She's 46, a movie freak who loves to travel, especially to New York. She's a freelance writer who also does store window displays and floral arrangements.

These women meet men every day in business. So, you ask, why are they having trouble finding men for companionship? I don't know, nor do they. Perhaps it's because they're so busy with work and raising children.

Please write me if you think you fit the description and you'd enjoy dining with these women. Tell me something about yourself and please include your name, age, address and, very important, your phone number. Then we can arrange the evening — five lucky guys and five interesting women.

More than 50 men wrote. Occupations included businessman, realtor, artist, lawyer, engineer, biologist, and physician. Eventually the women whittled the list down to five — a TV executive, a lawyer, a wholesale grocery executive, a financial adviser, and a business manager.

I set up the dinner by inviting the men they selected. The entire dinner lasted four hours and was a really comfortable way to meet. Everybody enjoyed the company and felt good about themselves when it was over. But nobody felt any instant and special connection. There were no romantic sparks!

The next day I asked their impressions. The men's comments:

- "The ladies were charming. They were definitely not boring. I'd like to get to know them better."

- "The evening was very pleasant. They were very personable, articulate, and capable. Am I romantically interested in any? No. Relationships are very magical. There has to be something very special. I didn't feel that."

- "They were very nice people but from a different social group than I am. They were more cultured."

The women's comments included:

- "It was a lovely dinner. But I didn't find any of the men worldly enough for the women, except maybe one. One thing about all the men — they didn't ask me anything about myself. One man was totally self-absorbed. The men weren't as dynamic as the women."

- "They were all very sweet but not interesting to me romantically. They were not my type."

- "It was a fabulous way to meet people. I didn't meet anyone I'd like to date but we'd like to get together again."

I'm sure all ten of these men and women will eventually find a suitable partner — if they continue to get out of the house, meet new people, and develop their social skills.

But what is that magic, that indefinable something that makes one person notice and want another? Let's look at the research.

Love maps

Sexologist Dr. John Money says attraction is largely a result of love maps. As early as age five, children begin to create their own individual love maps — a mental template of what makes another person a hunk or a nerd, a babe or a bowser.

Throughout childhood, all the appealing and disgusting traits of other people — family, friends, experiences, and chance encounters — tumble around in the child's subconscious. Included may be things like atmosphere in the home — be it peaceful or chaotic.

What pops out around adolescence is a sort of psychological guide to the ideal lover, complete with details of appearance, build, race, scent, manners, and temperament. It's a picture of your perfect man or woman, including the kind of conversations and activities that excite you.

That's why a woman with short, curly, dark hair might turn on one man, but means nothing to another. Or why one man must have a woman with large breasts, while another is far more concerned with a nice butt or shapely legs. It's why one woman's motor starts running when she sees razor stubble, but another might find the Don Johnson type totally unappealing. It's why one goes for the strong, silent type while another likes a man who's the life of the party.

We may be aware of some of the things we find attractive in the opposite sex. But many, many more are buried in our subconscious.

Brain chemistry

A good deal of infatuation may indeed be explained by brain chemistry. The euphoria, that incredible rush you get with romantic love, results when a natural amphetamine called phenylethylamine (PEA for short) floods the brain.

Awash with PEA, his heart flutters and his hands turn clammy. When her eyes meet his, their spirits soar. She feels a warm glow, a bonfire inside her breast, a completeness.

PEA is a neurochemical produced by the brain, similar in chemical structure and physiological effect to amphetamines or "speed."

It's an upper. PEA is responsible for feelings of exhilaration and giddiness. And PEA helps us to overcome our separateness. We feel so "understood," "identical," "incredibly close."

All we want is to be together constantly. We are deliriously happy and oblivious to the world. When we're apart we forget things, sit by the phone, long for our next encounter. And every moment we're apart merely feeds the frenzy.

We obsess. Our new love occupies our thoughts constantly and many of these thoughts are even delusional. We're apt to think things about him or her which in no way correspond to the realistic perception of others.

PEA can make hearts flutter and spirits soar.

Sigmund Freud once described falling in love as a short-acting, spontaneously remitting psychosis. But he had to admit later in life that he couldn't explain it. Yet we know a lot more today than we did then.

PEA, by the way, is the same neurochemical that gives skydivers a rush during free-fall and probably contributes to excitement in all sorts of situations. Come to think of it, I know two couples who met at skydiving classes and later married. Mmmm.

PEA is also contained in chocolate and that may be why chocolates are a traditional Valentine's Day gift and why some of us like to drown our lonely times in a chocolate binge.

The connection between chocolate and PEA was discovered by psychiatrist Dr. Michael Liebowitz, director of the Anxiety Disorders Clinic at the New York State Psychiatric Institute, and author of *The Chemistry of Love*. He and a colleague worked with "attraction junkies" — people who craved romance so much they jumped into ill-fated relationships with jerks. Their lives were a cycle of depression and elation as one love affair crumbled and another began. Many found solace in chocolate. Suspecting a lack of PEA in the lovesick, the psychiatrists gave them a drug that indirectly boosts the amount of PEA in the brain. Within a few weeks, one man started to make smarter choices in partners and even began to be happy without a lover.

Studies also show a correlation between PEA levels and sex drive. The higher the PEA, the higher the sex drive.

Over time, however, infatuation wanes, either because PEA levels drop or because the brain becomes so accustomed to high levels of the chemical that it no longer responds.

Liebowitz believes this second phase triggers the release of natural opiates called endorphins, which produce serene feelings. These endorphins calm the mind and allow us to feel not high, but pleasant. The lovers move beyond infatuation to deeper attachment, enjoying a secure sensation of general fondness leading to a more stable relationship.

But — and there's always a but — after three or four years, the relationship may become less serene. People begin to see the differences previously masked by PEA and other chemicals. At this point, without the relationship skills to get through, a couple may never reach the supremely fulfilling stage of deep, mature, and enduring love. Cynicism and emptiness may take hold. Then, once again, we are vulnerable to the magic of PEA.

Those with good communication and conflict resolution skills, however, are much less vulnerable. Their initial attraction becomes just the basis for a lifelong friendship with caring and continuing passion.

Still on the subject of chemistry, scientists wonder if there's any possibility that pheromones — minute chemical secretions (odorless "smells") released by the body — could be involved in the attraction process.

Scientists have been unable to agree on whether or not human pheromones exist, and, if they do, whether or not they influence attraction. But all sorts of animals and insects secrete pheromones and these do influence the physical and social behavior of their same species.

Some manufacturers do not intend to let this stone go unturned. You can buy pheromones in spray cans. An ad for one mail-order product says it will cause the most recalcitrant woman to swoon over almost any man. Another is supposed to send a reluctant male into an orbit of ecstasy. I'd have to see it to believe it.

In any case, biochemistry — whether it's PEA or the more dubious pheromones — isn't everything in the game of love. People's emotions and behavior modify their brain chemistry, and brain chemistry modifies emotions and behavior. Scientists don't quite understand how this all happens.

So perhaps this baffling thing called attraction happens when we meet a person whose love map and chemistry mesh with our own at the right time for each of us.

Timing

Timing is critical. Men and women are susceptible when they're ready to have a relationship or start a family, when they are looking for adventure, when they're lonely, when they're at a transition stage in their life, when they feel dissatisfied with themselves, or often when they're alone in a foreign country.

Infatuation can happen at any age past puberty and well into old age, continuing long after the need to sustain the species has ended.

Some cultures may try to convince people there's no such thing as romantic love. In some societies, romantic love either isn't recognized or is considered subversive because it undermines the tradition of arranged marriages.

However, a recent study of 166 cultures turned up evidence of some sort of romantic love in 147 of them. Dr. William Jankowiak, an anthropologist at the University of Nevada, Las Vegas and Dr. Edward Fischer of Tulane University, say the results suggest attraction and then love are part of the human condition and result more from biology than from cultural influences.

Also interesting is that people are rarely infatuated by someone they've grown up with. A study done in an Israeli kibbutz showed almost none of the children raised together married within the group.

As well, there's what's called the Romeo and Juliet effect: if lovers are kept apart by circumstance, these impediments tend to heighten infatuation, romantic love, and passion.

But there must also be some slim possibility of fulfillment. This is why infatuation and passion are often kept at a feverish pitch in long-distance relationships and extra-marital affairs.

5

*W*hy men and women aren't connecting

Attraction, love maps, chemistry. Fine. But how do you go about finding matching love maps or chemistry? It can be difficult, as these readers attest:

Dear Kathy:

Honest, I've looked hard. I can't figure out what men do and where they are. At 32, there's little I haven't done and hardly anything I wouldn't try. Occasionally, I'd like company. I'd have a better chance of finding the lost city of Atlantis.

Interesting, adventurous, single men are either 15 years too old or looking for someone 10 years younger.

Read the companion ads: If the person has travelled the world, skis, is a gourmet cook, and has blue-water cruised, it's a woman. If the person is into archery, kayaking, seeing plays, and the symphony, it's a woman. What do men do?

I went whale watching. All women. I took a photography course. All women. I learned to scuba dive. Almost all women. A friend took a motorcycle driving course. All women. Another learned to sail. All couples.

What do the men do? Where are they hiding?

All I want is a man, mid-thirties, adventurous, ambitious, and reliable. There must be a man who likes to ski, sail, scuba dive, bike, see a play, walk, who would take a trek on Anapurna, snorkel on the Great Barrier Reef, eat at the street stalls in Jaipur, or who likes to go to museums and concerts.

Daring To Go

Dear Kathy:

Where are all the men? Everywhere I go, it's women. I've even considered taking up golf. I hate golf. And the male golfers don't seem to socialize afterwards anyway.

I don't like bars (they're full of married men or men under 30). I've taken courses and classes of every description mainly for my own interest but also to meet people (preferably men). Only women take courses.

I give up! Where are the unattached men in their forties?

Resigned

So I conducted a survey asking for responses from men only. Where are you?

I asked single and single-again male readers. I told them that women join singles clubs and go to singles dances. And quite often they outnumber men there two to one. Sometimes, there are no men to be found at all. Some women leave swearing never to put themselves through such an excruciating experience again.

I asked men what they are doing, how they're going about meeting women, and whether or not they've given up on women. And, if so, why? Among other things, they were asked to answer the question: "On Friday and Saturday nights, I'm usually..."

The majority, yes the majority, of men said on a Friday and Saturday night they're *home alone!* This was the number one response from some 300 men in their twenties, thirties, forties, fifties, and even a few in their sixties. Most were in the 30 to 49 age group.

The answers were more than a little depressing. Most men said they're "ready for a relationship" and most disagreed with the statement "connecting with women isn't worth the effort."

But many men weren't looking and seemed confused, disappointed, or angry about women.

With all the women home alone just as confused, disappointed, and angry about men, is it any wonder we have a problem nowadays in connecting?

And what are the men home alone doing? Here's what they say they do: "Nothing in particular." "Reading, creative writing, talking to my cat, listening to music." "Working on my house or yard." "Housework." "Watching videos." "Watching TV." "Catching up on chores." "Working on my car." "Increasingly minding my own business." "At my computer." "Puttering in my shop." "Exercising." "Studying."

Reading and watching TV was the most common activity for the stay-at-home crowd.

For those men who usually go out on Friday and Saturday nights, their number one activity is to go to movies — alone. Some go with a male friend. The third most popular response was spending time with male friends or spending time with their kids.

A number said they go to bars, others to the gym, some play sports or go biking, some walk their dogs, others go to sports events, some do their shopping.

Quite a few are working on Friday and Saturday nights, especially if they're in the hospitality industry. A very few said they go to dances or nightclubs.

Fewer than one in ten of these single men belong to a singles club, even though that's a place they're guaranteed to meet women who are single. Most men said they do not belong to singles clubs because they don't know of any, they live in small towns or other areas where none exist, or because they don't know enough about them. So it's clear singles clubs are not doing a good enough job of advertising both their existence and what they have to offer.

So if the majority of men are home alone on Friday and Saturday nights, and if the rest are hardly making any major moves to connect with the opposite sex, what's going on?

It's pretty clear that not one man would rather watch TV. But a majority of men said they do not connect easily with women because they're shy; they don't know where the women are; or because women go out in pairs or groups and are unapproachable; and most common of all, they are afraid of rejection.

Some men also added they haven't the time and/or the money. Indeed, even if money were not a problem, a majority of men feel women are too concerned with a man's income, success, or the kind of car he drives.

And a number pointed out that even if they're not shy, and if they overcome their fear of rejection and make an initial connection, they have difficulty knowing how to keep that connection going to the dating stage.

But why are so many of the men not more motivated to overcome their shyness and fear of rejection in order to meet women? The answer probably lies in their answers to the survey question, "The biggest problem in connecting today is..." which indicated a great deal of ambivalence and confusion about women.

In their own words, the biggest problems in connecting are

- Not knowing if she's single.
- Paranoiac man-bashing typecasting.
- Time, money.
- Not knowing where to go. "Tell me where they are and I will come."
- Women judge men too quickly on looks and also distrust men.
- Women don't send clear messages that they are interested.
- Women want Tom Selleck with megabucks, even if the women are ugly losers.
- One must be professional and proper — it's too tough.
- Women worry about how rich a guy is.
- The confused state of public mores.
- Men and women have different expectations.
- AIDS and other sexually transmitted diseases.
- Missing on going with the guys.
- Meeting a non-smoking, non-drinking woman who has never been married.
- Meeting women who are not losers.
- Traveling distance sometimes too great to make the effort.
- Divorce law and its implementation and liability.
- Finding a woman who is honest and doesn't play games.
- Women are in such a rush to get serious.

- Fear of rejection, separation.
- Women's role in relationship — traditional or new age? Career or family?
- Over-expectations on both sides.
- Women are concerned with looks and race, but whether you drink or do drugs doesn't concern them.
- Women are too afraid.
- Meeting them in a non-threatening environment and picking up or sending signals.
- Afraid of rejection or possible commitment.
- Low self-esteem.
- Kids, money, and being accepted as you are.
- Women go for losers.
- Women my age (30 to 49) are so negative and defensive.
- Women look at younger men and I look at younger women.
- Myself — I have trouble trusting others because of letdowns in the past.
- Her kids.
- Women are too independent.
- Finding where the nice girls are hiding.
- Women are too bossy.
- Conflicting schedules/lifestyles.
- The confused borders of sexism and feminism.
- Men and women don't really like each other, don't trust each other.

How did women react when I published the men's responses? This letter was fairly typical of women's reactions:

> *Dear Kathy:*
>
> *Your column, "Where the Boys Are: Home Alone," really hit home! I found my head nodding in rueful agreement. I, too, talk to and play with my cat, read, listen to music, clean my apartment. I'm too shy and afraid of rejection to join a singles club.*

But when I read the multiple reasons men gave for not being able to connect with women, I got ticked off. That list read like an indictment of women in general. The men who responded to your survey seemed to be content to lay the blame entirely on women for their (the men) not being able to find a good relationship, instead of being willing to accept half the blame themselves.

There are still nice single women out there who are realistic about the differences between men and women, who are not perfect, and don't expect men to be either. Unfortunately, we've all been paralyzed by bad past experiences with the shmucks in life and are currently at home talking to our cats and lavishing love and affection on our house plants!

M.R.

Clearly a lot of the men who responded to the survey have an attitude problem. Certainly people who engage in either male-bashing or put-downs of women are unlikely to ever be successful in sustaining a relationship. People who build walls of pickiness or criticism or generalizations about the opposite sex are bad news, and boring in their complaints even to members of their own sex.

And if you operate from a belief system that women want only rich guys, or that you would have to give up too much for a relationship, or all the good ones are taken, or relationships are painful, or you usually get rejected, or you're not good enough — of course you're going to have problems meeting a special someone.

But aside from attitude problems, connecting can sometimes be difficult these days because of our fast-paced lifestyles and economic pressures. Time is at a premium and often so is money, especially for single parents and parents paying child support. Many men and women can't afford to go out more than once a week or pay for elaborate dates.

And women truly are concerned about safety, so they don't give out their phone numbers easily. Both sexes, it seems to me, are often poor at sending out signals that they're interested.

And some men are legitimately fed up with women who say they want equality but don't take any responsibility for approaching men. They say women don't take risks, they don't pay their own way, they won't start conversations, they won't make the first move, and they suspect all men of having ulterior motives.

So certainly there are things that do make connecting difficult and people's defenses get in the way. Both sexes need to look at what they are doing that makes connection impossible.

Len Macht who runs a social club for singles believes women have more guts than men in getting out of the house and meeting other singles. "Men seem to need an invitation," says Macht. "They need to be coaxed. Is it their perception of what a singles club is? A lot of men don't know it's Friday until about 8 p.m." But Macht says a man who joins his club has a shelf life of 1.8 months before "he's scooped." And as with all singles clubs, membership changes as people find a relationship and drop out.

"Eighty-eight per cent of life is just showing up. So I tell them to get out of the so-called comfort zone — it's really a misery zone. Get out of the house."

See the next chapter for tips on getting out of your shell.

6

*O*vercoming shyness

You die a million deaths waiting your turn to speak at an office meeting. You'd prefer brain surgery to attending a social gathering on your own. And making any approach to the opposite sex is out of the question.

When anxiety gets so bad it keeps you from finding a mate or enjoying life, it's worth finding a way to deal with it.

Many, many men and women share these debilitating fears.

Leslie, 38, couldn't speak up at office meetings. She also avoided any type of course where she was expected to participate. Leslie was nervous socially and feared others would see that.

But after joining a support group, Leslie found dramatic improvement. "I learned that the way I think I am is not the way I appear." Recently, she has been speaking up at work meetings and taking courses. "Now I put myself out more, initiating conversations," she says. "I think it's hereditary. I've seen others in my family with it. Some have dealt with it by using alcohol. Others withdrew."

Of all the traits that plague humans, shyness may be the most hard-wired into the brain. About 20% of people start life with neuro-chemistry that predisposes them to be shy, says Harvard University psychologist Jerome Kagan. The other 80% become either outgoing or shy, depending on their life's experiences.

An inhibited child seems to be born with what amounts to a hair-trigger brain circuit controlling heart rate and perspiration. It takes much less to stimulate than in other children. As well, inhibited children may have excessive levels of the neurotransmitter no-repinephrine, a cousin of the fight-or-flight chemical adrenaline.

In some people, shyness is not a primary trait but instead a means of coping with a learning disability. Dr. Larry Siever, of Mount Sinai School of Medicine in New York, says much social interaction is based on unspoken rhythms, cues, and pacing. Some people are actually victims of learning disabilities — they can't and don't read social signals that come naturally to most people. When they don't pick up on these, they often feel left out and alienated. A woman so affected can't tell from body language when the man she's chatting with wants to flee. After a number of these experiences, she responds by withdrawing.

Siever suspects the inability to process the information contained in rhythms and cues of social interaction arises from an oversupply of dopamine in the brain's emotional-control room and a shortage in the more rational cortex.

A support group led by a therapist trained in treating shyness can help people learn how to pick up on social cues and body language. A course in social etiquette may help as well. When you know when and how to shake hands, how to make introductions, it builds confidence.

Researchers are looking at drugs that can correct the chemical imbalance in the brain and these may one day be available. Dr. Sheila Woody, a post-doctoral fellow in the stress and anxiety unit of University of British Columbia Hospital, says shyness may be a result of either a lack of social skills or a result of fears. People who lack social skills don't know what's appropriate. For example, she says, a person might not know who to ask out and who not to ask out, "so he keeps getting rebuffed." Or without social skills a person may ask for something inappropriate. For example, a man might ask a woman to go away with him on a ski weekend as a first date.

Those who lack social skills might not know how to carry on a conversation, or how to keep the conversation going with questions. Socially successful people have a series of social scripts, says Dr. Woody. "They have a series of topics they ask about, not in a canned way. These might be, What do you do for a living? or Do you live around here?"

And if there's mutual interest, socially successful people might suggest a further opportunity for friendship by suggesting a time to meet for coffee, see a movie, or go for a jog. "It's a matter of starting off with things that are less threatening and less intimate, things you might do with friends or a co-worker."

But a lack of social skills doesn't always mean the person is shy and withdrawing. Sometimes a socially unskilled person is overbearing or too intense or invading another person's personal space.

Dr. Woody says people whose shyness originates in fears may tell themselves that they're too boring, or they're unacceptable. A shy man may think "I can't phone up that woman in my class because she'll think I'm boring."

"We ask him to look at the evidence for these beliefs," says Dr. Woody. "We encourage clients not to avoid social situations. We give them assignments. Begin three conversations with strangers this week. Or carry on a conversation with someone for 15 minutes without cutting out. Or ask for a date. The more you do something, the easier it gets."

In her 15- to 20-session treatment program, 70% of participants leave the program doing "a lot better" socially. "That doesn't mean they turn in to swinging TV personalities. But the program gives them a boost."

Shyness can be a vicious circle. A shy person can turn other people off and even create hostile reactions, which in turn makes the shy person even more shy. Sometimes shy people are so absorbed by their own self-consciousness, they don't tune in on the needs and feelings of people around them. There's no doubt that outgoing, happy people who react positively and with interest to others are very attractive.

Jim, 50, says he grew up in a family with shy, non-assertive people. Recently, he ended a six-year relationship with a "high-powered career woman" in which he lost his personality. "It was an incremental process of being squashed. I submitted."

He couldn't take assertiveness training because he was too anxious. But he found a group of people like himself less intimidating. "I learned we all have the same feelings and they're normal. Now I take advantage of every opportunity to socialize. I enjoy talking to strangers whereas it used to scare me."

In a future relationship, Jim says he would insist on being himself. "I wouldn't bend all the time."

It's important to realize that *everybody* feels some anxiety from time to time in social situations. Even politicians and performers, accustomed to being in the public eye, can fear embarrassment and rejection in unfamiliar situations.

For some, it's worse. One person can't eat in public, in case she spills some food. Another, fearing his hand might shake, finds it excruciating to sign a cheque while anyone is watching.

Help is available through individual counselling with a psychologist, social worker, or other qualified therapist. Support groups led by a qualified and trained counselor can help people put their anxiety in perspective. Others share identical fears and experiences — and overcome them.

Ask your doctor for the name of a psychologist or other therapist who specializes in this area or contact your nearest university or research hospital, which may have a stress and anxiety clinic. Or contact the psychology department of your nearest university, which may know of a clinic specializing in social phobia, social anxiety, or shyness — whichever label they use.

As well, you may wish to get information about anxiety disorders from the non-profit, self-help organization called the Freedom from Fear Foundation. It has support groups in Ontario and will be establishing one soon on the east coast of Canada. For information, write to the Foundation at 10 Lonborough Avenue, City of York, Ontario M6M 1X3 or call (416) 761-6006.

Another similar organization is called Recovery (phone 538-3399 in British Columbia). In the United States, phone your city's information line for a name and phone number. Look in the white pages under Information Services for your city or region.

In a support group, participants first look at what might be causing each person's anxiety. For some, simply avoiding alcohol, caffeine, and sugar helps a great deal. And for a few, anxiety comes from balance problems originating in the inner ear. But for most, social anxiety is an indicator of wanting to do well. Many very competent people suffer it.

In Vancouver, Erika Hilliard, a social worker in private practice, leads groups for shy and socially anxious people. She believes social anxiety is an inherent human trait, having served man well in cave-dwelling times when it was important to be aware of danger.

Today, social anxiety is most crucially felt during the teen years, when people are especially susceptible to peer judgment. Ordinarily, people grow out of it. But some don't.

Instead, they start becoming self-conscious about being anxious, which makes them even more nervous, and then the vicious circle begins. They get temporary relief by avoiding social contact, but opportunities are missed and loss of self-esteem often follows.

Hilliard says some people are more vulnerable than others for a variety of reasons. These people may have character traits of gentleness, eagerness to please, or be overly sensitive to the opinions of others.

Learn to overcome shyness.

As Hilliard says: "Anxious people don't thoughtlessly hurt or stomp over people. They happen to be sensitive and there's nothing wrong with that. It can be channeled in lovely ways. People with too little anxiety can hurt others needlessly."

Others learn social anxiety from parents who handled social situations in anxious ways. For Sophia, 24, anxiety was interfering in every corner of her day-to-day life. "Just getting on a bus was anxiety producing," she says. "I had trouble carrying on with school, jobs, and making new friendships. I had irrational feelings of worthlessness and inadequacy.

"Inside, I always had a voice saying, 'You can't change, you're always going to be like this, you can't make it, you're too sensitive, you're different, you're strange.'

"My mother was very anxious and depressed when I was growing up and I learned from her. Also, I felt abandoned because she wasn't there for me. My father just avoided everything. He stayed in his study." Sophia is learning to replace negative thoughts with positive ones.

Many socially anxious people have a distorted perception of self. They may have been raised in homes where parents destroyed their self-confidence by criticizing, by disapproving, by saying, "you're going to fail," "who can like you?" "you never do anything right." These children grow up giving themselves the same kinds of messages. They think in negative ways about themselves, they distort or over-generalize. They minimize their own good points while maximizing their shortcomings, just as their parents did. But they do the reverse with others.

Some socially anxious men and women grew up with repeated ridicule, humiliation, or criticism from other kids at school or in the neighborhood. Sometimes it was an intensely excruciating experience such as being reprimanded by a teacher and wetting his or her pants. That humiliation might have become the person's blueprint for shame, especially if the child was unable to confide about it with a supportive adult.

Socially anxious people may label themselves as failures, rather than saying they simply made a mistake. They need to develop a feeling of compassion for themselves.

As children, some people were deprived of social opportunities. I know of one man whose parents did not allow him and his brothers and sisters to mix with any other children in their rural community. This man grew up isolated and suspicious of others. He has overcome much of this childhood learning but still avoids some social situations. Never being allowed to have friends home as a child, today in his fifties he won't have parties at his home despite the fact that his wife is very outgoing and gregarious.

If you're shy, you need to honor this anxiety, realize it's a normal reaction, and not flee. Learn to be aware of your discomfort but focus on the task. Anxious people often are self-focused and need to concentrate more on other people or the task at hand.

Hilliard teaches her clients to replace negative thoughts with positive ones. She shows them how confident people think differently. A confident person will shrug off an error by saying, "So what? I made a mistake. It's not the end of the world. I'll do it differently next time." A confident person will think, "So she doesn't want to go out with me. Okay, not everybody has the same taste. There are other fish in the sea." A confident person says, "I'm going to give a great presentation to my colleagues. Sure, I'll be nervous at first but I'll get over it. I'm well prepared. I'm interested in what I have to say and they'll be interested, too."

By sharing their experiences, clients in Hilliard's support groups eventually learn to care less about what others think. They begin to picture themselves successfully, having fun in social situations. In time they make better eye contact with others and learn improved body language and voice. General confidence follows. (Read more about eye contact and body language later in chapter 9.)

Here are letters I've received from shy people, which illustrate some of the ways shyness and social anxiety play out in different people.

Dear Kathy:

I'm 19 and even though I'm told I'm sincere and funny, I have never been on a date or had a girlfriend. I'm not ugly, but I'm not Tom Selleck. I don't know what it is about guys like me but we always get overlooked. I'm also very shy. Even when I see a girl I'd like to talk to I can't because I'm too shy. What can I do?

Shy

I doubt he lacks physical attractiveness or great character traits. But shyness and lack of confidence are crippling. The terminally shy should be able to find a social anxiety support group in a big city. Even smaller communities often have a psychologist or other qualified therapists who can help shy people explore new ways.

Here's a slightly different look at the problem:

Dear Kathy:

I am 22. In high school I was too shy to date. Since then I have come a long way in being able to phone a girl, talk to her, and ask her out.

First dates seem to go okay and I always get a second date. But I just can't seem to get the courage to try and hold hands or kiss. Just last night I finally recognized a pattern. I was out on a second date. Finally, I excused myself, went to the washroom, and threw up. This has happened to me several times, each with a different girl. Are there programs that could help me?

Carl

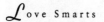

I told Carl he needed to establish real rapport with a woman first and forget holding hands or kissing on the second date. But sooner or later the moment of truth comes. Moving a relationship from friendship to romance is scary for everyone, even the socially successful. There's no way to eliminate this fear. It is scary when you take the person's hand or put your arm around her waist, for the first time. You're laying your cards out and making yourself vulnerable.

Here's a letter from a young man who worked on his shyness, but, as with most things in life, he found a new challenge.

Dear Kathy:

I am 21, male, and single. I have been shy all my life and have been too chicken to ask girls out. I suddenly realized not taking chances isn't going to find me love.

So I adopted a new attitude: Who cares if a girl says no when I ask for her number? I will probably never see her again anyway. I have nothing to lose and everything to gain.

With this in mind, on my recent vacation in the U.S., I asked girls for their phone numbers and attractive girls that I normally wouldn't bother talking to were giving me their numbers. I was shocked. I called some of them up and we talked for hours. Since I have come back, I haven't asked for anybody's number but I will soon.

Now to my problem: I am a virgin and an old-fashioned type of guy. I couldn't see myself having a one-night stand. I would like to get to know the girl well, build up to the moment. What would a girl think of going out with a 21-year-old virgin? Would it turn her off?

The More I Change, I Stay The Same

Dear More:

Pat yourself on the back for the tremendous progress you've made. There's nothing wrong with being a virgin at 21 or in wanting to know a girl well before your relationship involves sexual intercourse. A woman is going to be far more interested in finding out about your personality, your interests, and how you treat her than whether or not you're a virgin.

Once she gets to know you and decides she likes you well enough to make love, it won't matter to her if you've had sex before or not. And sex the first time with someone new is often a little clumsy and less satisfying anyway. It's expected.

After dating for a while you'll feel more comfortable holding hands — kissing and cuddling will come naturally. Wait until you feel some trust before you tell her you're a virgin. She may feel very special that she's your first. And, who knows, she might be a virgin, too!

Some people are only anxious with someone they're attracted to. With anyone else, they're confident. And sometimes to handle their anxiety, these people seem almost to go out of their way to be rude or distant. This, of course, is a defense mechanism. If you have it, work to get rid of it because you are turning away the very people you want to attract.

Being alive means taking risks.

7
Selecting a partner

If you're the parent of a teenager, the following conversation may sound familiar:

"Oh, mom, he's so gorgeous. He's got long, black hair. He wears the sexiest jeans and leather jacket. He's got great buns."

"But, dear, what's he like?"

"What do you mean, what's he like?!"

"Well, is he a nice person? Does he treat you well?"

"Oh, mommmm. Who caaares whether he's niiice. I'm not getting married!"

"That's good, dear."

Have you ever looked back at some of the people you've dated, even married, and wondered what you ever saw in them? That's because we change and what we find attractive differs at the different stages in life.

California psychiatrist Martin Blinder, author of *Choosing Lovers*, has identified eight different types of relationships. He says teenagers frequently seek *validating relationships*. A girl may want a boyfriend who belongs to a certain group — a banger, a preppie, a skater, or whatever. Or she may seek a guy who has a certain type of car. Or who is the most popular. The romance is expected to supply what is missing within herself. She wants to belong to a certain group or she's defining who she is by what type of boyfriend she has.

Unfortunately, some people, much older, also get stuck in this empty pattern. They go for superficial trappings, appearances, income level, position. A man may need a spectacularly beautiful wife, for example, to feel good about himself. A woman may seek a man to give her position and wealth, even though he may be a lousy lover and companion. These people, like the teenager above, seek a certain type of relationship in an attempt to make a statement about themselves.

Then there are *structure-building relationships,* says Blinder. These couples build for the future together, often following the model from their families. They save for a down payment, buy a house, have kids, and try to pay off the mortgage. But they are not very connected. The "form" has taken over. They act more like parents than partners and eventually start to question what they are doing. Sometimes couples recognize the dangers and improve closeness. Sometimes the emptiness can't be bridged and they split.

Experimental relationships, such as extra-marital affairs or liaisons with a person from a totally different lifestyle or culture, are usually short-lived. But experimenting can become a fixed pattern — he or she hops from one experimental relationship to another, over and over again.

The *healing relationship* is just that — therapy. These are often people who have just come out of a divorce and are looking for someone to heal their pain. When one or the other gets well, the relationship usually disintegrates.

Transitional relationships have something of past relationships but something new in them as well. Yet the person knows this isn't it. It's a stage of relationship growth.

Avoidance relationships are those in which the relationship allows the person to avoid real intimacy, real emotional closeness. One or both partners may be a workaholic or very busy elsewhere or even living in another community. If one of the partners wants more, the relationship is over.

Fusion relationships are ones in which each partner loses his and her individuality and each becomes an extension of the other. These couples may stay together forever and the death of one may be more than the other can survive. These relationships offer security but little personal growth. And if one partner starts to grow, it could kill the marriage. Or one partner may seek an affair and the other does anything to hang on, even tolerating open adultery.

By now, perhaps, you may be wondering: Is there such a thing as a healthy relationship? Yes, says Blinder, it's the *synergistic relationship* where both partners are mature and confident individuals. Their relationship may have evolved from one of the other types. Perhaps years ago they may even have been attracted by the other's "great buns." Or the couple may each have experienced other types of relationships but now are ready for this one. The synergistic relationship is two equals who have mutual friendship and shared interests.

While each partner is fairly independent, both are emotionally connected. They are not together mainly for the home or the kids. Their intimate connection enriches their lives.

I think Blinder's analysis helps explain how people's own neediness sometimes affects how we choose a partner for a relationship.

The following letter illustrates one of these types of relationships and the trap it creates for the single person who's interested in a committed relationship:

> *Dear Kathy:*
>
> *I've being seeing a woman for 15 months and while we have not yet made love, we are very close. We are the same age (22), have similar likes and dislikes, similar backgrounds and similar views on life.*
>
> *I am deeply in love with her and hope we'll be married some day. However, she does not yet love me. She doesn't know why. She says I'm the nicest person she has ever met and she feels guilty because she does not love me as I love her.*
>
> *She started going with me immediately after ending a very traumatic relationship with a boyfriend and as a result did not have enough time fully to get over the hurt. I do not make demands for intimacy. However, lately I have been wondering whether she will ever love me. Isn't 15 months long enough?*
>
> *Baffled*

> *Dear Baffled:*
>
> *The length of time it takes a person to recover from the breakup of a love relationship depends on how much that person's identity was tied up in the relationship and the length of that relationship. The rule of thumb is that it takes half the length of time of the relationship to get over it.*

> *Usually a person who's grieving will turn to another caring person who isn't considered a lover but simply a friend. So you may be a healing or a transitional figure to this woman. You may never be her love interest. You may be very helpful and rescuing for her and that is all she wants.*
>
> *Make it clear what you want and expect. Tell her you want a full relationship, with intimacy. If that's not what she wants, stop pursuing her (as difficult as that may be considering how you feel) and begin to distance. It's unwise to get involved with a person who is just coming out of a love relationship. They're best on their own without a significant love relationship for at least two years — time needed to become clear about who they are and what they like or don't like. You may well be in the right place at the wrong time.*

Hopefully Blinder's analysis of the different types of relationships will help you recognize some of the pitfalls in selecting the right person at the wrong time.

But how do you select the right person at the right time? You do it with a great deal of thought, not just hormones or neurochemicals.

Look at the foundations

People may spend hours, even days, selecting wallpaper, a car, a new outfit. Yet when they're buying a house, they often make their decision within a matter of minutes — without looking at the foundations, the wiring, or even flushing a toilet; they've fallen in love.

Many people select a lifetime mate in the same way. In only a few minutes they're sure this is it. They don't allow themselves to check the foundations, see the traits that may scuttle the relationship over time. Some people sustain their relationship, but too many aren't that lucky.

High standards or unrealistic?

Many people are choosy about unimportant things. A woman might say the man of her dreams *has* to be tall, athletic, and a professional — perhaps a doctor or an engineer. Then she meets a truly fine man who's less than average height, doesn't pump iron or do sports, and is a supervisor at a manufacturing plant. Instead of being outwardly powerful and exciting, he's a little shy and quiet.

Due to circumstances, the two are paired together. She has been telling herself she is definitely not interested and there will be no second meeting. Funny thing is, though, she has an exceptionally good time with this man. They connect in a very genuine way. And it becomes clear to her that this man has an inner self-confidence and strength. He knows himself well. And he is sensitive to the needs of others, including her.

She agrees to a second date, still thinking this man is not her type. He's too short, he works in a factory, and the only sport he does is hiking.

Two or three dates later, they're in love. This woman has fortunately given up her rigid ideas about what she wants and has broadened her expectations and chosen a man for the inner qualities that will serve the relationship so much better in the long run.

But many women never give up their rigid ideas. They're picky and highly judgmental and people they meet feel judged and guarded. Then these women wonder why they're perennially single. I know many women like this, but one in particular stands out in my mind. She's 33, attractive, in a good career where she meets men, and men are attracted to her. So why is she always bemoaning the "fact" that there aren't any good men?

When she asked me this question, I thought to myself impatiently, "Because you've eaten them all." I sense she's pretty superficial — more stuck on who's trendy or "important." I suspect she instantly and disdainfully eliminates good, intelligent, sincere men. What she wants doesn't exist and she wouldn't be able to see it if it did. She lives in a world of illusions. And I suspect she has a lot of insecurities she doesn't want people to see. She covers them with rather arrogant expectations and a workaholic lifestyle. Her dalliances with men feed her ego but leave her defenses intact. She doesn't have to be real or vulnerable.

Then there's the serial single — the man or woman who picks one loser after another. And oddly enough the picky types and those who pick losers, can often be one and the same.

I remember a dinner I had with a group of about eight women, all single, in their thirties, well-educated, attractive, socially capable with well-paid, interesting careers. Some had never married; others were divorced. All wanted to marry but wanted "an equal."

"The fact is," said one of the women at the table, "if we want to go out, we have to date down."

"What happened," said another "is when we were busy going to university and getting our careers going, other women were busy snagging the men."

Were these women indeed caught in some kind of twilight zone? Or could they still hope to marry? Yes — if they were willing to look at some of their assumptions and attitudes. It seemed to me all of these women were new women on the outside, but very traditional on the inside.

What would happen, I wondered, if they did what men for centuries have done? What would happen if they did (horrors) date down?

Why must a woman with a top-notch career have a man with an equal or better career? Does he have to be a CEO with a BMW? Could he not earn less and even be, dare I say it, blue collar? Could it be that the new woman is still essentially scared of not having someone to show her the way? That she's not really that independent? That she still defines herself by the status of the man she marries? We can, I believe, have our own status, power, finances. We can overcome the evolutionary programing that has produced instinctive behavior but which is no longer necessary for a satisfying and sustainable relationship.

Or could it be perhaps, that she's really just interested in a carbon copy of herself, except one in trousers? Is she only secure in familiar circles, eating the same kinds of foods and believing in the same things? One woman even told me that if a man wouldn't eat sushi, she couldn't stand that and wouldn't want him. Another told me she'd only date a Pisces.

And then how do we define intelligence or even status for that matter? Is it really more "intelligent" to be presenting a case in court than working in construction?

Is it more intelligent to be running a company or running a factory? What's better: a self-absorbed lawyer or a park maintenance man who makes you laugh?

I asked the women what "interesting" and "exciting" meant. It meant a man who liked to do the things they do. Obviously some shared interests are a good idea. But this can be taken too far. The best marriages seem to involve two people whose lives intertwine but who maintain their individuality.

As well, people, especially women, expect far more from a relationship than they once did. And sometimes it's beyond the capability of the opposite sex to deliver those things.

I'm not suggesting that women should seek men with widely dissimilar incomes, education, and belief systems. I am suggesting, however, that caring, loving men may be eliminated if women select by a set of standards that are meaningless for successful relationships.

It's often the woman who looks for perfection who ends up with a rat. Perhaps it's because rats often look perfect — strong, yet sensitive, heroic, yet tender, with energy for both romance and achievement in career.

How does the rat accomplish this miraculous feat? By being that way when she sees him, which isn't that often. And by not doing the other things that go with a relationship like arriving on time, being loyal, delivering on a promise, and being considerate over the long haul. A rat spins the illusion of giving everything without giving anything at all.

The fact is there are no perfect men or women. But there are a lots of really solid single people out there. People's best qualities usually reveal themselves over time. Men and women with flash may be intriguing at first, but usually they can't sustain emotional attachment. And men and women who seem too good to be true, usually are. (More about emotional exploiters in chapter 17.)

So think carefully what your type is and whether it makes sense. Screen people into your life rather than out of it. Don't eliminate people out of hand because they're too short, too tall, too blue-collar, too white-collar. Every single person you see is a potential mate.

Do you have unrealistic expectations? Many men of 50 want a woman under 35. But women under 35 are not usually interested in a man 50 or over. And today's woman in her forties often looks a lot better that her age sounds.

Someone called it the "I'm okay, you'd better be perfect" syndrome. She's five-foot four and wants a man over six feet. She's got a nowhere job, but is looking for the head of a corporation.

Over and over again men tell me that women overlook the nice guys. Here's how one reader put it:

Dear Kathy:

I have tried answering companion ads but rarely get a response because the writer has set her sights too high. I am not a tall, dark, slim, and handsome professional with a condo at a ski resort, an expensive car, a boat, and able to whisk you off for romantic weekends in the sun.

I'm an average looking guy with a receding hairline and a bit overweight and in good health who has a very enjoyable and fulfilling career but not a lot of extra income.

Anonymous

Both sexes need to get real. Many of the singles who stay that way won't admit it but they're looking for someone more attractive than they are. How many times have you overheard a guy with extra large love handles and an equally large bald spot say of his last night's date, "she's a bit on the heavy side" or "she looks her age." Men are notorious for seeing themselves as young and handsome and while thinking another guy or a woman are much older and less attractive when in fact they're pretty much the same. It's wonderful that such a man has such high self-esteem, but it's just unfortunate for him (and others) that he can't be more realistic.

Give up your fantasies and go for a person with whom you could be happy.

What qualities do you want?

To help you become clear about what kind of man or woman you want, write down 20 qualities you want him or her to have. Then think about the qualities you are seeking. Rank them in importance. Keep this list for when you meet someone. At that time, you can use questions, such as the following, as a guide:

- Do we have the same or similar values? (Remember, about the only thing that opposites attract is divorce.)
- Are our lifestyles compatible?
- Do either of us have any fatal flaws? Is this a fatal attraction?
- Can he or she give me enough of what I need? (Everyone has differing needs for closeness and distance. Usually people

brought up in closely knit families with other siblings, and where everything is shared, prefer a great amount of closeness. But among those raised in homes where many personal things were not discussed, where separateness was honored, or perhaps where that person was an only child, the need for distance may be greater. Problems can occur when one partner naturally needs more closeness and the other needs more distance.)

- Is he or she as interested and committed to this relationship as I am?

Fatal attractions

In more detail, lets look first at fatal flaws, fatal attractions. If the person drinks too much, you need to know now that this is a huge problem and it will likely get worse. It's virtually impossible to have a happy, fulfilling relationship with an alcoholic. The bottle will always be a better lover than you are. Most experts agree that the family of an alcoholic suffers more than the alcoholic.

The same goes for any of the other addictions — to drugs, other women, gambling, work. Eventually, addictions destroy relationships, no matter how much you love him or her or how many relationship skills you have.

Ask yourself whether you have a pattern of selecting partners who are bad for you in some way. Think about the men or the women you have been involved with. What were these relationships like and what ended them? Were any of these people alcoholics, still attached, womanizers, flirts, gold diggers, drug addicts, or gamblers?

Some women, and even some men, have such a bad track record in choosing partners that I figure researchers should be able to come up with a "jerkaderm patch" to help them first detect jerks and then resist them.

I've had men tell me that women must like to get hurt. "Go down to the [pub] any night of the week," one man said to me at a house party. "A guy slaps the woman around, calls her a bitch, and tells her to get lost. What does she do? She's all over him the next night. I tell you some women like to be treated like a piece of..."

I really don't believe women like to get hurt or that they consciously pick jerks. But some women, just the same, have a pattern of picking men who, at some level, feel familiar; they choose men that are like their fathers. In some emotional way the offhand or abusive man fits her original template of what a man should be.

If dad was rarely there for her, if he was often critical, controlling, non-supportive, or if he was commonly abusive, then as an adult she is often magnetically attracted to this type.

But not always. Some women consciously pick men unlike their dads. But many don't.

Read the following letter and see if you can spot a pattern:

Dear Kathy:

I'm a divorcee, 29, with two children. I got out of a mentally abusive nine-year relationship about two-and-a-half years ago. Just when I thought there was no man on earth who would interest me, along came one.

M. is 27, never married, and has no children. Before I met him he had a cocaine habit, which almost killed him. He crashed on a motorcycle while under the influence.

He's been clean for about a year. I do not do drugs or drink. I met him when I was moving out of a place where I didn't feel safe. M. was drinking and decided to moon me. I thought it was really funny he had the guts to do that. It was like it was meant to be.

I was in my new house about a week when I realized he had moved across the road from me again. He came over and ended up sleeping with me. I didn't mind because nothing happened that night. He was a perfect gentleman. Then he was supposed to come back over but for three nights he didn't. A friend from Calgary had come by to visit and she brought some cocaine. He had moved away from Calgary to get away from this crowd but they were moving here to find him again.

We saw each other again and again and talked about how much we cared for each other. Then, three months ago, he said he was going to do laundry and he disappeared. I found out he went home to Calgary.

I can't forget him. Is this situation hopeless or should I keep hoping? I've never had a guy tell me he cares for me and then leave town suddenly. I have this gut feeling he's not gone out of my life forever. What can I do to show him

*how much he means to me and how much I want him to
be a part of my life if he wants to be?*

Desperate

I suggested to this woman that she wake up. "You need this cocaine addict like you needed the nine-year, mentally abusive relationship or the home you didn't feel safe in," I replied.

"You've got a pattern of choosing people and situations that are bad for you. Start looking at that pattern. Don't write to this guy and resist him if he shows up. Then set up an appointment with a counselor."

I'm quite sure my advice went unheeded. Many people have these dysfunctional patterns. It seems that, once the bait is set, it takes just the slightest reward to keep a woman (and sometimes a man) hooked.

He calls for a date a whole month after romancing her off her feet and into bed. Rather than hang up on him as most women might, she's grateful he called at all. She instantly forgets all the bad stuff, she thinks about the few times he gives her something — and commonly she mistakes sex for love.

What is happening here? Psychologists have found that inconsistent reward or partial reinforcement can be more effective than consistent rewards to keep a person hooked. The person has learned to expect a resumption of the reward.

Psychologists Carl Hindy and Conrad Schwarz describe this phenomenon in their book, *If This is Love, Why Do I Feel So Insecure?* They describe an experiment in which three groups of puppies were given three distinct forms of treatment. One group got consistent affection, the second got consistent coldness and rejection, and the third group of puppies were sometimes treated kindly and sometimes coldly.

It was the third group of puppies that kept chasing after the experimenter, seeking his approval and affection. They were more attached to him and dependent on him than the puppies which were consistently rewarded or consistently punished.

"For the anxiously attached lover, positive feedback alternates with negative feedback (the man's inattention, neglect, disapproval, rejection, or greater interest in others). This is the pattern of reward and punishment that binds a person into an anxious romantic attachment."

Sadly, women who hang on to neglectful or abusive relationships or go back for more off-hand treatment have their energy and their productivity sapped. These are not women who reach their potential.

Short of a jerkaderm patch, these women need to develop some insight into their behavior (therapy is a good idea), learn to love themselves a great deal more, seek out a support group such as Women who Love Too Much, and discipline themselves so as to avoid destructive attractions.

But when I wrote about this in my column, I had men write me to say that they, too, sometimes need a jerkaderm patch. Said one man: "It took me six months of hard work in Adult Children of Alcoholics to realize I was in a relationship for all the wrong reasons."

Differences vs. similarities

Enough about fatal attractions. Are you ignoring other important incompatibilities? Are you dating someone who works halfway across the country? Very few couples can survive a long-distance relationship for many years. Most couples want steady intimacy. Still, long-distance relationships may suit a small minority of couples who lack intimacy skills and actually fear intimacy. One weekend a month is enough for them.

Is there a huge age difference, say 25 to 30 years? This may be okay now, but think about later when she's 50 and he's 75. She may be ready to travel or conquer the world. He may be ready for the old folks home.

Do you come from different sides of the track, very different religious or cultural backgrounds, widely different education levels? Certainly you don't need to be the same or agree on everything. That would be boring. But too many strong differences are a time bomb unless you both have extremely well-developed conflict resolution skills. Few people do.

Do you want children, while he or she doesn't or vice versa? Is he or she emotionally aloof, uncommunicative, and does that bother you? If you've been married before, does he or she resent or not get along with your kids? Don't minimize this problem. It can be deadly.

Does the person you're dating have a terrible temper? A short fuse should be a red flag. People who do not know how to deal with their anger, who fly off the handle, are bad news. Often marriage makes them worse. You don't want to walk right into a battering situation.

Is he or she still in love with a previous lover or mate? Are you not really sexually attracted to this man or woman you're dating? Sure, the sexual and romantic high of the infatuation stage will eventually wane, but it should be there initially and you should be able to say that you find your mate attractive and you enjoy sexual intimacy with him or her. If you can't say that, reconsider.

Is he or she a health nut while you're a couch potato, or vice versa? Eventually you may really resent each other. How does this person treat other people? Does that bother you? How does he or she spend money or save it?

If any of these areas are problematic, it's important you resolve them *now*, before you invest any more time in dating this person. Ignoring them, hoping they'll go away, or even thinking your love will change those things is unrealistic.

People who will be compatible over the long term have a strong central similarity, but are able to maintain their individuality. Differences give the relationship its variety, challenge, and opportunity for growth. But the differences should not be so fundamental as to threaten each other's integrity.

It's also crucial you agree on this: do you want a traditional relationship or an egalitarian one? If there's a mismatch here, it spells trouble.

Finally, ask yourself if the person you're dating is interested in a long-term relationship or marriage, as presumably you are, or is he or she in it for a good time, not a long time. If you hang in with someone who has a different level of commitment, you'll discover a growing imbalance of power and your life will become increasingly out of control. You will not be happy much of the time.

Two people must want a relationship more or less equally. They've got to want to work at it equally. Don't buy into some of those so-called relationship and personal growth organizations put on by unqualified people who are making big bucks telling women they are 100% responsible for good relationships. That simply isn't true and, indeed, it's a very dangerous idea.

Myths about mate selection

One of the problems in selecting a mate is that we've grown up on things Hollywood has taught us to believe about relationships. Dr.

Jeffry Larson at the University of Florida has identified the following unrealistic beliefs about mate selection.

First of all, there is no evidence to support the myth that there is a one-and-only right person in the world for each person to marry. Indeed, there are many you could be happily married to. This myth tends to foster a passiveness about finding a partner. When you think that one person will eventually come along, there is no pressure to date actively and get to know others more intimately.

A second myth is that you should wait to find the perfect person to marry. The fact is — no one is perfect. People who believe in the perfect person don't get to know their dates and relate to them, but rather evaluate and rate them prematurely. They develop a pattern of multiple short-term relationships. And, anyway, people change over time. The person who appeared perfect at the beginning will inevitably appear imperfect later. Pick people for qualities most important to you and compromise about the rest.

A third myth — that you should feel totally competent as a future spouse before deciding to marry — is also faulty. Few individuals ever feel totally competent to be a husband or a wife. Successful marriages require adjustments, cooperation, and effort by two people, not perfection in one or both.

Larson says some people believe they should prove their relationship will work before getting married. What if you prove it for now, but either of you changes in the future? The fact is, future stresses, crises, and challenges to a relationship cannot be accurately predicted. The most you can do is to feel comfortable. With trust, you should be able to adjust to each other over time and solve marital problems as they arise.

Another myth is that a person can be happy with anyone if he or she tries hard enough. It's not true, and you may end up picking almost anybody because you believe that with enough effort, it will work. Some people are simply poor marriage risks. This includes the addict (to drugs, alcohol, sex, food, or work) who is not in recovery. It also includes someone who is violent or emotionally abusive, a person under 20, someone who is sexually unresponsive, and someone with major religious differences.

Some believe you can change a person after marriage. You can't. It takes two mature and well-adjusted individuals to make a marriage work. So be reasonably sensitive and selective in the choice of a mate.

A prospective mate should be someone who is willing to give their fair share, to compromise, and to be sensitive to equity in the relationship.

Then there are those who believe being in love is sufficient reason to marry — that love is enough. Attraction and passion are great. But they won't sustain marriage.

Romantic love may actually be a strong sex drive, a flight from loneliness, a neurotic attachment (as in the case of an overadequate partner married to an underadequate partner), or an excuse for domination and control.

Although romantic love is important, especially in the early stage of a relationship, other factors are more important in marital satisfaction. Marital success is based on factors including similarity of values, similarity of backgrounds, age at marriage, readiness for marriage, realistic expectations, and happy childhoods.

Let's deal with the argument that a person should choose someone to marry whose personal characteristics are opposite from their own. Sure, opposites often attract! But marrying someone whose traits are significantly different usually leads to conflict and dissatisfaction. Eventually you'll want to change that person to be more like you. That is unless you truly learn to appreciate the person's differences and accept them totally. Unless you can, you should choose someone to marry whose personal characteristics are similar to your own.

Finally, some people believe that choosing a mate should be easy and a matter of chance. If it's accidental, these people maintain the individual has no responsibility if the relationship should fail, or for taking action to help the relationship flourish.

Choosing a mate should be carefully thought out.

To recap, make a list of the qualities you really value in a mate. These will help you to recognize what you want when you meet him or her. And remember that while opposites often attract, the things you immediately like about that person may eventually become irritating. So you'll need to be similar in many important ways. Either that or have a Ph.D. in handling conflict constructively and negotiating.

Give up the idea you can change someone or mold him or her into your perfect partner. You can't. What you see is what you get.

And think about what stage of life you're at and what stage the other person's at. Do they mesh?

Learn to be careful about the important things in your choices, but not picky about superficialities. Get real. And watch for any unhealthy patterns. Try to avoid making the same mistakes by discovering what it is within yourself that creates those faulty choices.

I hope these suggestions will prevent you from going down the aisle wearing rose-colored glasses, only to end up in family court some years later.

8

The single mingle

So you know the Texas Line Dance. You're pretty good at Karaoke. And you know your breath is minty fresh... but you still don't have a date. What you need to learn is the Single Mingle.

I've watched hundreds of attractive singles blow opportunities to meet each other, simply because they neglect to make the first move and talk to each other.

If you're the type who enters a room full of strangers and wishes for instant death, or someone who never leaves the safety of your TV, you need to learn how to mingle. Sometimes it's just a matter of doing things differently. That's the way it happened for Leila and Brian.

Leila, 32, had been separated a year, going to university, working full time, and raising her daughter when she noticed an ad in *The Province* newspaper for a singles show I was hosting. At that point she didn't see having a man in her life. She was too busy and enjoying single life. "But I felt like some fun and this show looked good," Leila recalls.

Brian, 37, of Kelowna, also saw the ad at about the same time. "Hey, I need some of those seminars and I need to get away," Brian recalls telling himself. "I was quite shy about asking someone for a date." So he was attracted to two seminars on the subjects of shyness and flirting.

Leila lined up a girlfriend to go to the show with her. Brian lined up a hotel room in Vancouver.

"It was at the Friday night mixer," Leila remembers. "I was really nervous. I was amazed, however, at the cross-section of ages. There were kids in their twenties to people in their sixties. Hey, I thought, this is really great. People from all walks of life. I was people-watching like crazy. A couple of men approached me and I talked to them but nothing further.

"Then, all of a sudden, Brian walked by. What a wonderful face, I thought. He has these sparkly, dancing, mischievous eyes. There's just something about him."

Brian says he walked by, noticed Leila, but couldn't think of anything to say. Then he heard someone use the word "buzzwords" and he just started talking to Leila and her group, giving some more examples of buzzwords.

Says Leila: "We all started talking, then just Brian and I. He explained the seminar he had just been in. He was easy to talk to. We found similarities. He loves to cook; I love to cook. He reminds me of my father, who's a contractor. Brian's really handy that way.

"After talking for an hour and a half, he said, 'I guess we should mingle some more.' I thought, oh great, that'll be it. Then Brian came back and I thought if I let this one go, it'll be a mistake.

"I needed to find a washroom and he escorted me there. He asked for my phone number. Then a group of us, including him, went up to The Roof [of the hotel where the singles show was held] and we kept talking."

Leila and a girlfriend offered to drive Brian back to his hotel. He called her the next day to meet at the singles show again and go to dinner.

Brian says he and Leila seemed to get along really well right from the start. Friends told Leila they were obviously smitten and surely would end up together.

"Actually, he was not what I had ever dated. Normally it was fair-haired ones. He was dark-haired and balding. But when he took my hand I just melted. He is very kind, very honest, with no pretense. He made me feel special."

That night they talked until 3 a.m. On Sunday, he had dinner with Leila and her daughter before going home to Kelowna. A week later, on Valentine's Day, he left a message on her answering machine: "Will you be my Valentine?"

Later, there was another visit to the coast. "It was a weekend that turned into a week," says Brian. "I had a very good idea she might be the one. Actually I knew I was dead meat by Tuesday night when we went for a walk." The pair have been dating ever since and plan to marry.

Leila and Brian's story tells us a lot about successful connecting. Both of them took risks: Brian got out of his rut and booked a hotel room. Leila decided to chance going to the show. Brian seized the moment when he overhead the term "buzzwords" and started talking with Leila. Leila realized it would be a mistake to let this one go.

Both were risk takers. They hadn't always been. But this time they were, and now they're together. People who risk nothing may avoid some embarrassment, even some pain, but they lose out because they don't really get to live and grow.

As a reporter who's had to go to countless gatherings over the years, I've had to learn how to mingle and take some social risks. Not all reporters are as hard-boiled or nervy as you might imagine. Many of us are quite shy. Mingle-phobic in fact.

The important thing to remember is, whether you're at the fitness center, seminar, convention, or party, strive to meet as many people as possible. The more people you get to know, the more chances your life will open up... and one of them just might have a brother or sister who's a hot babe. Of course, you can always go back for another conversation with someone you've just met and to whom you're attracted.

So how do you start? First you psyche yourself up. As you stand frozen against the wall in a room full of people you don't know, pretend that you're self-assured even if it's hard to do so. Try this, even for ten minutes, and you will begin to actually feel that way. Breathe in deeply. I used to think taking a deep breath couldn't possibly help allay my terror. But I tried it in desperation and found it most helpful. Whenever I go on TV or radio, I start shaking five minutes before I'm on. Then it gets worse. My top lip sticks to my teeth and may even start to twitch, which is excruciatingly embarrassing if the camera is rolling in for a close-up. But several really deep breaths definitely do calm me down and then once the first 30 seconds have passed, I'm okay.

At a gathering, you can use several tricks of the mind to feel less awkward. You can pretend everyone else there is naked, except for you. A lot of people use this one. Or you can pretend you're invisible. I pretend I'm with a friend, but he or she is just not with me at the moment. That works really well.

Okay, you're ready to begin. So who do you approach?

Your first mingling possibility should be someone who looks a little lost too and will be relieved to talk with someone. Be honest: "Excuse me. I don't know anyone here. My name is.... Are you enjoying this?"

A little more difficult but also good is to move quietly up to a group of people, as Brian did when he heard the group talking about "buzzwords." Listen carefully to all that's being said. Then contribute to the conversation as if you had been there all along.

Or try flattery: "Hi, I've been admiring your earrings. Where did you get them?" or, "Hi, you people seem to be having a great time. What's the topic?"

Here are some more openers:

"Hi. What's your connection to the party?"

"I just can't believe how lovely it is here, can you?"

"Excuse me, but what is that deliciously sinful-looking stuff you're eating?"

You've made the opening line and if the person isn't a complete nerd, he or she will respond. But what do you say now? Here are a few conversational follow-ups:

"Did you come here directly from work?" (This gives you an opportunity to learn what the person does for a living and what he or she might then be interested in discussing. It also gives you an opportunity to share what work you do.)

"Did you hear on the news that...(something that has just happened or something big that's been going on for a while)?"

"I love watching people. How about you?"

"The energy is really good at this party. How do you know the hostess?"

"You know, you remind me of a very good friend of mine."

"Isn't this a nice area?"

"Isn't the rock in the fireplace interesting."

"I wish we didn't have to yell."

"Man, this place is so crowded. Have you been able to find a chair anywhere?"

"Have you talked to that person over there? She and I were just talking about..."

"See that man over by the door? Do you know who he is? I think I've met him somewhere, but I can't remember."

"Are you having a good time?"

Or coyly, "We've got to stop meeting like this."

If you're at a party or function connected to work, it's okay to talk shop. But if you're in a job you want to keep, avoid gossiping, whining about your boss, or drinking too much.

Make a point of talking with people who may be from another department. "Have you taken any holidays this year?" People love to talk about their plans for a vacation. They often love to talk about their kids, if they have kids. The economy is another good topic, especially how it's affecting your work. Ask about a specific project. Talk about sports, movies, books, or new restaurants.

There are several other ways to meet someone you particularly want to meet. Use the old accidentally-on-purpose bumping in to him or her routine. I know a couple who met this way and are now married.

And eye contact is very important. Look straight at anyone who is speaking to you. Use the time when you are speaking to look away and see what else is going on.

But what if you get stuck with a bore or a boor, a drunk or a talkaholic, a lecher or a joker who isn't funny or who doesn't know when to stop? Or what if it's someone who wants you to get them a job (or in my case, some free publicity)? You can take several exits:

"Gotta go, I promised to help the hostess." "Excuse me, I need to use the washroom." "Excuse me, I must find my friend."

Other exits include: "Oh, I have to make a phone call." "Excuse me, I just spotted my boss." "Oh no! My wallet (purse)!" "I'm not feeling well. Please excuse me."

If you're at a gathering, bring something others can enjoy too — like a pitcher of margaritas, or a plate of fortune cookies, or whatever is appropriate for the occasion. You can meet people as you move around serving them. And with the fortune cookies, the sayings, proverbs, or jokes inside are a great ice breaker. And how about writing your phone number on the cookie meant for the person of your dreams?

A variation of offering food around the room, is to offer to get something for someone from the buffet or the bar. Also make use of the time you are in line there to talk to people about the party, the food, the ambience, the hostess or host, whatever.

Remember, *people love to talk about themselves.* It helps a lot in mingling if you truly are interested in people. Ask questions, not too personal at first. Get good at asking questions and listening. Be interested in other people's lives and opinions. And if you like truly interesting conversations, don't avoid politics and religion. But be respectful of other people's different views.

If you discover a possibility of meeting that special someone, after awhile you may try some romantic opening lines: "You have the most extraordinary complexion." "I really like your smile (energy)." "Did anyone ever tell you you are pretty (handsome)?" "Do you want to go for a quiet coffee so we can talk?"

Remember, a mingling opportunity doesn't have to be a party. One of the best places to mingle is in a line up — store checkout lines, ticket lines, restaurant lines, or lines at the bank or the movies.

"How do the reviewers rate this movie (restaurant)?" "This better be worth it!" "The sign says five minutes. I think they left off a zero."

Finally, realize everyone feels afraid to initiate a connection. But with practice it gets easier. Sooner or later it becomes a pleasant task giving you an opportunity to meet new people with charm and confidence.

Take small steps at first. Smile at people you don't know on the street. Chat at the bus stop. Then build up to go to a bigger gathering. You don't have to be the life of the party to start with. Just be there, and pat yourself on the back for how far you've come.

9
Flirting and other smooth moves

I was one of three guests on a radio show recently. The other two guests were young women, both of whom had only recently entered into serious relationships after months of not being involved.

Chrissi said one of the reasons she'd been single for so long was that, over and over again, she'd meet a man, they'd have a good conversation, he seemed to be interested in her, *but he just didn't ask her out!*

Countless women tell me this and I've had it happen to me. There's an initial connection but no follow-through and consequently no relationship.

A couple of days after that radio show, a good friend of mine — a single father of four — told me about a "girl" of 32 taking a class he's in. He's been single for five years, mainly because he just hasn't found any women in his small town who are single and appealing to him.

But he found this one attractive and felt there could be something special between them. "I have a feeling she might be interested in me," he confided. "I'm probably imagining it. I talk to her a lot. Last time when I was out of the classroom I came back to find she had my jacket on. She said she was cold. But it seemed like a thing someone wouldn't do if we were strangers."

Of course it wasn't. The woman was interested. I told him about Chrissi's comments. His response: "I'd almost rather dodge a machine gun than ask a woman for a date. I guess I just need to find the courage."

Darn right he does!

I suggested he ask questions that will increasingly put their relationship on a more personal footing. I suggested he should find out why she moved recently from Ontario and how she became interested in working in construction. She'd given him all these openings to get to know her better, but he had not seized on one of them!

It's clear many, many men need to develop their social skills and realize that most women still expect the man to at least make some of the moves.

Is it okay for a woman to make the first move?

As well, more women need to overcome their reluctance to initiate a connection. In a recent letter to my column, "Marie" asked me, "Is it okay for women to make the first move? Or is it the man's prerogative?"

That question drew many response from readers, both male and female:

- "Should a woman make the first move?" wrote one man. "Absolutely! I'm hesitant for these reasons. I've just left a long relationship and am out of touch at asking for a date. I'm new here and find it tough to meet people. I'm so turned off by leeches preying on women and I fear, by approaching an attractive female, I might be labelled a leech. If a guy like me is out there and you'd like to say 'hello,' please do."

- "If a woman will let me know she is interested, I appreciate and welcome it. Remember, we guys can't read your minds..."

- "I love women to make the first move. Use the direct approach, like 'Maybe we should have lunch or coffee sometime.'"

- "I'm 26, a female, and have been seeing a guy for five months. I pursued him — totally. This is the 1990s. You want something, you go get it — no matter what it is — job, goal, dream, friend, lover. Make it reality. Like the saying goes, You snooze, you lose."

- "I have been single for about three years and have dated about 20 men. I've found most men like women to take the initiative. I think a lot of men are quite confused about their roles, since our society has changed so drastically in the last 20 years. As to being rejected, it's not the end of the world. The reason you've been turned down may have nothing to do with you personally. It could be the wrong time for him."

- "I'm a single male, 41. Often I find women looking and smiling at me, appearing to want to speak, but not doing so. Hindsight tells me I could have made a move, but often the chance comes by and is lost so quickly. I think it would be a refreshing change to be approached by an interested female."

- "As a 60-year-old father of two daughters, I tell them a young man is not only unskilled, but scared. He would accept ten more zits on his face than face the dreaded rejection. To solve the dilemma and anguish my two daughters had, I tried to tell them about men, that they are shy too and will procrastinate by saying, 'Why would a lovely girl like her want to go out with a guy like me?'"

So it's clear men and women must act on these moments. Indeed, a global survey of women by Harlequin Enterprises, publishers of Harlequin romance novels, found 79% of American women and 82% of Canadian women said it is okay to ask men out on dates.

One reader who works in a store asked me how she could let a regular customer know she's interested: "Where I come from, a girl should not run around telling guys her feelings because guys would think she is a slut and cheap. They would treat her not as nice as they would treat someone who they think is hard to get. How would I approach him so he would respect me and not think I'm cheap?"

I suggested there's nothing cheap about a woman letting a man know she finds him attractive. By showing interest in him, she would not be saying, "Take me, I'm yours," but rather, "I'd like to know more about you so I can determine whether or not I'd like to spend some time with you."

She may still be hard to get — since presumably she's after a sustainable relationship. Sustainable relationships are usually built slowly on emotional, intellectual, and spiritual compatibility, as well as physical urges.

I suggested she show some interest in his life and his activities when he's at the store. At the same time, she could reveal something of her own life and interests. If she found some common ground or mutual interest, she may then be able to direct the conversation to something they could do together: "Would you like to join me next week at the (gym, movie, whatever)?"

The man would likely be relieved, since he's probably been trying to think of a way to invite her out. What I'm suggesting is that single people need not be aggressive, but social.

I also suggested, "Flirt, just a little. There's nothing wrong with flirting. It's an age-old art, involving subtle eye contact and body language, which lets the other know his or her advances may be welcomed. Eventually, if he's interested, he'll pick up on your signals. If he doesn't, assume he's not interested or already attached."

How to flirt

How do you flirt? To some people it just comes naturally. To others it doesn't. Children seem to flirt naturally, just as they dance, naturally. It seems to be inborn. So I suspect those who don't know how to flirt (and don't dance) have somehow had it knocked out of them, perhaps by a misguided parent or teacher. And that's a shame.

There is nothing wrong with flirting — with being sexual, emotional, physical, and intellectual all at the same time. There is nothing wrong with enjoying our natural attributes and abilities. Flirting is just one of those ways we express ourselves.

Here's how one male reader described those first moments when he is attracted to someone:

"I first notice the eyes and face. If eye contact is made, I look again at the eyes, the face, taking in the picture above the shoulders. Hair style, skin tone, mouth. Physical stature comes next. The whole package right down to her feet. This happens in two or three seconds. [Then], I again catch her eyes and have her watch me give her an appreciative once over. An eye flutter or hidden smile will acknowledge my attention.

"Depending on circumstance, I will either look away and go about my business with a smile, or I may make further eye contact — suggesting that I am approachable or asking through the eyes — 'are you approachable?' Once initial mutual attraction is established, then voice contact is made.

"Attraction is reinforced by coyness and unspoken mutual interest. Or by friendly flirting and innuendoes. And touching. The electricity in the air keeps us together, at that time. The sparks that fly with a touch suggest future involvement."

It's universal

The man above has accurately described the mating dance. Indeed, when it comes to courtship, everyone, across all human societies, follows the same unwritten rules of flirting, body language, and courtship.

German ethologist Irenaus Eibl-Eibesfeldt discovered a universal pattern of female flirting by secretly filming flirting behavior in Samoa, Papua New Guinea, France, Japan, parts of Africa, and Amazonia. He discovered that women around the world use the same signals to let men know they're interested.

Anthropologist Dr. Helen Fisher describes the ethologist's findings in her book, *The Anatomy of Love*. "First, the woman smiles at her admirer and lifts her eyebrows in a swift, jerky motion as she opens her eyes wide to gaze at him. Then she drops her eyelids, tilts her head down and to the side, and looks away. Frequently she also covers her face with her hands, giggling nervously as she retreats behind her palms. This sequential flirting gesture is so distinctive that Eibl-Eibesfeldt is convinced it is innate, a human female courtship ploy that evolved eons ago to signal sexual interest."

Dr. Fisher says other gambits people use also come from our primeval past. "The coy look is a gesture in which a woman cocks her head and looks up shyly at her suitor...Animals frequently toss their heads in order to solicit attention. Courting women do it regularly; they raise their shoulders, arch their backs, and toss their locks in a single sweeping motion."

Men, too, speak the same body language everywhere — stretching, thrusting out their chests, swaggering, swinging from side to side, and preening to attract women, says Dr. Fisher.

"Men also employ courting tactics similar to those seen in other species. Have you ever walked into the boss's office and seen him leaning back in his chair, hands clasped behind his head, elbows high, and chest thrust out? Perhaps he has come from behind his desk, walked up to you, smiled, arched his back, and thrust his upper body in your direction? If so, watch out. He may be subconsciously announcing his dominance over you. If you are a woman, he may be courting you instead."

According to Fisher, the chest thrust is a basic postural message used by men and dominant creatures across the animal kingdom — head erect, stomach sucked in, and chest inflated. "It's not uncommon to see men and women swell and shrink in order to signal importance, defenselessness, and approachability."

This is why police instruct women to carry themselves confidently, tall, and boldly when walking alone. The message then is not one of approachability. It's one of strength and power.

Eye contact

Dr. Fisher says the gaze is the most striking human courting ploy. "In Western cultures, where eye contact between the sexes is permitted, men and women often stare intently at a potential mate for about two to three seconds during which their pupils may dilate — a sign of extreme interest. Then the starter drops his or her eyelids and looks away.

"Eye contact seems to have an immediate effect. The gaze triggers a primitive part of the human brain, calling forth one of two basic emotions — approach or retreat. You cannot ignore the eyes of another fixed on you; you must respond. You may smile and start conversation. You may look away and edge toward the door. But first you will probably tug at an ear lobe, adjust your sweater, yawn, fidget with your eyeglasses, or perform some other meaningless movement — a displacement gesture — to alleviate anxiety while you make up your mind how to acknowledge this invitation, whether to flee the premises or stay and play the courting game.

"Perhaps it is the eye — not the heart, the genitals, or the brain — that is the initial organ of romance, for the gaze (or stare) often triggers the human smile."

And for those of you who wonder whether a man or woman is single and available, what he or she does with the eyes is a pretty good indication of interest. If he or she returns your gaze, after looking away, and if he or she smiles, there's some attraction and message of availability. One word of caution, however: he or she may be available, but may not be single. That's something you'll need to determine in conversation or if the relationship develops. More about that in a later chapter. For now, we'll assume he or she is single.

Smiling

Dr. Fisher says there are 18 different types of human smiles. The upper smile is used in friendly contacts, including flirting. In this smile, she says, you expose your upper teeth and combine this with a momentary eyebrow flash.

But it's the open smile, in which the lips are completely drawn back and both upper and lower teeth are fully exposed, that is used to pick up one another.

Couple this with the sequential flirt, the coy look, the head toss, the chest thrust, or the gaze — and the intentions are sexual.

With their exaggerated antics and pickup lines, it may seem that men are taking the lead. But cross-cultural studies show it's usually women who initiate connections with the opposite sex, perhaps by walking up to the male or taking a seat beside him. Perhaps this has been the problem for Chrissi and all the other women who say "he seemed interested but then he didn't ask me out." Perhaps people are missing their cues and need to do what once came naturally.

Here's what biologist Dr. Timothy Perper found in his studies of the American singles bar scene — the subject of his book *Sex Signals: The Biology of Love.*

With subtle but deliberate cues — smiling, making eye contact, or shifting position — women started two-thirds of the bar pickups that Perper observed. And the women he later interviewed were quite conscious of having coaxed a potential lover into conversation, touching him carefully here or there, enticing him ever forward with coquettish looks, questions, compliments, and jokes.

But it's clear the man must respond to the woman's overtures if the liaison is to proceed.

Let's look at the process from the beginning.

Attracting attention

Each sex finds a place and then begins to attract attention to themselves. Men tend to pitch and roll their shoulders, stretch, stand tall, and shift from one foot to another in a swaying motion. They exaggerate their body movements. They laugh loud enough to attract a crowd. They may swagger. They adjust their clothes, tug their chins, or perform other movements that diffuse nervous energy and keep the body moving.

Older men may use different things, like expensive jewelry and clothing that spell success.

Young women also use smiling, gazing, shifting, swaying, preening, stretching, moving to draw attention to themselves. They also twist their curls, tilt their heads, look up coyly, giggle, raise their eyebrows, flick their tongues, lick their upper lips, blush, and hide their faces to say they're there.

Some also strut. And with their high-heels, eyes, brows, lips, and their swaying, they signal their approachability to men.

Voice

When eyes meet eyes, one or the other acknowledges with a smile or body shift and they'll move into talking range. They'll engage each other in somewhat meaningless conversation, starting with an ice breaker like "How's the food?" or "Where did you get the boots?" It's the tone and inflection that are most important.

As Fisher writes, "a high-pitched, gentle, mellifluous 'hello' is often a sign of sexual interest, whereas a clipped, low, matter-of-fact 'hi' rarely leads to love. If a prospective mate laughs somewhat more than the situation calls for, she or he is probably flirting too."

A lot about each other can be learned just from the sound of the other's voice — background, education, and other subtle things which may attract or repel. The mating dance may be killed right then if the two do not like what they hear.

Touch

But if they do, then the next step is touching. This begins with intention cues such as leaning forward, resting one's arm toward the other's on the table, moving one's foot closer if both are standing, or stroking one's own arm or face as if to stroke the other's. Cues must be returned if the encounter is to progress. If, for example, he remains impassive or refuses to turn his shoulders toward her, the ritual will stall and she will likely move elsewhere.

But if moves are reciprocated, the flirting progresses until the climax — when one person touches the other on the shoulder, the forearm, the wrist, or some other socially available body part. Normally the woman touches first, grazing her hand along her suitor's body in the most casual but calculated manner.

According to Dr. Fisher, "the receiver notices this message instantly. If he flinches, the pickup is over. If he withdraws, even barely, the sender may never try to touch again. If he ignores the overture, she may touch once more. But if he leans toward her, smiles, or returns the gesture with his own deliberate touch, they have surmounted a major barrier well known in the animal community.

"If our pair continue to talk and touch — bobbing, tilting, gazing, smiling, swaying, flirting — they usually achieve the last stage of the courtship ritual: total body synchrony. They pivot or swivel until their shoulders become aligned, their bodies face-to-face. After a while they begin to move in tandem. When he lifts his drink, she lifts hers. In time they mirror each other more and more. When he crosses his legs, she crosses hers; as he leans left, she leans left...they move in perfect rhythm as they gaze deeply into each other's eyes. Couples that reach total body synchrony often leave the bar together."

Dr. Fisher says people woo each other slowly and cautiously. At each stage, the responses must be returned for the mating dance to continue.

It is when the pair leave the bar together, says Perper, that a shift in leadership must occur. The male must make his moves — put his arm around her, kiss her, woo her and eventually maneuver her into bed.

But let's not get the idea that what happened in the American singles bar of the early eighties is what most people do today. That is a most telescoped version of the ritual today. For one thing, many people today avoid the bar scene and bedding down merely hours later is comparatively unusual.

Before our couple ever touches the sheets, there's usually the dinner date, the flowers, the small gifts, in which the two "feed" each other as do many animals in the mating ritual. In most cultures, music is part of the mating dance.

So if you see a stranger across a crowded room, and you make eye contact, naturally you will look away. But then if you're interested, return the glance. Smile. Remember, a little of the right eye contact (no lascivious stares or up-and-down "elevator" glances) and there's a chance. Even if you cannot yet say hello, you can make eye contact. Eye contact creates a bond. It conveys your interest in communicating further.

Move into talking range, smile, and initiate conversation. There are all kinds of pickup lines. But I'm not a proponent of this approach. The best way to break the ice is to say something genuine. "I notice you seem to be having a good time here and I just want to introduce myself." Even a comment about the weather, a compliment (I like your tie or earrings) or "What time is it?" is okay. Especially if you have a second question or comment ready so the conversation doesn't end. Certainly, those are a helluva lot better than "If I could be anything, I'd be your body lotion" or "I'm a morning person, so why don't you spend the night?"

Have you ever noticed how some women just seem to attract men like bears to honey? What is it? It's that these women let men know that they like them. A woman like this has a warmth and acceptance of a man and this creates chemistry. This is a woman who likes herself and *likes men*. She makes them feel good about themselves. She listens to them. And she is enjoying herself, and not thinking about outcomes. She is living in the moment. She is being expressive and alive. She is being whatever she is at the moment — curious, silly, arrogant, excited, sad. Her aliveness helps others to feel freer and more able to express themselves — which is what most people want to do.

And men who are magnetic to women also are not afraid to be who they are. It's kind of disarming when a guy has the self-confidence to admit when he's a bit nervous!

Flirting errors

Often, women and men give out defensive vibes. Afraid of rejection or of appearing eager, they actually appear to be not interested. And who's going to approach them then?

This is one of the biggest complaints from men — that women are cold and unfriendly. But men who are successful with women realize that women are wary with any man they don't know. These men realize that women are attracted to men with unflappable self-confidence. The confident man ignores a woman's initial disinterest and gently persists by being genuinely warm and friendly. However, if a woman gives a man a clear directive that she's not interested, or if she fails to respond after a reasonable effort by the man, he should make himself scarce.

Besides giving up too soon, men can make other mistakes. For example, a man sees a woman he fancies at a seminar. But instead of finding a way to chat with her so she has an opportunity to assess him, he simply walks up to her and gives her his card asking her to call him. Fat chance she will. Or at a nightclub, close to closing time, he asks a woman to dance. No conversation first. The man is working under his own imperative — he's attracted by looks alone. But women want far more information than looks. Trying to short-circuit the mating dance usually doesn't work.

Here's an interesting letter that reveals how the mating dance can get screwed up:

> *Dear Kathy:*
>
> *As a 36-year-old divorced man with several attractive, professional, and platonic women friends (no, I'm not gay), I would like to share some observations that may be helpful to women writing you for advice on how to meet a man.*
>
> *My 30-plus female friends seem to still think that a man likes "the chase." They tend to act and react according to this belief when relating to men and they remain, of course, without male companionship because nothing could be further from the truth.*
>
> *Twenty years ago, this may have been true as we believed in our superiority and women, whether believing it or not, encouraged this belief. We had the edge and considered it our responsibility to make the first move.*
>
> *Today, many of us work for female bosses, accept female co-workers as equal, and we are tired of being expected to travel back in time when it comes to dating.*
>
> *Think of the last guy who came on to you. Did he turn out to be egotistical, chauvinistic, and very temporary? This is typical of 90% of the men who still believe in "the chase."*
>
> *I have heard more women brag about their witty (and devastating) response to a poor guy's effort and I never hear about a woman's initial efforts to meet a man she is attracted to. If you, as a woman, are not prepared to take the same risk as a man in meeting and developing a relationship, then you should not consider yourself to be equal.*
>
> *Gary*

Gary makes a good point. Don't be afraid of appearing interested. And don't be afraid of making some first moves. Many men wish women would be less passive. They wish women would ask them for their phone numbers. This would also solve the problem of women who are reluctant to give out their own number for safety's sake. But if you make the call to a man, there's no such worry. Men don't worry about safety with women. In that sense, they're very lucky.

One guy says the challenge is not where to meet men but "to initiate a conversation, to be the first to say 'Hi,' to ask men if they are single, to ask friends to introduce her to singles, or to finally bite the new-age bullet and join a dating club."

Another man says, "In waiting for Prince Charming to ask, a woman should remember that he might be unaware or he might be as human and as shy as she is."

And women, realize that most men have difficulty approaching a woman who is with another woman or a group. Nobody wants an audience when they're risking rejection.

There's no harm in developing a conversation, and eventually asking that person to join you and your friends at some activity. If you're in a class, for example, invite several members of the class for coffee, including the one you're interested in. That's a low-key way to get to know each other and then you can always suggest something for just the two of you.

Another letter from a reader:

Dear Kathy:

I'm nearing a personal crisis. I'm turning 30 and I don't have a special person in my life. There is a certain redhead I've been trying to get in touch with, but I seem to be having difficulties. I have tried subtle hints, and not-so-subtle hints (like taping messages to my office window). What am I doing wrong?

Reid

Dear Reid:

Have you tried the direct (telephone) approach?: "Hi, this is Reid. I'm the guy who (works at..., tapes messages to windows, or whatever). I find you very attractive. I'd like to take you out for coffee (or lunch). Could we meet at (name the place) tomorrow at (name the time)?"

All she can say is yes or no. Remember, guys who get dates are guys who ask and who figure it's the girl's loss if she turns them down.

If not only at first, but always, you don't succeed, you likely need to get some feedback on what, if anything, you're doing wrong.

By the way, a friend of mine says his 34-year-old son has just discovered new duds make a difference. Apparently his son normally wears jeans and looks pretty scruffy. But recently he got dressed up for a social gathering and found himself being "hit on" like crazy. Clothes may not make the man. But perhaps they help make a first impression.

10
H andling rejection

Men's number one reason for finding it difficult to connect with women is a fear of rejection, according to my survey of readers. (See chapter 5.) And women don't like rejection either.

Whether you're 16 or 60, this fear is common among many, many people. But the risks you don't take are often the things you regret in life when you look back. Both sexes need to overcome this fear if they're going to make a connection. Finding someone with whom to share life is worth the risk.

If you're waiting until you're not nervous, you're going to wait a long time. You may hear a lot of no's, but eventually someone you like is going to say yes. Those who actually do make a move, eventually succeed.

Here's one man's view of handling rejection:

"Mike" is a nice-looking, 46-year-old businessman who's a divorce survivor. He dated for nine months between the end of his 18-year marriage and the beginning of his current serious relationship.

He says he had to learn never to take rejection personally. "It doesn't bother me because I know not everyone will like me. Now I find rejection is not terribly difficult to swallow. Every no is one step closer to a yes."

Mike says it helps if you know what type of woman you're looking for before you venture out. Then figure out what activities you like and where this kind of woman might be.

Mike and a male friend organized brunches every four to six weeks with other men friends. "We each invited a woman who was simply a platonic friend. But that person may well be suited for someone else.

We made sure to get an equal number of men and women — about eight to 12 people altogether — and picked a restaurant for mid-Sunday morning.

"We mingled and talked. If we wanted to, we could ask somebody out." Biking, hiking and skiing trips became a spinoff from the brunches. Although Mike didn't meet his current sweetheart this way, some of his friends did. "It does work," he said.

Here is Mike's advice on how to handle an initial encounter with a woman you may be attracted to:

"You have five to 15 seconds to make an impression. So pay a compliment: 'I've got to tell you I like your earrings (your jacket, your smile).' After she replies, talk about something mutual such as, 'Did you enjoy that seminar?' From there, a man could say something like, 'Let's have a coffee some day.' Then give her your card and ask for hers. Follow up with a phone call. If you ask her out for lunch, give her a choice of, say, Tuesday or Friday."

On the first date, Mike suggests giving the woman "a single rose. It's a simple gesture but you'll be remembered." After the first date, call her the next day and let her know you had a nice time."

Here's some women's views about that survey and about rejection:

Dear Kathy:

I've been a single parent for 13 years and have also spent many Friday and Saturday nights at home — mostly by choice but sometimes not.

I have gone to singles dances, joined clubs, put a personal ad in the paper, and met some very nice men through these methods. Even though none of these turned into "true love," we have remained good friends and do stay in touch.

After reading some of the comments made by some of those men who answered your survey, I felt they deserved to be home alone. The ones I am referring to are the ones who made comments like "Women want Tom Selleck," "Women go for losers," "Women are too bossy."

Does the male population realize that most women share those same feelings/insecurities (men are only looking for slim, gorgeous blondes)? Not every woman is into the bar scene. Women fear rejection, too.

One night, I went to a dance with a bunch of single women from my co-op. It took me half the night to get up the nerve to ask a gentleman (and I use the word loosely) to dance. Instead of politely saying no thanks, he laughed at me and tried to push his friend on me. I was very embarrassed and humiliated. I went back to my seat and sat down and unfortunately I let that person ruin the rest of my night.

It is not easy being single today and not all the singles' functions are for everybody. I have tried a few and I usually enjoy myself because I go to have a good time. If I meet someone I connect with, then that is a bonus. If that is not for you, why not join something non-threatening like a co-ed fitness club, dance club, or take up golf, whatever.

I am still looking for a companion to share my life with, especially now that my children are almost grown. I don't judge a book by its cover (looks don't count with me) and when I go out I have just as many fears as the men do.

So, guys, don't give up and stay home. There are a lot of great women out there in all shapes and sizes looking for the same thing you are.

L.W.

The letters I've had about rejection are countless. Here are a few more:

Dear Kathy:

I'm a 49-year-old male who hasn't had any luck with women these past seven years. I was married 15 years to a woman who didn't want any physical contact with me, but, out of wifely duty, let me have sex with her. Previous to that, I did hold hands, kiss and cuddle with a few women.

Now, these past seven years no woman has wanted any physical contact. They just want to be friends.

Initially I came on strong and was rejected. After about two years and 50 rejections I decided to let women come on to me. What a joke; it never happened.

I have been through so much therapy aimed at this issue that it's difficult to have any hope. I've become a social recluse. My dog is my best friend. I see a hooker once in a while and watch exotic dancers often. But I'd like to have a girlfriend. Is there any way that you can help?

Anonymous

Dear Kathy:

I'm 27 and never had a relationship or even been out on a date. All through school, I tried asking a few girls out but always got turned down. I think it's because I wasn't the most desirable guy around and I was a few pounds overweight.

Since leaving school my luck hasn't changed. If I go to a movie and I see a couple getting it on, it gets under my skin. At times I've been so upset that if I had an AK-47 I would have used it just to relieve frustration.

The few times I've tried to talk to anybody about it, I've got the impression they don't care or it's a source of amusement. I feel so alone that I want to do something or die, so please help.

Angry and Frustrated

Dear Angry and Frustrated:

Difficulty in forming relationships is an extremely common problem — a constant theme in therapy. The first thing you need to address, however, is your depression. You need to see a therapist before you get into self-destructive behavior.

It's unfortunate that, when you've tried to talk to others, they've been unable to help you. Many people simply feel inadequate in this role and don't know what to say, and consequently you may feel they don't care or are amused. That's often a cover for being unable to cope.

What's probably happened is that the rejection you have suffered has undermined your self-esteem. A therapist will guide you to recovering your self-esteem and teach you the conversational and social skills to get you into dating.

Dr. Sheila Woody, a post-doctoral fellow at the stress and anxiety unit of the University of British Columbia Hospital says it's important to expect rejection. "Accept it as a certainty," says Dr. Woody. "It happens to all of us."

She advises her clients to consider all the reasons why a person might reject him or her. "That person might have somebody else or not want a relationship right now or you may remind her of an ex-husband. Also remember the times in the past when you rejected someone. And that person is still worthwhile."

After being rejected, Dr. Woody suggests people surround themselves with friends, relatives, and others who value them. And then after licking your wounds for a while, get out there and meet some more people.

Other therapists have suggested it pays to expand your social skills. Go out and learn to be good at things you're not good at right now, like dancing, which is an invaluable skill in meeting the opposite sex. Becoming a reasonably good dancer will increase your self-esteem and make you more visible at dances.

Singles clubs may seem depressing if you hang dog it. Be prepared to be turned down nine times out of ten and celebrate the one time you're not. It's really a numbers game.

But if rejection is the only thing that happens, it's time to look at yourself and your approach. Make an appointment with a psychologist. Ask for some straight answers.

Do you have B.O.? Do you look uncared for or perhaps as dreary as your life is? Are you so quiet and give so little of yourself that nobody even knows who you really are?

You might even try asking your friends, your relatives, or your work colleagues for the brutal truth. It may hurt, but at least you'll have something to work with. Then when you've made any necessary improvements, go out and try again.

But what if you're not the one who is rejected, but the rejectee? There will be times when a person is interested in you, but you don't feel any interest. The key is to say no, kindly but firmly.

Here's an example:

Dear Kathy:

You frequently write about women who love too much, but what about men who love too much? Most of my girlfriends and I have, at one time or another, had to deal with one or several men who feel they can pester us endlessly. We say no, but they don't give up. They feel women are like jobs — if they keep calling, they'll eventually be hired!

These men are difficult to get rid of because they usually belong to an organization we can't quit or live next door or work with us. Behavior ranges from leaving 20 beeps a day on one friend's answering machine to attempting to reach us on our vacations in Cairo, to buying us expensive gifts, which we never accept, of course.

What is wrong with these men? Most of them are professionals with power, money, and anything else a girl could ask for. Why do these men not have any semblance of pride? Most of them could probably find someone if they would just cool the ardor.

Puppies Aren't A Girl's Best Friend

Dear Girls:

The men you are describing wouldn't necessarily fit the description of men who love too much, although indeed there are such men — men who are so needy for love they will put up with all degrees of abusive treatment in a relationship.

The guys you describe sound like men who chase too much and I'm not sure what's going on with them.

I'm wondering how assertively you tell these guys no. Do you make some feeble excuse? Do you give mixed messages? Do you try to be so nice about turning them down that they end up confused?

A polite "no, thanks" is appropriate the first time. The second time say something like, "I have already said 'no.' I am not going to change my mind. Please don't call (ask) again." After that, treat the guy like an obscene caller. Don't speak; simply hang up. With no satisfaction whatsoever, he will usually give up.

If that doesn't work, get tough. Tell him his behavior is harassment and you will be taking appropriate action.

At work, report his behavior to the boss. Most companies have policies on sexual harassment and those that don't may be caught legally unaware. At home, tell your landlord if harassment from within the building is out of hand. At your club, lodge a complaint with the executive.

For more information or to make a complaint, call the government department that deals with human rights.

11
Looking for love in all the right places

Okay, you're saying, I've got a life, I've expanded my circle of friends, I know what kind of man or woman I want, I've even overcome some of my shyness and armed myself with some social skills for approaching the opposite sex.

But *where* do I find this person?

Robert Riordan, a Statistics Canada demographer, says maybe you've been looking for love in all the wrong places. You might improve your odds of finding a mate by going where the boys — or girls — are.

I've had readers tell me the same thing. One man said women should try the mining towns or other places outside the big city where men work. Another guy out in the sticks said: "I have a better chance of meeting a moose on the road than a woman."

In Alaska in 1991 there were 212,540 single men and 187,691 single women, giving that state a reputation as a place teeming with bachelors.

Under the age of 35, single men outnumber single women. After age 40, however, this reverses. Here are some statistics from Riordan by age group:

- The under-30 crowd. In Canada, unattached men in this age group outnumber women by about 120 to 100. There isn't a single Canadian community of significant size where the opposite is true.

Looking for love in all the right places.

- Ages 30 to 49, the baby boomers. There are more singles aged 30 to 49 than occur in any other age group. And there are 98 unattached males for every 100 females.

- Parents of the baby boomers. In the 50 to 64 age group, mortality factors begin to influence the ratios, and women outnumber the men.

- Grandparents of the baby boomers. The older the age group, the wider the gap between the sexes. Across all communities studied, senior women outnumber senior men three to one.

It's the same in parts of the United States. Doris Bass who teaches at the Elders Institute at Florida International University, says senior men can marry women 25 to 30 years younger than themselves. The ratio of widowed women to widowed men in Florida is more than five to one. Not fair, but fact.

There is only one community among those studied in Canada with a sex ratio among seniors that is even. In Yellowknife, Northwest Territories, there are the same number of unattached senior men as women. Women in Canada can expect to live about 81 years compared to 74 years for men.

But because women are adopting more roles previously associated with men — working, drinking, and smoking, women's life expectancy grew only 1.66 years from 1981 to 1991, while men's grew 2.71 years. Men are starting to take better care of themselves. Still, there are 25 times more women aged 90 or over than men.

But if you think these figures are tough, think about being a young single black woman in the United States. There are only seven black men for every ten black women, says Dr. Larry Davis, author of *Black and Single: Meeting and Choosing a Partner Who's Right for You.*

The reason? A high rate of infant mortality, imprisonment, and homicide among black males. And of the seven, many are considered unsuitable as romantic partners by black women, says Davis, because they don't have enough money or aren't educated.

The statistics are grim for blacks: most are single. Two out of three black marriages end in divorce. Only one divorced black woman in three ever remarries. More black men are in prison than in college. And black men have been losing economic ground relative to everyone else, including black women, making them less desirable.

In one chapter titled "Dating White," Davis advises blacks to apply their criteria on physical attractiveness, income, education, and social status across racial lines. And like me, Davis advises singles to be realistic, be positive, be your best immediately, get out there, and date someone who is already happy.

So if you're not ready to chuck in your job and go where the ratio is good, what else do you do to find that special someone?

Well, you don't hang around outside divorce court. The freshly single are often too emotionally strung out or screwed up to be good bets.

What you should do is open your eyes to what's around you everywhere. Anywhere from the bar to the bus is fertile ground for meeting people. Everything you do on a regular basis — cashing your paycheck at the bank, getting stamps at the post office, maintaining your car, going for a second helping at the salad bar, buying a toilet plunger at the hardware store — is part of his or her life too.

In the right frame of mind — if you are open to meeting someone, outgoing and genuinely interested in other people — you can meet a special someone almost everywhere.

So it's a matter of developing that frame of mind, having good self-esteem, and the confidence to open conversations with strangers.

Smile. Ask a question. Flirt a little. And if you do have a conversation with someone who appeals to you, whether you're a man or a woman, it's a good idea to introduce yourself by your first name. Give him or her your business card and say you'd like to meet for a coffee at some future time. Ask for her or his first name. A word of caution: women should be careful not to give a card with their home address and phone number. That comes after you're sure he's not weird.

If you're a woman, start fixing your own car and browse at the auto supply store. Be brave and ask the guy next to you whatever you might have asked the store clerk. Unless, of course, the store clerk is the hunk of your dreams.

If you love music, start up a conversation at the sound store. Try to have a second question ready to keep the conversation going.

Start making time for finding a mate on a regular basis. Take your appointment diary and each week have things to do where it's possible to meet someone.

And learn to go out alone. Men find it very intimidating trying to connect with a woman who's in a group of other women.

Get some new hobbies popular with the opposite sex. Join a chess club. Playing there will help you upgrade your skill, but ask questions. Take a course in film making or script writing or acting or animation.

Really hot are martial arts classes. These classes are mixed, the age range is 16 to 60, and there's a very real opportunity to get to know others well. One man about 35 told me: "If I were single, that's the way to go." He said classmates help each other to stretch and give each other pointers on movement. There's a lot of physical contact and, in concentrating on the task at hand, men and women become less self-conscious and quite friendly.

If you love reading, browse the bookstores. Increasing numbers of bookstores are creating a relaxed atmosphere for singles to meet each other. Bookstore owners who cater to this market say it's a calm and sophisticated setting for singles to strike up a conversation.

More bookstores are offering author readings, singles nights, classes, and social activities — turning themselves into community centers to attract young spenders and fight the encroachment of large-chain bookstores. They're like cerebral Club Meds. And if your town's bookstores don't cater to singles this way, why not speak with the manager and suggest it. Point out the number of singles in your community and how catering to their needs will be good for business.

So look for the bookstore in-store cafes and coffee bars — the intellectual equivalent of the fitness center. They're warm. There's usually some background music. And it's easy to strike up a conversation while browsing the shelves, then continue the conversation over a cup of coffee, all without leaving the store.

How do you make a move in this situation? If you're a fan of thrillers, sidle up to the brunette perusing a book by John le Carre and tell her you love le Carre's latest novel. In the psychology section, ask him if he's read Dr. Barbara De Angelis's *Are You the One for Me?* Or in the travel section ask if he's ever been to Italy and if he can recommend some good restaurants in Rome. In comedy sections, share a chuckle and if you get a conversation going ask his or her name, or another question, and invite him or her for a coffee in the store.

Looking for love in a place like this can be better than telepersonals because you see the person as well as talk to him or her, so it's easy to assess the chemistry. You can see the other person in action, what he or she wears, how he or she interacts with others, and what he or she is interested in.

Use the same approach elsewhere. Although not quite as relaxed an atmosphere, computer stores are usually full of men; kitchen shops are often full of women. Who doesn't need some expert advice sometimes? Ask the guy you notice with the thick, dark hair who's just your type, if he knows anything about printers. "Excuse me. Do you know if a bubble jet is as good as a laser?" you might ask.

And if you're in a market-type place where there are coffee bars and delis, become a regular — same day, same time, same stool — you'll start to know who the other regulars are and soon there will be opportunity for conversation and introduction.

And don't forget supermarkets. If the person picking out mushrooms beside you looks interesting, take a peak at his or her cart. Does it spell single? If so, ask him or her the difference between white mushrooms and brown ones (other than the color). How does he cook them? Share recipe ideas.

The same general approach works at sporting goods and video stores. Have you seen this movie? is a good opener. Was it good? Gee thanks, it looks like I'll be home again tonight. He or she might suggest going out together to the theater instead.

And for heaven's sake, if you find the person is already married or doesn't respond, *don't take it personally!* That's just the luck of the draw. Smile and go about your business.

Men tell me that women who want to meet men should get on to the ski slopes or play golf where the ratio of men to women is ten to one! And ball games are apparently good places to meet men as well.

One man suggested bowling or curling leagues. Indeed, one woman I know found her special someone after she joined a curling league. They married a year later. "All you do is call a curling club and ask which leagues are looking for curlers," she told me. "I joined a mixed league and they generally have equal numbers of men and women. Curling is quite a social activity. Unlike golf, you have a lot of people in a small area and everybody finishes curling at the same time."

Most curling clubs also give lessons, usually starting in September. Most Canadian cities and their suburbs have a dozen or more curling clubs. On the Prairies there are many more. And every small town usually has one curling club.

Anything to do with boats is also good. When I was single, I first took a sailing course and later a Canadian Power Squadron beginners' course on boating safety, just prior to buying my own small power boat. The course was full of gorgeous men and I got to know a few. As well, once I had my boat, many a man was more than willing to become my boating partner for a day or offer to show me how to install this or that on my new boat. It was a wonderful sport, even on days I didn't get out of my marina and only spent the afternoon cleaning or fixing my boat. Marinas are full of interesting men, even if some of them are married and out of bounds.

Incidentally, selling my boat wasn't the end of my boating. I met my sweetie, who has a 34-foot yacht, at a marine pub. I had dropped into it for a coffee as I was early for an interview at a nearby hotel. I was feeling very outgoing that day and was joking with the waiter. Sweetie entered the conversation and we got onto the subject of boats, even though I had already sold mine. That led to lunch and then dinner and eventually we went out on his boat for a weekend. Two years later we built a house together and have been living together for about four years. Boating was a sport I got interested in just a year or so after my marriage ended and it eventually led me to sweetie. We continue to enjoy this mutual interest.

Men are everywhere. One man suggested the local auto raceway is an excellent place for women to find men. "There's six guys to every girl." He suggested more women could join private clubs or get involved with business or professional associations.

I was a guest speaker recently at a Rotary Club lunch and noticed only a handful of women members among a group of 60 or 70 men. Certainly most of the members were married but some were not.

Single parents can meet each other at their kids' sports activities such as hockey, soccer, and football.

Another man suggested swim clubs, scuba lessons, dance classes, cooking school, language classes, extension programs at colleges and universities, outdoor clubs, literary readings, folk cafes and blues bars, or a season ticket to football, hockey, baseball, or other games.

Most young single people rely on school, college, university, workplace contacts, and their friends and family to meet someone. What are some other right places to look for love? One survey found the number one best way to meet is through friends, followed by singles bars, social events such as parties and picnics, singles organization events, and on the job.

A lot of young people do meet each other at bars. But if you're single again and just re-entering the dating world, you'll likely feel positively geriatric at most singles bars. The music will be loud. You'll be jostled. You won't be able to talk. You may not be wearing the appropriate muscle shirt or mini skirt. Nor should you be.

Don't depress yourself this way. Find something suitable for your age group. And don't give up because you made a mistake and started looking for your special someone in the wrong place.

Love at work

For a lasting relationship, another survey found there is a four times greater chance of marrying if you meet the person through your job rather than some other way. I'm one of the 57% of people (according to a 1991 Gallup poll) who think dating in the workplace is acceptable. It's a very good place to meet a prospective mate because you learn so much about the person even before the first date. I've known some people who actually choose their careers because they like the idea of working at something where there's a good "sexual mix." For women this might be the police force, an engineering firm, or a trucking company. Men are less apt to think in these terms but jobs in the food business, real estate, in fashion, education, or health, for example, are full of women.

And in the workplace, relationships can start quite naturally. People can become friends. Pressures are understood and shared. And shop talk eventually turns to pillow talk. Sometimes messages are sent in bits and bytes. Indeed these steamy electronic love letters, which are becoming more common by computer or fax, can be a delight not only for the lovers involved but hilarious for everyone else who knows how to access your e-mail.

So start expanding your social network in the workplace. Reach out, for example, to new people. Introduce them to work mates when they first start. Help them to become familiar with the cafeteria, the lunch places nearby, anything peculiar about the workplace that they may otherwise take weeks to find out. Ask a new colleague about where he or she comes from, previous jobs, and talk about things that you are involved in within the community. Invite a new employee to join you on the company bowling team or a union committee or when your group goes to the pub after work or dinner. At the very least, you may make some new friends this way. And perhaps a husband or wife.

But you don't have to wait until someone new joins your company. Get involved in teams and outside work activities that are organized at work. Volunteer. Put some effort into things. If you see a need at work, do something about it yourself.

So don't reject the workplace. It's still one of the best resources. You just have to know the pitfalls and be prepared to deal with them, should they arise. The point is to be social and friendly, but don't be overbearing. Never interfere with another person's ability to get his or her job done. Do not make personal remarks unless you get a very clear message that the other person is interested in more than a working relationship. It's important for women to understand that, at work, a man is not as likely to make the first move, especially in these days of sexual harassment laws. (More about that in chapter 20.) Of course, going for coffee together at work is not a problem and if your interest seems mutual, there's no harm in asking the other person out for lunch or dinner, outside the workplace, where the relationship could be moved onto a much more personal plane.

Once a personal relationship is established, the two of you must make some rules. Agree not to fraternize at the office. Agree ahead of time that if you break off relations, there will be no scenes or attempts at contact while in the office. If you do not think you can handle the possibility that a romantic relationship started at work may break up, or you feel the other person couldn't handle it, don't get involved with anyone at work. What I'm saying is work can be a good place to meet people because you can learn a lot about the person first. But whether you can handle a romantic relationship started there depends upon your emotional maturity as well as that of the other person.

Clubs and associations

That special someone may be a work colleague or someone you meet in a store. But there are many other ways too. Most cities have social clubs and professional associations. If you're athletic, sports clubs are a natural. If you're a man and like to dance or would like to learn, join a dance club where you'll be in very high demand. Wine clubs are good too. So get out your Yellow Pages and look under Clubs or under Associations or under Dance Clubs. Check out the shopping mall or community center bulletin boards. You'll be surprised what exists in your town.

Join a political party and get interested in current events if you are not already. Go to political meetings. Volunteer. When you get involved in a project, you meet people and over time get to know them. This is an excellent way to expand your social life.

If the environment is your passion, get involved in environmental clubs, issues, and recycling efforts.

Perhaps local community government is your cup of tea — volunteer for park, recreation, and other civic programs.

Volunteer at one of the many immigrant centers and societies that help new people adjust to their new country. This is especially good if you're a person of color and can offer your insights from both perspectives.

If you are religious, get involved in your church. Or look what needs to be done in your neighborhood. Get involved in your strata council, become a volunteer with Big Brothers or Big Sisters or Meals on Wheels, arrange an open house in your apartment building, or hold a street party.

Finally, if you're looking for a mate, take heed of this letter:

Dear Kathy:

Gorgeous men are everywhere. Go with the attitude that every man is eminently lovable and interesting and just as fearful of rejection as we women are.

Then get out of the house! Attend as many meetings, trade fairs, and gatherings as you can stomach. Get involved with something that interests you — sports, politics, or even car repairs.

By far the most successful way to meet available men I've found is with a singles club. They do a lot of non-threatening activities such as sailing, potlucks, skiing, the theater, dining and dancing, to name a few.

I met Mr. Wonderful recently at one of the potlucks.

Carolyn

But some women don't want just gorgeous. They want rich!

Dear Kathy:

I am 42 and doing a perfectly good job of looking after myself. But after more than 20 years, that's becoming tedious. Even though my friends all dubiously talk about "sugar daddies," when I mention the idea, I think that for a change I'd like to be kept.

Let's get right down to brass tacks — how do you meet rich men?

Bored With Earning My Own Paycheck

Dear Bored:

Tsk. Tsk. You probably know it's as offensive to look on men as sugar daddies as it is for men to look on women as sex toys. And about as fruitful. What you're bound to get is a rich guy who makes love while wearing his beeper, or, worse still, one who doesn't make love at all.

That said, the only way I know to find a pool of possibly rich men is to join a high-rent district golf or tennis club. Either that or quit your job and go work for a millionaire (study the business newspapers and magazines for names)

and then inveigle yourself into his heart and American Express Card.

Another possibility is to follow Jackie Kennedy Onassis's lead. As I recall, she wanted to meet John Kennedy and used her job as a writer to make the connection through an interview. The catch is, Jackie was rich herself — she had the money, clothes, family etc. to present a political advantage to Kennedy.

Going the country club route, even if you have the money, it may take years before you get a membership — waiting lists are usually long or suspended altogether. And you'll need a proposer, seconder, and references, all from club members.

By the way, you'll most likely have to do something about your wardrobe. You'll need clothes — good ones — for all occasions, especially play. It also helps if you look healthy and rich and speak well, even if you don't have anything to say, which may or may not be a requirement.

Frankly, I think you'd be better off plotting the capture of a new job and a good man.

12
Playing the odds

Many of us enjoy a great deal of personal control in our lives. We choose which groceries we want to buy, what kind of car we want, which movie we'll see and when, what style of clothes we like. Many of us, but unfortunately not all, can set out to get a good education, go after jobs and careers, find an apartment or a house we feel comfortable in, and explore whatever hobbies, sports, or creative pursuits interest us.

But finding a suitable partner often doesn't feel quite as certain. Often it's the one area of our lives we just can't seem to control. And because people are marrying later in life, after they leave college or university, and as more close friends get married, it gets harder for single people to meet other eligible singles.

The pace of change has made our lives more hectic. We work more hours and spend more time commuting. We are more alienated. With the pressures of a career, and for single parents, there's not a lot of time and freedom to make the search.

But I believe many people can do a lot more than they're doing now. And one of the things you might consider, if you don't want to leave your social life to chance, is the potpourri of businesses that exist to help you connect.

Most large cities have a great number of singles clubs, dating services, introduction services, singles magazines, dance clubs, sports clubs, courses, classes, and special interest clubs. Look through the Yellow Pages under the heading Dating Service. This will connect you to the various matchmaking and video dating services.

Unfortunately, most non-profit singles clubs are not listed in the Yellow Pages. Look for these under the Coming Events section of the classifieds in your daily or weekly newspapers. Peruse shopping malls, community centers, and other bulletin boards wherever you go.

Visit your library and look for special interest magazines that may contain a directory of clubs and associations. Once you really get into researching, you'll be surprised how much there is. Keep a special notebook to list all the clubs and events for singles with their phone numbers.

But you must conquer your initial reluctance. Don't be like Lester, a man around 70. Lester thinks of singles clubs as "used car lots." Because he doesn't want to think of himself as a used car or anyone he dates as a used car, he doesn't go anywhere. Lester's negative thinking is his worst enemy. Despite the fact that the odds are in his favor (the ratio of women to men is high in his age group), Lester lives alone on his boat. He would dearly love a wife or constant companion to share his life. "I would settle down with a woman," says Lester. "I want a full, long-term relationship. I'm a very lonely man. I'm not happy on my own."

But still he says, "The singles thing is not my cup of tea. I went once. I think, somebody else has already dumped them, otherwise why would they be out there?"

Of course, most men and women, either at singles functions or home alone watching TV, have been either the dumper or the dumpee. But they've conquered their false pride and they're willing to risk and love again. They're not the couch potatoes. They know a relationship is something they value and they go after it.

So let's look at the various types of singles organizations you can try to find the man or woman of your dreams.

Singles clubs

At one of the three-day relationship seminar shows my newspaper and I put on in our city, I asked one audience of single people: "How many of you belong to a singles club?" Out of more than 100 men and women in the room, fewer than a dozen hands went up.

Clearly a lot of single men and women are missing a good opportunity by not finding out about the many singles clubs that exist in most cities. Many singles are simply unaware of what's out there. Some at the show said they'd tried one but it wasn't what they were looking for and hadn't tried others.

Singles clubs are usually non-profit, so they're an inexpensive way to connect. It's important, however, to realize that it takes a little experimentation to find a club with your kind of people, in the right age group, with activities you enjoy and an atmosphere you feel comfortable in. Giving up after trying just one is like judging all movies by the only one you've seen. And often a club grows on you as you start to know people and participate more.

Don't try just one thing and conclude singles clubs and events are useless because you didn't meet that special someone right away. That's silly.

Some clubs cater to the under-30 age group. Some to those aged 30 to 49, etc. Some clubs mainly have dances. Others have house parties and barbecues. Still others are sports-oriented.

Phone first. Find out the age group, the ratio of men to women, the type of club it is, and the annual membership fee. Ask to be sent a newsletter.

When you find a club you like, get involved in some of the volunteer work so you'll really get to know other people. Don't leave all the work to others.

Here are some examples of singles clubs and organizations that are available in most major North American cities (for more names of singles groups, see the Appendix):

- At Toastmasters' clubs you learn the skills of public speaking, have a good laugh, and make new friends. It's not expensive.

- If you're among the 2% of the population with an I.Q. of 132 or above, especially if you're a woman, become a member of Mensa. Two-thirds of the members are male and 52% of all members are single. Mensa Singles Special Interest Groups publish newsletters. The Mensa Bulletin accepts personal ads.

- If you want a traveling companion, many travel agencies have singles travel clubs.

- Science Connection is a singles network bringing together unattached science professionals, amateur science enthusiasts, and naturalists. Currently 565 men and women belong from across North America. About 70% have science-related jobs. The others are lawyers, teachers, and other professionals.

- Parents Without Partners is an organization throughout North America for single parents with or without custody of their children. Most members are in their forties.

- The Single Booklovers' Club is an international club for singles who like books and want to meet book lovers of the opposite sex.

You'll find that some singles clubs aim for equal numbers of men and women. Some, mainly those catering to the parents of baby boomers, have given up that quest. Here's some correspondence that illustrates the latter:

Dear Kathy:

I read your column several weeks ago about the man who wondered if his baldness would make it difficult for him to attract a woman. I can already hear women screaming at you: "Kathy, really! As if any MAN need ever be lonely?"

I belong to a singles club for widowed and divorced people and (as always in such clubs) it's usually three women to every man at our parties. A frequent pattern is for a little bald-headed gent to come to a meeting, answering in monosyllables to every proffered greeting by date-hungry ladies, and later tell the person who brought him as a guest that he's disappointed the ladies were all over 40! (Some over 50 with grown children. Horrors!) Then he adds with a twinkle meant to sound very original, "I was hoping they'd be younger."

One such man recently married a woman 24 years his junior, who was evidently his choice of the widowed, divorced, and single women he met at the various singles clubs and dinner parties which filled his life.

Our club is a great lot. We're like cousins and have great times, but the constant quest for more male members never ceases. And every new man finds himself surrounded by people urging him to join. Our oldest male member is 84; the youngest, 53.

Articles like your recent one cause me to think: "We'd like to go on a picnic, but I don't know if we're good-looking enough to attract any ants."

P.S. I won't tell you the name of our club for fear you'd mention it and we'd have another 75 ladies on our waiting list!

Anonymous

This imbalance is a fact of life among parents of the baby boomers. There are about 25% more women than men and by age 90 — 25 times more women! That's because, of course, men on average die younger than women.

However, several male readers responded to the above letter saying there's no reason singles clubs for older folk need to be lopsided. "Where are these clubs?" was the key question. And that's an important point. Too many men — in all age groups — are simply unaware of the singles clubs that exist. But another problem is that, outside the big cities, few singles clubs exist — as this letter illustrates:

Dear Kathy:

I'm a single man, 42. Like so many other men in my age bracket, the small, industrial, smelter town that I live in is a nightmare if you're single. I'm too far from the big city, too old for bar scenes, and disappointed in personal ads.

What about the rest of us out here in the boon docks? Where is the nearest dating club?

Anonymous

And then some people, like this man, want specialty clubs that also don't exist — yet:

Dear Kathy:

I'm a single guy in my early thirties and a little under average height for men. I would be interested in finding a singles club for shorter people.

Unfortunately, there are too many people in society who look down on shorter people in more ways than one. Can you help?

Down to Earth Guy

I suggested this man start a singles club for shorter people. So the message is, if you determine that the kind of club you want just doesn't exist, form it yourself. You'll have a great deal of fun doing this and meet a lot of nice people in the process. Simply put an ad in the coming events or companion section of the classifieds. Say what your club is about. This man for example, could ask single short men and women to join him at an upcoming meeting at his home or perhaps arrange a community center discussion on being short and single. I haven't heard from him but I hope he took my suggestion.

Introduction services

Introduction services are convenient for people who don't have a lot of time to do their own screening. Someone from the introduction service will meet with you, ask you to fill out a questionnaire about your lifestyle and interests, what you want in a partner, and then try, sometimes by computer, to make matches approximately compatible with other clients on file. Fees range from several hundred dollars to several thousand.

But some agencies really don't do much screening or can't produce as many likely matches as they promise.

Make sure you choose an introduction service that has been in business for a reasonable time. There are fly-by-nights in this field, who come and go.

One thing to remember about dating services is they often charge a lot of money and may not be able to find suitable matches. No one is able to predict chemistry.

Video dating services

Video dating has the advantage of allowing members to see the other person's looks, mannerisms, and perhaps some personality as presented on a video. While you do the choosing, rather than the company, people who are not photogenic may lose out as the camera fails to capture their attractiveness.

The responses from my readers has been mostly negative to video dating services. Here are two letters which illustrate the problem:

> *Dear Kathy:*
>
> *I joined a video dating service several weeks ago. It seemed like an effective way of meeting other singles through the use of photos and videos. They really push the two-year membership ($1,400, plus taxes) which I bought.*
>
> *They take photos, some history, and do a video of you. Then you're supposed to make up to five selections of other*

singles you'd like to meet after viewing their photos and videos.

After carefully selecting five ladies, you submit the form and they contact them to come in to view your photos and video before you agree to meet.

Only one of the five ladies even bothered to come in to look at my photos and video after three weeks. And she did not want to meet. That's fine; that's life sometimes. But I think the other four could have come in to say yes or no. How much more effective this system could be if the people acted more responsibly.

I don't know whether or not I will bother to try to meet someone this way again.

Anonymous

I spoke to the president of the firm. "We contact a person twice," she said, "and, if they still don't come in, we send them a letter asking about their status. There's a possibility that he selected four who are 'on hold' — that is, there's a little heart applied to their photo file which indicates they are currently in a relationship, traveling, too busy with work, or otherwise temporarily unavailable.

"We don't want to have an unhappy member. We'd like him to inform us of this problem because it's hard for us to keep track of 2,000 members."

Dear Kathy:

Two-and-a-half years ago my husband walked out on me for another woman, leaving me with two children. After 19 months of counselling, my self-esteem was once again on the way up. But I was really missing male companionship. I don't get many opportunities to get out.

Hating the bar scene, I joined a hiking club. I made new friends but felt I needed more options. So I went to a video dating service. The salespeople told me I was quite attractive, men absolutely loved to be picked, having kids is no problem whatsoever, and this is the place for me to be.

I put up $1,200 for a two-year membership. Well, after 12 months I have only been selected once. We met a couple

*of times and knew nothing was going to come of it. He
wanted much more from me.*

*I chose 15 men and they have all responded no for 15
different reasons. They tell me at the service to just keep
coming in and picking men. Well, after 15 no's my self-esteem is not that great anymore. When they tell me at the
service that 15 is not that many, it does not make me feel
better.*

*I feel I was lied to just to get my money and I would never
recommend this place to any of my single friends. It can be
incredibly devastating to one's ego. And why didn't they tell
me at the beginning I could be rejected 15 times?*

*I will not go back, even though I have one more year on
my membership. I am just going to add this onto my list of
ripoffs.*

Still Alone, Just A Little More Broke

So, a few words of caution. Video dating services, introduction
services, and other businesses helping singles connect are a growth
industry. But it's consumer beware.

There have been several cases of people who paid for extremely
expensive dating services — only to find they were being matched with
people who were generally unavailable or totally unsuitable.

Peter Crocker, a Wilfrid Laurier University graduate, is working
on a consumer guide to dating services. His company, Consumer
Satisfaction Research Associates of Toronto, plans to rate dating
services based on prices and level of consumer satisfaction, after
interviewing hundreds of consumers of these services.

Crocker, who is completing his Ph.D. in clinical psychology,
worked for one introduction service for ten weeks. "I saw a lot of things
that disturbed me." That's what prompted him to start working on his
consumer guide to dating services. (For a copy of his guide or if you
would like to give him your feedback on dating services, write to him
at the address given in the Appendix under the listings for Ontario.)

Crocker says he's found the experiences of people using these
services varies enormously. Some were happy or relatively content with
the service they got. Others were deeply disappointed.

Depending on the type of dating service, he's found prices vary from $35 to $4,000. He hasn't found much correlation between how much people paid and how satisfied they were. Indeed, he says the $35 service is quite a good one. One of the problems for consumers is that it's very difficult for them to comparison shop. Many consumers have "mismatch after mismatch after mismatch," says Crocker, and get so frustrated they end up taking the service to small claims court or just giving up.

Crocker said those who are most likely to be well served by dating agencies are young women and older men, simply because there are lots of young men looking for young women and the older man is a rarer commodity than the older woman.

He said some unscrupulous services claim very high success rates. "One woman who ran a service claimed that 98% of her members ended up in a relationship. Soon after that her company went out of business and she kept the money."

Crocker said a good agency will match from 15% to 40% of its clients so well as to result in a marriage or long-term relationship.

He said dating service owners told him some men and women are impossible to match simply because they have unrealistic expectations. Crocker agrees: "You've got to be realistic. If you are short, fat, bald, ugly, and poor to boot, people who look like runway models are not likely to be interested in you."

But sometimes it's the dating service that creates unrealistic expectations in order to get the person's money. They won't tell a very overweight woman that her weight may lessen her chances of being matched.

If you find a company giving you the hard sell, that should be the red flag. Take the contract home, without signing it. Think about it carefully. Check the firm with the Better Business Bureau — have there been complaints?

Singles fairs or shows

Many major cities hold a fair specifically designed for singles. These fairs are often held around Valentine's Day. This is an excellent opportunity to get information on the various dating services, singles clubs, special singles travel clubs, etc. in your area.

And people have been known to meet a special someone just by attending these fairs. Loretta, 34, and John, 51, met on Valentine's Day 1988 at a large singles fair held in Vancouver and married a few years later.

Loretta had split up with her husband when her daughter was only six months old. She felt socially isolated by single motherhood, long working hours at two jobs, and very little money. Realizing she needed to take charge of her life, she was at the fair to contact Parents Without Partners.

John was at a booth advertising a singles discussion group. He had already been involved in the group and volunteered to man the booth for a few hours.

They were introduced. John, fearing he'd never see Loretta again, asked for her phone number — and got it.

They might not have ever met had both not taken action to end their isolation.

"I wanted some social outlet and support from people in the same situation as myself," says Loretta. "I needed a group where people would understand I couldn't go out for pizza on five minutes' notice." As well, Loretta realized she had to do something instead of waiting for someone to save her from being a single parent. "The prince isn't riding up to my doorstep, so maybe I should get on with my life."

John had been separated and divorced for seven years, Loretta for five years. Both were teachers.

"I thought he was cute. I was hoping he would call. Finally he did." They went for coffee and then saw each other every weekend. John now advises other singles to join a group that reflects their interests, such as hiking or camping that gets them out meeting people regularly. I really like his further advice: "Don't put too high an expectation on any one time or event."

Loretta advises single moms not to wait for someone to "save" them. "Do something to get your life together again."

Singles discussion groups

Whatever town or city you live in, without fail, you'll hear single people say it's the hardest place on earth to meet a mate. But I believe meeting the right person is often a matter of making changes.

Rick and Liisa, a couple in their thirties, might not have met and married, were it not for conscious decisions to get out of their ruts. Indeed, for Liisa it was a New Year's resolution.

Both had read about a weekly discussion group for singles in my newspaper column. Rick had just ended a long-term relationship. To get back into the swing of things he'd tried companion ads, going to nightclubs, and working out at a gym. None of this appealed. Liisa had just ended a three-year marriage. She had tried singles parties, boat cruises, and going to bars with girlfriends.

Both felt like fish out of water. They didn't want to be alone but weren't sure how to change that. Each saw the singles discussion group as a good first step. The groups were not designed as a dating service but rather as a way singles can share problems. Yet Rick and Liisa found the comfortable atmosphere of a group not designed for dating made connecting easy.

"I quit focusing on meeting the right person and started becoming more of myself," says Rick. "I found I could talk about everything without worrying about not showing weakness or my negative side." Before he went to the group, Rick says he was artificial, always trying to look as if he had no problems. "At first I looked around. Were there any women I'd want to ask out? Then I quit sizing up and started listening."

People shared their broken relationships, their feelings about the futility of mating rituals, and asked questions of each other about how the opposite sex thinks.

Liisa had been out of the dating scene for six years when she and her ex-husband split up. She had one very disillusioning relationship after that. "I felt totally lost. I didn't know what people were doing to meet each other."

She signed up with the discussion group to find out. At first nervous about going, she found herself more at ease each week. When Rick showed up, she was attracted to some of the things he said in the discussion. "I started responding because we feel the same things. At a distance, we were discovering things about each other. We were both just saying what we felt and letting the chips fall where they'd fall."

Part of the group met afterwards for coffee, giving Rick an opportunity to ask Liisa out for dinner.

Looking back, Rick says, "when I didn't have self-esteem, I wasn't meeting anybody. When you have a positive belief in yourself, when you know it's not a matter of being the richest, or the most successful, or a real good talker, or the captain of the softball team, it's different."

Says Liisa: "I always knew I was a good person even though I didn't stand out. But very few people saw the good in me. I'm not really outgoing." The discussion group was a way for people to get to know Liisa beyond the pretty-but-not-outgoing face.

Both Rick and Liisa say they feel an equality, an honesty, and a feeling of being understood with each other that had eluded them in other relationships.

Billboards

Believe it or not, some daring singles with a lot of cash, advertise for mates on billboards.

In Chicago one billboard read: "Four professional middle-class women, ages 29 to 31, seek husbands. P.O. Box 175 B, Chicago, Illinois 60614."

"We're not hogs. We're not losers. We just want to meet men who are ready, really ready, to meet Ms. Right," one of the four told a Chicago newspaper reporter. While the four women received a stack of replies, who knows if this was any more effective than a companion ad, which of course is a lot cheaper.

In the city where I live, a 33-year-old woman by the name of Erika T. Love, who claimed to be a university fine arts graduate, paid $2,000 for a billboard which said "Fine Arts graduate seeks wealthy husband." She gave the postal box of a downtown hotel.

The billboard featured an eight-foot photo of herself. But it only drew about 30 replies in the month it was up. Efforts to track her down since, to find out if she found the wealthy man of her dreams, have been unsuccessful.

13

*L*et your fingers do the dating

Telephone personals

Telephone personals, computer dating services, and newspaper companion ads exist because many people in big cities are too busy for the more traditional rituals of courtship.

And the trend is worldwide. In Paris, for example, where the French claim seduction was invented and where love — so the tourist bureau would have you believe — is supposed to be the national obsession, there are 48 dating agencies in the central Paris Yellow Pages.

Madeleine Ghertman, director of Ion International dating agency says attitudes have changed. "Everyone distrusts everybody else nowadays, so it is just not on for people to start chatting each other up in the street." Not surprising for a city of almost nine million people.

In a country where some consider the extra-marital affair to be a fine art form, those seeking a fleeting encounter can turn to Minitel, the computer network linked to the French telephone system.

Christophe, a 32-year-old married man from Lyons, advertised for "cuddles in the afternoon," apparently while his wife would be out at work. His message was one of 1,235 on a computerized bulletin board called Cum (Latin for "with"), which can be reached through Minitel.

Here in North America, personal ads by telephone, computer, or newspaper have become a way of life for people with busy lifestyles. Why bother with more time-consuming ways when personal ads are a one-stop-shopping love catalogue? We've come a long way, baby, since 1727 when Helen Morrison, a lonely spinster living in Manchester, England, became the first known woman to place a newspaper companion ad. The mayor promptly committed her to a lunatic asylum for four weeks.

Today it's a recorded message saying something like: _"Welcome to telepersonals. Male callers, press 1. Female callers, press 2. Couples seeking partners, press 3. Women seeking women, press 4."_

Letting their fingers do the dating, customers record amorous want ads, browse through other people's ads, and leave messages for any voice that catches their fancy.

You need a touch-tone phone. First, you receive your own box number and place your ad. Many telephone personal services are free to women, but men must pay both to pick up messages from their voice mailboxes or to leave messages in women's mailboxes. Look in the Yellow Pages under Dating Services for local companies.

Let your fingers do the dating.

Telephone personal services have revolutionized the dating scene. It seems every single man and woman I know is using them because they're an easy way to make a connection. Readers tell me telephone personals are fun, too. No letters to labor over or long delays in awaiting replies. Many, many men and women find this method successful. This letter is typical:

Dear Kathy:

Friends have often found it difficult to believe I couldn't meet someone nice over the past six years since I have been divorced. I am dating a wonderful man. My friends and co-workers all think I met him at a pub because that's what I told them. Actually I met him though one of those free (for women) companion phone lines. We talked for several weeks before we actually met.

I felt very secure meeting him after a number of intimate conversations on virtually every subject under the sun. This was so non-threatening for me. I would encourage others to use this service.

Unfortunately, I feel embarrassed about having had to resort to this to meet someone. I would like you to remind other singles this is not only a non-threatening way to meet people, but it is also a lot safer than handing out your phone number in a bar, restaurant, or other social gathering.

Anonymous

This woman needn't feel embarrassed. Most people are quite open about using these services. Telepersonals may give you a better and even more honest idea of the other person than printed ads alone. You may detect a great deal from a person's voice — education level, social background, and even attitude. You may tell how old the speaker is, what country he or she is from. You may recognize other qualities from a person's voice such as strength, shyness, warmth, insincerity. And later these and other qualities are revealed or confirmed during conversation.

Smart liars avoid fibbing on the phone, where subtle inconsistencies in emphasis and intonation are easily discerned. Most of us are unconscious of the power of the voice. As a columnist who spends hours on the phone, I feel I can almost tell you what a person looks like on the other end of the line. Certainly education, social background, and sincerity, or lack of it, are immediately obvious to me. My impressions are often confirmed later when I meet the individual.

I believe telepersonals may give you a better opportunity to relay your inner self first, not just the superficial exterior. When I think about it, how many truly super people we know — prime ministers and presidents, artists, inventors and astronauts — would actually have projected well in a written companion ad?

It's important when you place a voice personal not to speak only about the kind of person you wish to meet. Say something about yourself as well, so that those who are hunting through the many other ads can get a feeling of who you are and whether or not you might be someone they could feel compatible with. After all, if you place an ad to sell your home, you wouldn't simply say House for Sale. You'd offer some detailed description.

Saying you like walks on the beach or listening to music by the fire really means very little. How many people don't like those things?

It may also be a good idea to discuss the wording of your ad with some close friends. They may have excellent suggestions about how to describe yourself. Indeed, in the search for that special someone, it's a real plus if you have good friends who will give you encouragement.

Telepersonals, just one of the companies offering voice companion ads, has received more than ten million calls. The Toronto-based company has offices in Vancouver, Calgary, Edmonton, and Montreal in Canada, as well as San Francisco and St. Louis. At last word, it was also scheduled to open in New York City. In 1994, one hour of phone time on the system costs $36; six hours, $142.

Most big-city newspapers and alternative weeklies have similar services. The newspapers print their recorded ads in the form of traditional classifieds, allowing readers to choose a specific ad before calling into the system.

Women find telephone personals reasonably safe. You can change your name or meet the person in a restaurant. If you don't want to see the person again, you don't.

Many users of the system are single parents or people who don't have a lot of free time to meet people in other ways. Many are professionals in their late twenties or early thirties, and even seniors are getting acquainted with this technology. And papers have found the phone-dating services generate more readership and increase the print run.

Despite the efficiency of telephone personals, there's no getting away from the fact that you may have to meet many people before you find your special someone. Still, they seem to be a good way of making an initial connection to find out. And with telephone personals, you never need to be without a date!

A word of caution: If you don't want your phone number to be read on the other caller's identification phone line, call your telephone company to activate the "call blocking" feature.

I'm told some of the telepersonals' members in Vancouver have recently been arranging group dinners through the system and that these have been a pleasant, unstressful way for people to meet. "It's quite cute," said one of the members. "People could be overheard asking each other 'What does your ad say?' or 'What is your box number?' Instead of being just a group of singles meeting for dinner, there was a commonality and something for people to talk to each other about."

On-line dating

By linking your computer to phone lines through a modem, you can enter the world of computer dating. Computer users contact bulletin boards in many ways. They may tap into local-access services that charge nominal fees. Among them, more expensive commercial services like Prodigy, CompuServe, and America Online serve millions of users.

Mike Godwin, on-line counsel for the Electronic Frontier Foundation in Washington, estimates there are 40,000 to 60,000 electronic bulletin board services in operation in the United States. "Lots of marriages began on line," he says. "For people not on-line, it sort of astonishes them that people would start a relationship in that way. But actually, for on-line life, it's not strange at all. When you are on-line, you can write whole essays that perhaps say more about you than you would ever say in a face-to-face conversation. So to that extent, the medium enhances intimacy."

On-line users may begin to feel they've known each other for years. Some begin a flirtation. And that can lead to phone calls and eventually to visits.

If you're on-line, here's one: The Electronic Matchmaker is a free, worldwide matching service that can be used through electronic mail. To participate, on your computer keyboard you'll need to type "perfect@match.com" with Send Form on a single line in the body of the message. You will receive a copy of the Electronic Matchmaker questionnaire which you're asked to fill out and return.

But like anything else, be aware that scum bags can be found on-line too. For example, there are some people who use several different names and contact the same person using a different persona.

So all the care you'd use in meeting someone through a companion ad should also be used when meeting someone on a bulletin board. You may wish to sign on using initials instead of your name.

To learn more about computer chatting, speak to the experts in your local computer store.

Companion ads

"Hey, look," whispered the gorgeous 30-year-old brunette. "More than 20 letters just in the first week. Seven of them look really good. Don't tell anybody."

Many people still use the traditional newspaper companion ads, preferring them, where they still exist, to the phone personals or computer services. Yet, as newspapers switch over to voice personals, the old style companion ad, without voice personal, will likely disappear in time.

You can usually pay by credit card number. You may have the replies to your ad mailed to you or pick them up personally at the newspaper office.

Some companion ads ask for a photo, but personally I think this is counterproductive. Photos can be quite deceptive. Some people look great in photos but may be a big disappointment to you in real life. Others are not photogenic, so you may eliminate good possibilities.

Asking for a photo seems rather superficial to me. I know some very dynamic people who wouldn't rate in a photo, but are considered desirable in person.

When replying to an ad, be sure you are addressing the person individually and not sending a photocopy of a standard reply letter or even your resume. Explain why their particular ad sparked your interest.

Companion ads do work. Many people have met their partners this way. They simply won't admit it.

U.S. researchers Aaron Ahuvia, professor of marketing at the University of Michigan School of Business Administration, and Mara Adelman, assistant professor of communication studies at Northwestern University, found that between 5% and 20% of people who place singles ads or use dating services succeed in finding serious relationships.

Meeting people this way can be time-consuming, even stressful, until you get into the routine. Both in print and sometimes in voice personals, some people are less than honest. Some will lie about almost everything, especially their age, their weight, and their height.

Exaggeration and selective truth telling are common. False claims about appearance create the greatest dissatisfaction with personal ads.

Don't assume that all people who advertise for companions are looking for marriage. Some people simply want a lot of dates; some are still getting over a past relationship and aren't ready for anything serious; some are looking for extramarital affairs.

Most people to whom I talked had positive experiences even if they didn't meet "the one."

One woman who gives workshops on how to do it recommends immediately eliminating prison inmates, married men, and anyone who's written a sexually explicit letter.

By the way, you may not be able to tell if someone is a prison inmate because the return addresses are only box numbers in a geographical area. It's wise to know where correctional facilities are located!

Then she recommends getting on the phone and asking, "What was it about my ad that appealed to you?" A little conversation, she says, usually reveals whether the guy is a jerk. You shouldn't have any qualms, she adds, about saying "I don't think you're the person I'm looking for."

If the phone conversation is positive, she suggests meeting for coffee in a public place and being careful never to give out your full name or address until you're sure you're interested. (Read more about safety in setting up encounters in chapter 20.)

After meeting for coffee she recommends either "I'd like to see you again" or "I don't think we're suited."

Placing a very generalized ad, she said, may result in more than 100 responses. When you are ready for a serious relationship, make your ad more specific. Then, she says, you'll get fewer responses, but they are more likely to be what you want.

Other advice she gives:

- Men should not specify they want a "slim" woman. They should say "fit" instead because too many women, even skinny ones, don't see themselves as slim.

- Don't be too narrow about age. You may well eliminate people you'd find really compatible.

- Don't list the things you like to do unless one or two of them are really important and you really would not want someone who doesn't share those interests. Rather, give general categories such as creative, artistic, or athletic.

Derek, a 39-year-old professor, says companion ads work "if you're lucky." He hasn't been. After two ads, at $100 a shot, and 100 replies, Derek did not find a suitable companion.

Instead he encountered one woman who promised to turn up at his home in the middle of the night wearing only a fur coat — if he would send her his house key. Another wanted to get him into bed as soon as possible but broke down in tears, confessing she had tried to commit suicide the night before.

Derek says two other women could have been right for him. But one returned to her old boyfriend. The other moved to San Francisco.

What hit him hard about companion ads was the time and energy involved in meeting just the most likely prospects.

He also found:

- Some who said they were slim "weren't even close."

- Several were not over previous relationships.

- Two changed their minds and said they couldn't meet because "you might be a rapist or something."

- One was into "new-age healing, crystals, and purple flames."

- One wrote an upbeat letter describing herself as a 38-year-old sun goddess but turned out to have "skin like old leather." She also had a small apartment neurotically crammed full of furniture and confessed that she answered ads just to be taken out for dinner.

Will Derek place another ad?

"No. I think I'm more comfortable meeting people in the natural course of events. But I have a friend who put in 20 to 30 ads. He's married now. Maybe you have to approach it like finding a job."

There, Derek hits on the crux of the matter. Finding a job can be important to financial health. Though having an intimate partner can be equally important to some people's emotional well being, few people make as much of an effort in their search for a companion as they do in looking for a job.

Dirk said he got exactly what he wanted when he advertised for a "morning person" who was "attractively buxom." Dirk courted Sally, one of a dozen women who replied to his ad, by letter for two months and then they dated for two months before marrying five months later.

R.K., a divorcee, placed ads three times, finally finding a husband: "He described his attributes as somewhat plump, which caught my attention. I found it endearing. What's more cuddly than a live teddy-bear type anyway! He sold me over the phone with his upbeat, optimistic, ambitious chatter. We clicked right then and there, sight unseen. We are looking forward to our eighth anniversary this summer."

Some people never find the right one. They criticize. They are looking for commitment too soon. The perfect person doesn't exist.

You have to be able to overlook some faults. You have to give and take a little bit. Accept change — be flexible and able to communicate.

One man says using the companion ads means meeting lots of people before the right one comes along.

"Some people get 20 replies and go out with one. If it doesn't go so well, they give up and don't even see the other 19. And a lot of people don't have much confidence. I'm in sales. You get used to rejection and make another phone call. As well, some people aren't open enough when they do meet. I worked hard at that."

14
Traveling alone

As I've implied in previous chapters, there'd be a lot more hanky panky going on if singles made the extra effort to get out of their homes, out from behind their desks, and took advantage of all the events set up especially for them.

Travel is a case in point. Tour operators and others get a little exasperated with the singles market sometimes. Singles are notorious for not committing to travel arrangements, yet most travel must be pre-arranged if it's going to be at a reasonable cost. The tour operator has to pay hotel and transportation deposits well in advance.

Maybe you're in the waiting-for-a-better-offer style of thinking. You don't get off your butt to plan and consequently you don't do anything or go anywhere. Boring!

As well, perhaps because men have been socialized not to treat themselves to extravagances, there's a shortage of them on travel tours and cruises. While women on cruise ships and tours have fun anyway, they'd still like to have more men along. Another factor may be that men tend to prefer more adventurous trips to taking cruises.

Many frustrated travel operators and agents find singles too much bother. But those who have hung on despite these frustrations are beginning to come out on top, as the singles travel market is now growing rapidly. In the majority of larger North American cities you can fairly easily find travel agencies that cater to you if you're single and that will match you with other singles for trips, tours, and cruises, with either the same or opposite sex.

Look for a travel or vacation supplier who offers "guarantee share" options. The guarantee share option is for singles who are willing to share accommodation. Some tour organizers and cruise lines pair up individuals and guarantee that a single pays no more than the per-person double occupancy rate, even if a roommate cannot be found.

In contrast, most packaged holidays are normally priced so that each of two people pays a per-person rate for shared accommodation. A single participant who either cannot find a roommate or wants to occupy a room alone must pay an extra "single supplement."

A girlfriend of mine who travels the world alone every chance she gets, says meeting men while traveling is "dead easy" but the question is quality. Because she travels alone in underdeveloped countries she has had to develop techniques for getting rid of unwanted attentions gracefully.

"In these countries you are constantly being hustled. What the men are looking for from a white woman is either wealth or sex, not friendship as we know it. I don't want to insult anybody, so I often say my husband and children are back at the hotel. That usually heads things off. Or I say I'm meeting a friend and I must be on my way."

She says she loves traveling alone because it is the way to meet lots of people. "I don't go on package tours and resort trips because adventurous, interesting people are usually scarce and the norm is couples letting themselves be herded around in groups. Having a passionate interest in photography and scuba diving has led to some pretty interesting people and places. It certainly gives a single woman an excuse to be in places that might feel awkward otherwise."

My friend says safety is always a concern and recently she has made a point of choosing only those countries reputed to be safe for a single woman travelling alone. "Research on the crime rate and cultural traditions is mandatory because travel in a hostile environment is really restrictive. There is too much you can't do. I experienced this in Papua New Guinea and in Turkey and quickly found it necessary to link up with other travelers for safety reasons. This seems to be easy enough to do if you are outgoing and friendly."

Diane Redfern, a colleague of mine at *The Province* newspaper, writes a travel column and puts out a very useful semi-monthly news-letter called *Connecting — News for Solo Travelers*. She travels by herself all over the world and says there's lots of opportunity to meet people when you go alone, especially if you leave your inhibitions and fears at home. "But you need to learn to speak up," she says. Ask questions. "If you're alone you tend to attract people because you look like a tourist. People want to help out and fellow travelers attract one another."

She says activity-oriented holidays are a great way to meet people. For example, if you're interested in a computer graphics or a desktop publishing course, consider taking it in another city so that you can combine it with a holiday. Or perhaps improve your art skills with a seminar in some other part of the world. Universities run all kinds of educational programs combined with trips. There are also spas, ranches, and holidays that can be combined with learning a new language, photography, studying wildlife, or carpentry.

The list is endless. You just need to find a good travel agent or subscribe to a newsletter like Redfern's *Connecting* (see the listing in the Appendix). In one recent edition, not only were there many travel opportunities for singles, but also numerous travel companion ads (free to those who subscribe to her newsletter) like these:

"Ben (50s) SM, is off to Costa Rica for the third time. Looking for compatible female."

"Bill, a 50-year-young adventurer, is anxious to travel to Russia with a compatible female."

"Betty, 51, wants to cruise the seven seas with a fun male or female."

Redfern says most people who want travel companions prefer the opposite sex. And when she surveyed her newsletter readers she found that one-third want group tours and cruises, especially singles-only tours. Their first choice was adventure holidays, followed by sightseeing holidays.

Gallivanting is a New York-based tour company now in its fourth year of providing soft adventure holidays for singles aged 25 to 55. In 1993, it had more than 100 departures covering five continents.

Relationships and even some marriages have developed from Gallivanting groups. Women nearly always outnumber men, but most of the participants are just happy to be traveling with friendly individuals instead of feeling out of place in a group of couples.

Michel Le Goaise of Singles Bicycle Tours says the best group he ever had was one with the widest age range — from people in their twenties to those in their fifties.

Backroads in California — another singles pioneering tour operator — has added half a dozen singles trips to its yearly schedule of biking and cross country ski trips. To contact these and other tour operators, look in the Appendix under Travel.

The biggest area of growth in the singles' travel market is among young and affluent vacationers who don't want predictable holidays at family resorts. Many of them are looking for high-energy vacation packages with everything from sailing trips to wilderness hikes.

Some travel agents are now organizing specific cruises for young and middle-aged singles, sometimes around a theme or a person. I've heard about relationship counselors who offer their courses as part of a singles' cruise in the Caribbean. One travel agency approached me to host such a cruise but I had to decline because of work pressures.

The older crowd is also a staple of the singles' travel market. To illustrate the opportunity men over 50 have in meeting women through travel, I just have to tell you about this: The travel industry actually hires single men over 40, who are good dancers, as cruise hosts. They don't get paid as such, but their travel is free. Phyllis Zeno runs The Merry Widows, an organization for women who love to dance, formed in 1977. She is also creative director for the AAA Auto Club South in Tampa, Florida. And since 1977 she has been organizing dance tours and cruises for women and supplying dance hosts to escort them. Now some other cruise lines are doing the same thing. These include Royal Cruise Line, Delta Queen Steamboat Company, and Royal Viking Line. In addition to being single, over 40, and a good dancer, a cruise host must be physically fit, a moderate or non-drinker, and a good conversationalist. In other words, the ideal man! On a cruise he must socialize with all single women over 50 and refrain from favoritism. He must remain courteous, participate in games and activities, assist with shore excursions on request, and have an adequate cruise wardrobe, including a black tuxedo, white dinner jacket, and appropriate sports clothes. Hosts must be absolutely discreet and not get romantically involved with any women while on the ship.

One cruise host suggests you do not do more than one month at a time to avoid burnout. But, he says, "You could make a career of dancing your way across the seven seas. It's tough but somebody has got to do it!"

So men, if you're interested, contact your local travel agent, or Redfern at —

P.O. Box 29088
Delamont Postal Outlet
1996 West Broadway
Vancouver, British Columbia
Canada V6J 5C2

Or contact Zeno at —

AAA Merry Widows Dance Cruises
Box 31087
Tampa, Florida 33631
Tel: (813) 289-5923
1-800-374-2689 (U.S. only)

Finally, women who travel should not be as naive as this woman who wrote to me:

> *Dear Kathy:*
>
> *I'm a divorcee, 48, who has not met too many bachelors. A year ago I met a little wild Hungarian. He loved to dance, cook, fish, and drink.*
>
> *I went heavy-duty with him but at every dance he flirted with every attractive woman. If I went out of town, he dated other ladies.*
>
> *So I dumped him. Then I went on a cruise to Mexico and met a senior officer who has been phoning weekly from L.A. He told me he fell in love at first sight. Yet he told me he has a wife but would like to move to Canada after he straightens this out.*
>
> *I can't get him off my mind. I asked him if he cheated on his wife. He said no. His marriage was arranged and he spent the last 11 years cruising and going home for two months a year.*
>
> *I am searching for a nice partner. I hate being alone in this pensioner town. What would you do?*
>
> *Anonymous*

> *Dear Anonymous:*
>
> *I'd forget the senior officer. I suspect he romances at least one woman on every cruise and then keeps them hooked by phone.*

15
H olidays

By and large, many people find being single okay most days of the year. But there are times such as Christmas, New Year's Eve, and Valentine's Day when you tend to feel something's missing. Advertising creates the impression that everybody who is happy is part of a couple and is receiving gifts, flowers, and words of love.

To avoid holiday-induced depression, it's wise to plan ahead for some activities with friends. Throw a house party. Or go with a group to one of the events you may find listed under Coming Events in the classified section of your local newspaper. Or put some money together and reserve a ski resort condo.

I will never forget my first Christmas a couple of months after my husband and I split up. I felt so alone.

Fortunately, my daughter and I were invited to visit relatives. We didn't eat Christmas dinner alone but I was acutely depressed. I cuddled my seven-year-old daughter as she sobbed herself to sleep Christmas Eve. I tried very hard to have a nice tree, some gifts under it, and to fulfill our Christmas morning ritual. But, of course, her dad wasn't there and it was so painful. For us, getting through the Christmas season was a matter of surviving one hour at a time.

New Year's Eve was also difficult at times during the eight or so years I was single. It's one day, aside from Valentine's Day, that you really feel alone. I think I went to a friend's place the first New Year's Eve. But the most painful was one seven years later. New Year's Eve came after another important relationship had ended days before. I had made no plans because I had expected we'd spend it together. So, faced with staying home on New Year's, I decided I had to do something or I'd cry all night. I made bread.

The whole procedure lasted about six or eight hours. I can't remember. But I do remember being totally miserable, eating a whole loaf of fresh bread on my own at midnight, and sobbing my heart out.

So if you're alone on one of the major holidays, please realize there are many others going through the same thing. Whether you're newly single, new to the area, or have not yet established a network of other singles of the same or opposite sex, holidays can be hell.

If you're suddenly on your own, it's natural to be pretty depressed and have very little energy. This too will pass. With time, your energy level will pick up. You will be depressed for shorter and shorter periods and eventually you'll be your old self and ready to plan fun things with friends for these holiday events.

If you're over the worst and know someone else who is alone and feeling blue, reach out and include him or her in your activities. You already know what it's like. Few people understand as clearly as you do the profound pain a newly single person may be suffering.

On Valentine's Day, think of your single friends — especially those who are newly single. Make sure you send them a card. You can make a big difference.

You might organize a Valentine's Day brunch or a dinner and invite all your same-sex and opposite sex friends and ask them to bring a friend. You can rotate the seats with each course.

If you're not in a relationship, on special holidays you can host a party for all the people you love — your parents, relatives, and friends. It's important to learn how to invite people into your life. Don't always be the guest, but be the host. Create your own fun instead of waiting for it to come to you. It can be enjoyable to prepare for parties and other events if you get others involved in the preparation.

An excellent Christmas event is a tree decorating party. You can invite friends or relatives or ask someone of the opposite sex to help: "The tree's a little big. Would you mind coming over and helping me set it up? I don't think I can reach the top to put the star up." Or a man could suggest "the tree really needs a woman's touch."

At some point after a divorce, you may want to throw a survival celebration party. Invite everyone who helped you get through your breakup and ask each person to bring a guest. It's a way of saying thank you and expanding your social circle at the same time.

So it's really important to work on developing friendships with other singles, not just focusing on finding a mate. Friends can go a long way in helping you combat loneliness and maintain a healthy social life.

Don't give up your married friends, though there will be times when you feel like a fifth wheel.

If you have few same sex friends, work on creating a better balance. If you're a single mother, a good way to connect with other women in similar circumstances is to join the Singles Mothers Network of the YWCA. YWCAs exist throughout North America and most cities have these networks. In Vancouver, for example, there are 40,000 single-parent families in the city and surrounding suburbs. Almost 90% of these single parents are women. And in Vancouver they've had an annual conference each fall for 15 years. It's a day when mothers share challenges, solutions, and survival tips. You'll meet new friends and have a support group of other single mothers who meet monthly.

16
$\mathcal{D}$ating has changed

For teens, the very term "dating" is out of date. It comes across like "courting" or "going steady." It's through a network of friends that many teens and twenty-somethings make their connections nowadays. When they go out, it is more often with groups of friends than just one person.

It's been called group dating, pack protection, group identity. It is a way of forming the early bonds that sometimes lead to relationships.

Platonic relationships with members of the opposite sex are common. A lot of older people wouldn't believe this but I have seen it with my own eyes and it's true. The one who turns out to be a boyfriend is sometimes a friend of one of the friends in the group.

Parents often feel more comfortable that their kids have a group. These young people watch out for each other. Before they get involved, they already know something of each other's background. It seems a lot safer.

I think older adults could learn from this method. I'd like to see more people inviting their friends of both sexes to meet with their other friends and their friends, say over brunch. Extending the group to include your best friend's friends creates the potential for several intimate love relationships.

If you're single again, it's important to realize that the basics of the dating game have undergone an overhaul. For one thing some people have several relationships on the go at the same time. If you want a monogamous relationship it's wise to check out the intentions of the other person quickly.

For example, one woman I know has a steady, intimate relationship with a man she has known for years. But it's only for sex — safe sex. She doesn't love him and doesn't really share much else with him. But she trusts him. He's very conscious about AIDS and other sexually transmitted diseases and presents her with no complications.

A man I know is seeing four women. One is an ex-girlfriend he sees occasionally. They are friends but no longer sexually intimate. Another, he sees casually and they do have sex, but not exclusively with each other, which, of course, is risky these days. This man also sees another woman casually who is more interested in him than he is in her. They don't have sex and he thinks they'll remain just friends. At the moment, he's most interested in the fourth woman. He figures this could be a steady sexually intimate relationship if it develops as he plans. This one could be exclusive. But he doesn't want to reach that point in his life yet. He doesn't feel he's ready for commitment.

Those interested in one special person for a committed, monogamous relationship and marriage, need to keep the above in mind. You can get burned by not understanding that others may not share your point of view and goals. I think it's a good idea, if you're marriage minded, to talk about this with the person you're seeing fairly early in the relationship so you don't waste time and don't get hurt.

Preliminary dates

Meeting briefly for coffee or lunch, you and your date can find out if you have anything in common. Can you talk for half an hour comfortably? Is there any possibility of chemistry? As the woman, do you feel safe?

When you go out for dinner on a first date, there can be unspoken expectations. One woman I know doesn't like to go out for dinner with a man until she's met him for coffee or lunch several times. The first few times she meets him at a restaurant and doesn't let him know where she lives until she's fairly confident he's okay. Then dinner is far more relaxed because she already knows him a little. This approach also works well for many men who don't want to blow at least $40 for dinner, only to discover there's no basis for a relationship.

When you go out on a date, try not to have preconceptions. Keep a sense of freshness and spontaneity. Relax and simply be with each other. This will free both of you to reveal yourselves and be a lot more interesting. When we're trying to be perfect, we tend to be boring.

Unless you feel unsafe, or the person is a complete and utter nerd, go out at least twice. Even if things don't seem right immediately, you may change your mind. But if you discover he or she really isn't good material for a relationship, cut the association early. Or, if you find out this person doesn't ever want a long-term relationship or marriage, and you do, cut your losses. Tell him or her what you want and end the dating. That will free you to start meeting others.

The first date

Dear Kathy:

I'm a 41-year-old divorced male who has been out of the dating scene for 20 years. There is a woman in my office building whom I find very attractive. I think the feeling may be mutual.

I am working up to asking her out but need a little advice on what would be appropriate on a first date. Do I ask her out to dinner, to a play, or invite her for [a game of] squash?

Out Of It

Dear Out Of It:

Any of the above ideas sounds great to me. But perhaps it would be a good idea to first ask her out for a coffee or a workday lunch. That would give her a chance to get to know you a little first so that she feels some comfort and safety with you before you ask her for a real date.

My inclination would be to make the date fairly casual. If your intention is to develop a friendship and possibly a love relationship, it's important to present yourself with truth and create a comfortable atmosphere. It should focus on something other than gazing into each other eyes, which is a bit too pressured and intimate for a first date. But it should also present an opportunity for conversation so you both get information about what you may have in common.

All three of your ideas allow for unpressured getting-to-know-you. However, it may be wise to ask her which option she would prefer, since for all you know she may have a strong dislike of racquet sports or theater, and maybe she's on a diet.

It's also wise to limit the first dates to four hours or less.
To develop a truly intimate relationship, take it slowly.
Sexual intimacy before real intimacy is usually a big mistake.

Dating seems to be a lost art. And it's not just the newly single who have trouble knowing how to do it. Even college students can be lost. At the Florida Institute of Technology, for example, orientation includes a mandatory seminar on dating. One seminar leader says students need dating instruction because most students have forgotten how. A college student's idea of a great date is typically go to a movie, adjourn to a bar, get plastered, and make out.

Dating methods need to change for various reasons. Movies and dinners out are not affordable to many students; there has been growing awareness about date rape; and making out with a virtual stranger isn't safe because of AIDS and other sexually transmitted diseases.

The point of going out on a date should be to get to know each other better. Nowadays, maybe rent a bicycle built for two and then afterwards go for a coffee. Or study together. Or invite some friends over.

Who calls?

This is another question I'm often asked. As I discussed in chapter 10, most men like to be asked out on a date and most women say it's okay for a woman to ask a man out.

Calling a man is certainly okay initially and when a relationship is developing. I see no reason why, if a woman wants to speak with a man, she should not assert herself. Certainly, waiting by the phone for him to call is disempowering and nonsensical. However, there are circumstances where calling is inappropriate in the mating dance, as illustrated by the following letter:

Dear Kathy:

I'm a 20-year-old attractive female. I recently ... went out on a date [and] we got along great and had a lot in common.

I called him about two days later and we talked awhile on the phone. He hasn't called back. He has been all I have thought about since. Should I call again or would I be too pushy and scare him off?

Too Pushy?

Dear Too Pushy?:

Don't call. The ball is in his court. If he's interested, he'll call you. If you call again, you're giving away your power.

And here's some dating advice in general from Doris Wild Helmering, a clinical psychologist and columnist for the *St. Louis Post-Dispatch*. Helmering says the following behaviors will keep you from forming a long-lasting relationship:

- Sending flowers and candy immediately after the first date. While it's nice to get flowers and candy, most people feel uncomfortable if someone comes on too quickly with too much too soon.

- Baring your soul and telling everything there is to know about you. Telling too much in the beginning is a turn-off because it assumes the relationship is deeper than it is.

- Always resisting a change of plans.

- Thinking he or she "owes it to you" to report everything he or she is doing each day. *Memorize that one.*

- Talking about prior relationships, with intimate details.

- Expecting that the person will ask for another date (or will call the next day to set up a date) and being resentful if he or she doesn't.

Who pays?

My sweetie and I have always shared the cost — both when we were dating and even now we live together. After all, we both work and have income. Perhaps it's why he's kept me around so long!

In his previous experiences, many women didn't share expenses. I'd always assumed that most women today share equally. But do they?

In preparing this chapter, I spent some time re-reading letters from single men about dating. Many men said women were just too demanding, too picky, and too unrealistic. Some said women are opportunistic — looking not for love but for the guy with the most assets. Even if women are pitching the equality line, said some of the men, they don't put their money where their mouths are.

"Where are all the ladies who want a sincere relationship, someone who loves you for who you are, not what you have?" one man wrote.

"I'm 33, financially secure, but I don't own a BMW or a condo at a ski resort. I love things that are real and important, like love, friendship, caring.

"I have a mortgage so I don't always have the cash to be spontaneous (it costs) but I do live for romance and plain good times. The ladies that wrote you about all the things that they like to do, but can't find men to do them with, expect their date to pay for them. They're always around as long as the money's there but when it runs out, so do they."

How much of this is generalized bitterness resulting from a few bad experiences? And how much of it represents the way it is? What happens if the woman earns more than the man? Or don't women date men who earn less? Are women only interested in rich guys with BMWs and ski condos, as the above man and others have claimed?

Do women date as equals or not? Can they? Should they? Who should pay on the initial dates? Many readers, both men and women, said both sexes should share dating costs equally or at least in proportion to their incomes. But a few, possibly reflecting generational differences, felt men should pay. And some said young women they know don't share dating costs.

The issue of "who pays" can cause tension on a date.

Here are some excerpts from readers' letters:

- "Six years ago, I dated a professional. She grossed $72,000. I grossed $21,000. She insisted I pay for everything because I asked her out. Five years ago, I started dating the woman who is now my wife. I insisted and she agreed that we share everything equally. Her gross salary was $39,000. Mine dropped slightly to $20,000. This arrangement continues, except that I now earn the same salary as she does."

- "I'm 29, attractive, earning $35,000, and I do ask men out. My approach is that the person who asks pays. This principle works if women ask men out on a similar frequency. For more regular relationships, I try to pay my half. This is only fair in a time when many women are at similar pay scales with men. It is also important in the power balance between the sexes."

- "I'm a woman, 28, single and I gross $25,000. I think who pays depends on how long you've known someone. I was burned for thousands of dollars when I was 21. There are men who look for suckers to put them through school. If a man asks for a date, he pays. If I know a man is sincere, I treat once in a while."

- "I'm 42, a professional aviator, salary $50,000, no BMW, divorced, popular enough with the ladies, and I enjoy my life. I have always earned more than my partners, so I have always felt I ought to contribute more financially. Naturally, there will be those who will insist on paying, those who take advantage of them, and those who must pay — husbands of wives who must stay home and look after a family, for example."

- "I'm a 35-year-old single parent. I can't afford to pay half when I date. But I do cook a nice meal as my contribution."

- "I never expect a man to pay for me unless it's a special occasion. I have many girlfriends who think men should pay everything and don't realize they have to live as well. I can keep a man around longer, usually, because I'm being fair."

- "I'm a 43-year-old male, currently living on investments. My annual income was in excess of $100,000. The custom of men paying for the meals and entertainment on a date is still a very real romantic notion. I do not find the custom even slightly romantic but simply a throwback to the days when men were considered superior to women. And there is also the implication of a trade off — the man pays for the date in return for what?

Men can refuse to date women who won't pay their equal share but I think it is more incumbent upon women to call upon their personal dignity and integrity and insist on picking up the tab on an equal basis."

- "I'm a 64-year-old female. My husband wanted me to stay home so I never worked out of the house. For almost 17 years, I have been alone and worked for small wages. Should a gentleman like my companionship and take me for dinner, yes, I expect him to pay. No, I am not out for his money. But I still like to be treated like a lady, with respect, and do not want to have to repay him with a 'romantic' encounter. Should a friendship develop and more outings, of course, I will show my appreciation and pay."

- "I think it's obvious that the rules have changed a great deal. Gone are the days when a man asked and a man paid. An increasing number of men want women to ask and to share the load. In the fifties and sixties, men paid for everything. Now, if a young man is going to college or has only part-time employment, he often can't afford to pay for two and have a car on top of it all."

Other men in their late twenties and older, may have the money, but are fed up paying for everything, especially if the woman also has a job. And a lot of women too feel they're equal. I feel strongly that, if I expect to be equal in all aspects of my relationship, I should pull my own weight financially.

The Harlequin survey of women found 42% of Canadian women and 60% of U.S. women still prefer the man to pay for everything, but I wish their survey had included men. It's important to talk about this issue with the person you're dating. That can help to avoid a lot of confusion and resentment. On the first date, however, before you can really discuss this, it's usually the one doing the asking who pays. After that, don't hesitate in advance to say, "Is this your treat?" or "This is my treat" or "Shall we split this?" Many women today like to share the expenses and the decisions equally, unless they are financially unable to do so.

Chivalry in the post-feminist world

The Harlequin Romance survey of women found 75% of Canadian women and 85% of American women prefer the man to open doors for her. On helping you on with your coat: 68% of Canadian women prefer that, 78% of American women prefer it. Asked if their escort should plan the location and activity for the date, 59% of Canadian women said yes, 68% of U.S. women said yes. When asked if they prefer their date to order for them in restaurants, 93% of Canadian women and 79% of U.S. women said, "No Way!"

When it comes to opening doors, personally I do it for men, women, or children if I'm there first. And a man, or anyone else for that matter, who lets a door close in my face, is a boor. I don't expect a man to open my car door, although I appreciate it when it is done. I do expect a man to help me on with my coat. Yet if he unilaterally picked what we were going to do or what I was going to eat in a restaurant, he'd be toast.

When sex?

In the old days, sex came after marriage. Sex was an accurate indicator of the seriousness of the relationship. Today, it certainly is not. Although some women still equate sex with love, men rarely do.

If there is no regular pattern to the times you see each other and you're not sure the other person feels any real emotional involvement, sex should be out of the question — unless you only want to get your rocks off too. But if you think you'll become emotionally involved, it's better not to sleep together in the first month or so of a new relationship. Sustainable relationships are usually built slowly.

Sex intensifies and accelerates the psychological processes that make up romantic relationships, say Carmen Lynch and Dr. Martin Blinder in a paper entitled "The Romantic Relationship: Why and How People Fall in Love, The Way Couples Connect and Why They Break Apart." Sexual intimacy dissolves boundaries and facilitates the mirroring — the reflection of what and where we are. That is why it is often so difficult to be "just friends" after the romantic phase of the relationship has run its course.

Sex will intensify a person's needs, bringing them to the surface. It elicits our best, our most positive feelings, such as appreciation and attractiveness, and our worst character traits, such as the need to be in control, to be right all the time, and possessiveness, say Lynch and Blinder.

"Sex so accelerates the relationship process that erotic union is an excellent way to find out a great deal about someone in a short period of time, provided that one's sexuality is not split off from feelings and behavior. Of course, people with little link between what they do and what they feel are able to have sex with individuals for whom they have no affection. Their partner's character or personality — even their gender — may be totally irrelevant."

There are few things worse than having sex with someone who leaves afterwards and you never, ever see him or her again. And if you have to ask, "Do you still respect me?" you became sexually involved too soon.

And while on the subject of respect, please turn now to the rating test for guys on page 157. Worksheet #2 is a love quiz that made the rounds among highschool girls. While I don't like rating people, I do support the idea of promoting the value of mutual respect. Perhaps because teenage girls usually become interested in relationships long before guys do, there's a tendency for girls to tolerate the most off-hand treatment in order to have a boyfriend. Even some adult women do the same thing.

I'd change the quiz slightly: I'd give an automatic fail to heavy alcohol/drug problems and to forcing you into drinking or sex. Acts of jealousy and name calling would also be a red flag for me and earn many more penalty points. On the other hand, I don't think buying major gifts or paying for a date should earn him extra points. I favor paying your own way and not valuing the relationship on a material basis.

The Harlequin survey asked women what behavior is guaranteed to turn them off on a date. Canadian women said they were most grossed out if the date drank too much (29%), if he was too aggressive about sex (21%), by loud boisterous behavior (17%), and flirting with other women (17%) as well as he does all the talking or he's too quiet and conservative.

American women were most upset with men who are too aggressive about sex (29%), followed by too much drinking (26%), loud boisterous behavior (18%), and flirting with other women (15%).

In Harlequin's survey of men, 24% said they are turned off on a first date if the woman flirts with other men. Another 21% said they don't want to be with a woman who's too demanding and "acts like a princess"; 13% don't like a woman who's loud and boisterous; and 12% don't want a woman if she drinks too much; 10% say they're turned off if she's too quiet and conservative.

Only 2% said they're turned off if she dresses too sexily.

WORKSHEET #2
LOVE QUIZ

Here's how the quiz works:

1. Start your boyfriend off with 100 points.

2. Deduct points for each bad act (see below).

3. Add points for each good act (see below).

4. Apply the test for two full weeks, three if he's borderline.

5. You may add other good/bad acts and attribute demerits or credits as you think relevant.

6. Do not combine two acts into one (e.g., rudeness to family and mean comments). Pick one and apply appropriate points.

7. Do not provoke or trick him into committing an act in order to give him more or fewer points.

8. Pay attention to every detail but be kind. Remember, he is only human.

9. Do not be too lenient.

10. Above all, do not let him know you are giving him this test.

FINAL SCORES:

0 to 25 — Bail. He's not for you (or anyone else either).

26 to 50 — Watch him like a hawk. You may have to dump him.

51 to 75 — Basically a good guy. Could either screw up royally or improve immensely. Encourage the latter.

76 to 100 — Sounds like a sweetheart. Keep him if you can.

Bad points (remember to deduct from 100):
* Very late phone calls. Deduct 8.
* No phone call when it was promised. Deduct 12.
* Being stood up. Deduct 25.
* Act of jealousy. Deduct 5.
* Physical abuse. Automatic fail.
* He dumps you. Automatic fail.
* Name-calling or mean comments. Deduct 10.
* Going out with his friends when he's made plans with you. Deduct 15.
* White lies. Deduct 8. Harsher lies, 12. Major lies, 25.
* Forcing you into something (e.g., drinking, sex). Deduct 15.
* Act of disrespect (e.g., embarrassing you in public). Deduct 15.
* Cheating. Automatic fail.
* Minor drug/alcohol problems. Deduct 20 to 25.
* Heavy drug/alcohol problems. Deduct 50.
* Rudeness to you, friends or family. Deduct 8 to 20, depending on severity.
* Making fun of you. Deduct 8.
* Inconsideration in bed. Deduct 15.
* Taking off for evening or day without telling you. Deduct 20.
* Neglecting or ignoring you at a social function. Deduct 15.
* Purposely going against your wishes (e.g., drinking and driving). Deduct 20.
* Forgetting important occasions such as anniversaries, social functions. Deduct 20.

Good points:

* Giving you small gifts, such as flowers, for no reason. Add 10.
* Picking you up, driving you home. Add 10.
* Taking you out for the evening (including dishing out the cash). Add 10.
* Opens doors for you. Add 3.
* Making daily phone calls (not 5 points for every day). Add 5 points.
* Act of affection for no reason. Add 8.
* Buying you big gifts such as clothing. Add 25.
* Putting his interests or preferences aside for you (e.g., going where you want). Add 15.
* Remembering anniversaries or important occasions. Add 15.
* Showing concern when it's obvious you are sad or upset. Add 10 to 20.
* Small (cute) act of jealousy. Add 5.
* Sticking up for you — verbally, add 8. Physically, add 12-20.
* Good bedroom manner. Add 12.
* Act of sensitivity — minor, add 8; major, add 12.
* Act of sacrifice, minor (e.g., giving up last smoke). Add 6. Major (e.g., giving up evening with the guys for you). Add 10.

How to tell your lover it's over

It's sad, but there may come a time when you realize the person you're seeing is not for you. I think you need to tell that person gently but firmly that the relationship isn't working for you and that you're sorry that you must end it.

Realize that while you may have been aware that the end is coming, your partner may not. Do not put the person down. His or her reaction is likely to be very emotional. Listen quietly. Be respectful and caring but do not put out any hope for a future together. That is cruel.

Pick a weekend to burst his or her bubble or other time when the person has a couple of days to deal with the shock before going to work. He or she may want to see you again as the reality of the situation sinks in. You may do this a couple of times. But do not do anything to raise the person's hopes that you'll change your mind. Be kind, but firm.

What to do when you're dumped

Unless you're extremely lucky, there will be times when dating leads to a relationship that eventually ends. When a relationship is about to break up there may be some early signals. Perhaps he or she is distancing. You call and she's always busy. He sees you only at your urging. He never suggests getting together anymore. When you are together, there's not a lot of connection.

Perhaps you are always finding something wrong with him. You constantly want him to change. Or one of you is cheating.

Whatever the signals are, if the relationship meant a lot to you, you're going to feel devastated when it's over.

The pain that comes when a relationship ends is among the most wrenching of human emotions. Tinged with anger, numbness, despair, self-doubt, and loss of love, rejection by a lover is the stuff that half the world's songs are about and most of the crimes of passion.

You're dead tired, yet you can't sleep. You may not be able to eat either and your weight will drop. The days of crying, the feelings that you're losing your mind, the self-pity, the plots of revenge and even thoughts of suicide seem unbearable. All this is normal — a natural reaction to traumatic stress — and part of healing.

Personal relationships are central to our identity. You may obsess about why the breakup happened. I think partly this is a form of denial, an inability to let go.

Reach out to your friends for support, including your platonic opposite sex friends who are helpful in restoring your ego, your desire for approval. Try not to say too much at work about the breakup. You're there to work and your colleagues may be upset. Talk with them at lunch or coffee, if you must.

Try not to lose yourself in food or booze. Instead, baby yourself with soothing music, a warm bath, a long walk — whatever gives you comfort.

Try to limit your obsessing over him or her to three ten-minute periods a day and gradually reduce these times. Try to think more and more about aspects of your life that will improve without him or her. Fantasizing about getting back together may occur, even months later. Eventually you'll realize that it won't happen and it's not meant to be anyway.

And realize that no matter how intense your grief, how unmanageable your life seems now, you will heal. Don't worry that your recovery is faster or slower than someone else's. You are an individual and you will do it at your own pace. And even if life doesn't seem worth living now, it will eventually.

Keeping a journal, writing down your thoughts, doubts, and feelings will help. Try to let go of feelings of revenge. They will only prolong your unhappiness. Don't get even; get ahead.

17

E motional exploiters

Con men and gold diggers

"If You're Rich, I'm Single" reads the bumper sticker on the young woman's sports car. Not too surprising really. There have always been gold diggers looking for a free ride. But now, with more women getting their share of good careers and good money, there are also plenty of con men looking for sugar mommies. The problem occurs so often that a police officer recently asked me to warn my readers about it.

Dear Kathy:

I feel a responsibility to write you about Don Juan cons. There are probably hundreds of single women whose lives are being manipulated by con men. Every day, the numbers of victims increase. Yet for every one reported, probably 25 or more, for fear of retribution, embarrassment, or denial, never report the huge sums of money lost.

Most of these con men have no criminal record. If confronted, they acknowledge involvement but plead that a poor investment resulted in the loss of money. An arrest or conviction is next to impossible.

The women's hurt is doubled knowing that they weren't loved but used. These con men come in all shapes and sizes. They usually prey on the over-forties, but not always. They do not have to drive flashy cars or wear trendy clothes, and they are not necessarily fast operators who go after the big bucks quickly.

They have charisma, are astute assessors of women, have a gift of the gab, and know the women who have money. (Most of the women will tell them.) These men enjoy the slow pursuit, where the ultimate conquest results in the women falling madly in love. They also get off on the sexual encounters.

Most are described by the women as "perfect gentlemen." They seldom make the first move. They fill up their "owe you" box every time they see the woman. They arrive with wine, chocolates, or flowers. She receives cards, letters of thanks, and appreciative phone calls.

Many evenings she's embarrassed by how much she's talked about herself, but she sees this relationship as the most positive thing that's ever happened to her. After all, women "die" for a man to treat her this special. He builds up his "trust bank" then begins his real purpose.

The con routine takes many forms but the mode of operation is similar, as are the con's ultimate goals. One that's worked goes like this: Early in the courtship, he reveals his knowledge of the stock market. He says he's investing heavily in a stock, arrives one evening, and gives the woman $500. He explains that he invested $1,000 "for her" and that is her profit.

Another time, he gives her $1,000 from another "investment" he's made. Then one evening he painstakingly outlines the inside information he has and asks her to go 50-50 with him. She needs to come up with $50,000 or more.

Now, unless you have been in this situation, you have no idea how difficult it is for the woman to refuse. She trusts him, loves him, sees a future with him, and the risk of refusing may mean losing him. He may hint at proposing marriage after they "strike it big." She seldom consults family, friends, or a lawyer. She goes with her heart which says "yes," and gets him the money.

She might never see him again but usually does. He says the money will come soon (even after considerable time) and she believes him. When she subsequently gets dumped, she inevitably blames herself and doesn't turn him in.

Will a woman who reads this confront her lover? Will she stop seeing a potential con man? Not likely. The good con man will convince her, embarrass her, for even considering he'd do such a thing. But take my advice: If the man in your life asks you for money — even for his sick child — run to a lawyer, a family member, a friend, a counselor, a police officer. Be sure not to go through this alone.

Where do these men meet the women? It's usually not at a $5 singles dance or a bar. More than likely, it'll be at a high-priced seminar, a dance at a high-class nightclub, an aerobics class where women outnumber men ten to one, a high-priced fat farm, or the weekend companion section of the paper.

Con men know the scent of money. Amazingly enough, there are Don Juan cons on record who have courted as many as 18 women at the same time. No wonder many of them don't work for a living — how could they?

Encourage women who have been conned to write you. I believe you'll find the results staggering.

Police constable

I did just that, and this is just one of the many responses:

Dear Kathy:

I, too, was conned by a man who, after only a few dates, said he was falling in love with me. I was going through a bad time after separating and was very vulnerable.

Boy did this guy suck me in. He lived in an old basement suite and drove a very old car, but always bragged about his $1,200 silk suits from Hong Kong. When I asked him about his living arrangements he said he did not want people to know he had money!

He was very generous, buying me jewelry, clothes, etc. After eight months of dating he started traveling a lot but said he could not get charge cards as he was being sued by a bank for some bad investment not his fault.

Like an idiot, I gave him authorized use of two of my charge cards. When we broke up, they were at the limit. He sent me a note saying he would pay them off. But after three months of only making minimum payments on bills totalling $10,000 he missed a payment. When approached, he went crazy on the phone.

I have since gone to a bank and got a loan, co-signed by my wonderful father. When I made up my mind to forget what happened I felt I'd shed 260 pounds. (That is how much this guy weighed!)

He is not good-looking but the charm was unbelievable. He made me feel as though I were the only person in his life. Later I found there were a lot of other women.

Whenever he felt there was a problem, the gifts would come and he could make me feel so guilty I'd give in and do whatever he wanted. A few months later I became so angry about this sleazebag I went to small claims court, garnisheed the one bank account I knew about and got $2,500 put into trust in court, and have a settlement conference set for November.

Unlike some people I'm lucky to have a lot of documentation in my favor about him. I have also sold the jewelry and clothes to pay my loan down.

I was too trusting and ignored the warning signs and I want other people to learn by my mistake.

Burned

Another woman said she had been ripped off and many of her female business clients had had similar experiences.

Sandra, 45, said she felt used, stupid, and angry when a lover ripped her off for $600. She put the bill in the hands of collection agency.

But after she heard even worse horror stories from her clients, she realized she wasn't stupid, just in the wrong place at the wrong time. Some men, she said, make a career out of taking women to the cleaners — romantically and financially. If you're single, you may meet one of them one day.

Typically, says Sandra, the woman is in business or in a good career, divorced, alone, and wanting a little fun in her life. Enter a man, often a little younger, always very sincere, and usually quite a bit of fun.

"These guys are really smooth. They play you. I met this man and at first felt he was too young for me. But he was fun, full of energy. After a couple of months of dating, I wanted to go to Las Vegas for a holiday. He said he didn't have the money because he was trying to pay off a couple of bills. So I offered to put it on my charge card and he said he'd pay me back. He wasn't interested in keeping costs down. It had to be the best of everything, the best rental cars, the works.

As soon as we got home, I found out it was not just two debts but $10,000 worth and he was on the verge of bankruptcy."

Sandra stopped seeing the man, never received the money, and he's now living with another woman, she says, "probably ripping her off."

A short time later Sandra got taken by another man. "We were out and he said his cash card was broken. I lent him the $60 for the bill. When I didn't see the money or him, I phoned his boss. I did get my money back."

One of Sandra's clients — a woman who sells real estate — fell in love and six months later lent her boyfriend $50,000 to start his own business. He used it instead to date other women and buy cocaine.

Another woman signed over part of her expensive house to her boyfriend.

Sandra said it's not uncommon for women who work in the stock market to make loans to male colleagues and never see the money again. "One girl lent $12,000 and then the guy said that Revenue Canada had frozen his bank account and he couldn't pay her back. These men are always waiting for their big deal to go through and it never comes."

To avoid a man pulling both your heart strings and your purse strings, here's some advice:

- Realize you may be emotionally vulnerable.

- Be wary of men who like to live high, seem too good to be true, or are perhaps too much fun. Trust, rather than deny, your gut feelings.

- If he has no charge cards, they may have been taken away.

- Don't give your trust. Make him earn it.

- If a man suggests you make an investment, asks to borrow your credit card, wants to borrow money, or makes any other financial move on your cash or assets, get advice from a lawyer, friend, or family member.

- When smitten, people have a tendency to ignore or minimize details and facts they don't like or which don't add up. Try to resist this tendency.

- Try to learn as much as possible about the history and friends of someone you're dating.
- Call him at his place of work to confirm that indeed he is employed there.

To be fair, let's also talk about women who are gold diggers. Here's a letter from a man:

> *Dear Kathy:*
>
> *It's not only women who get ripped off. I became enamored with a woman who moved in with me last winter. She persuaded me to buy her a car, which I put in her name. She often wanted me to go shopping with her and each trip cost me several hundred dollars.*
>
> *Then, almost as instantly as she appeared in my life, she was gone one afternoon and never called or wrote to say what happened. There was no incident to provoke her leaving.*
>
> *A month later I discovered she had moved in with another man. She appears to be doing the same thing to him.*
>
> *Ripped off*

Psychopaths

To give you a healthy appreciation of how singles may be preyed upon, Dr. Robert Hare's book, *Without Conscience,* is a good read. Dr. Hare is a world expert on psychopaths. He says psychopaths number one in 100 people and most are not in prison. While we usually think of psychopaths as cold-blooded killers, most are operating freely in business, in the professions, in the stock exchange, in politics, and in relationships. There's a good chance, he says, that everyone will encounter a psychopath at some time in their life.

"The callous use of the lonely is a trademark of psychopaths," writes Dr. Hare. "Some psychopaths, particularly those in prison, initially contact their victims through the lonely-hearts columns. Letters often lead to visits and, inevitably, to disillusionment and pain for the victims.

"Psychopaths have an uncanny ability to spot and use 'nurturant' women — that is, those who have a powerful need to help or mother others."

Later on Dr. Hare sums it up. "Psychopaths have little difficulty in making use of people who feel physically or psychologically inadequate, or who feel compelled to hold on to a relationship no matter how much it hurts."

Here is a brief outline of Dr. Hare's description of the characteristics of psychopaths:

- Glib and superficial. Entertaining, clever conversationalists who are slick, smooth, and tell unlikely, but somehow convincing stories.

- Egocentric and grandiose. They feel entitled to live by their own rules and they love power and control.

- They lack remorse or guilt. They rationalize their behavior and shrug off responsibility.

- They lack empathy. They are unfeeling.

- They are deceitful and manipulative.

- They have shallow emotions. They don't experience love, grief, fear, joy, or despair. Love is equated with sexual arousal. They learn to act emotions when they're useful.

- They're impulsive, have poor behavior controls, may be short-tempered, and respond to frustration or criticism with sudden violence, threats, or verbal abuse.

- They need excitement and are easily bored.

- They're irresponsible.

- As children, they typically torture pets, lie, cheat, steal, bully, and set fires.

- As adults they commonly engage in questionable business practices, spouse or child abuse, and victimize acquaintances and strangers.

The married man or woman

While on the subject of dangerous liaisons, let's look at involvement with a married man or woman.

If you're single and lonely, you may be exceptionally vulnerable to the flattery, the ego caress of the opposite sex, married or not. And for a single mother, for example, an affair with a married man may be a convenient and time-efficient answer to her need for male companionship.

Married men often see the single mother as ideal because they expect her demands will be few.

If you're the single in this affair, you're opening yourself up for turmoil. Most likely you're going to become emotionally involved whether you expect it or not. If you fall in love, in the vast majority of cases, you will be hurt.

Dr. Don-David Lusterman, a New York state clinical psychologist who specializes in treating people who've been involved in an affair, says the majority of these liaisons don't work out.

Most often the married person will not leave his wife or her husband. While, occasionally, some lovers beat the odds, statistically only 2% of marriages that result from an affair are successful.

An affair is often exciting and often sexually addictive. But sooner or later most affairs come to an end, leaving at least one victim. The depression at the end is often profound.

Lusterman says the "other woman" often lives in la-la land, thinking the affair will go on forever or that it will end in marriage. She is usually devastated when eventually she is dumped, as happens in the vast majority of cases. And before that happens her life is often out of control, largely because she's in an unequal relationship. One person is pulling most of the strings. Instead of being a threat to marriage, an affair often makes it tolerable and keeps the marriage going.

I have met too many single women riding the emotional roller coaster of an affair. Their lives are chaotic, their loss of self-esteem is enormous, and when it's over they feel used and self-destructive.

Don't get sucked in. You deserve a whole relationship, not just a bit of a fantasy. While you're involved in an affair, you're not open to the possibilities around you.

And if you're already in an affair and reading this book, do yourself a favor. Make an appointment with a psychologist who deals with relationship issues and possibly join a group for Women Who Love Too Much. At some point you'll need this kind of guidance and support.

Here's a letter from one woman who's wasting her time:

Dear Kathy:

I am involved with a man I met eight months ago. He's in his early forties and I'm in my mid-thirties. He is married.

I tried everything in the beginning to keep a relationship from developing. He was very persistent and, although I knew there would be no future in this, I stupidly fell in love with him.

He is a successful businessman and quite wealthy. I had no knowledge of how wealthy when I met him, and it wasn't and isn't something that attracted me to him. He seems to genuinely care for me and often tells me how much he loves me. But with his business, children, and wife, I am last priority. He says he tries to see me as often as possible. But I need more quality time with him.

I have become resentful because I'm not exactly a spring chicken and time is running out to have children. I feel so torn and know I should go on with my life and perhaps meet someone of my own.

We've sat down and talked about my feelings and he says there just might be a chance for a future. But I'm not prepared to sit around for two or three or even 12 years before he's ready. What can I do? I feel incapable of taking charge of things and do what is right by letting go of this relationship.

I'm A Flake

Dear Friend:

You are not a flake. Your letter is among many from women who feel hopeless, helpless, and hurt because they are involved in affairs. They realize they've made a big mistake.

Most women start affairs because they want to love and be loved — and there's nothing wrong with that. Often their self-esteem is low and they need the attention. They also tell themselves they won't get emotionally involved. Big mistake.

They fall in love and start to want more because, indeed, they deserve more. You deserve more. Ask yourself if you really want a man who hasn't the guts to face what's missing in himself or in his marriage and fix it. Ask yourself if he loves you or is simply "in love."

Love is when you care about someone as much as (not more or less than) yourself. Love is giving you what you need or deserve. Love would make you a first priority, not a last.

This relationship is not equal and therefore basically faulty.

Do not be sucked in. He is not going to leave his wife. He has established a life with her, has children, and loves her, or so he thinks.

What's missing is true intimacy. But instead of seeking that, he's regressed to the first stage of love — the excitement and romance of being "in love" — which he gets with you. The man is emotionally immature.

Love yourself. Tell him it's over and don't give in when he pursues. You likely will need help. Confide in a friend who will back you as you take charge of your life. And make an appointment with a counselor. You might start with your local YWCA which is likely to offer a counselling service.

18

Herb, and other dates from hell

It was like a date with the living dead. She wondered why he ever had invited her out for dinner in the first place. He never asked her anything about her life, her work, her kids, her home, her trip to Europe the previous month, or her plans. He didn't notice anything about her; nor did he seem interested in her, either physically or emotionally.

Instead, he spent the entire evening talking about investing in foreign condominiums. He could just as easily have been talking to an empty chair. She felt as though she was sitting through a long, boring college lecture: Male Egotism 101. She fell asleep, literally, over dessert.

Then there was Alex. He also had no idea what he was letting himself in for. His was a date with Ms. Bitter. She talked all afternoon about her ex-husband, "the jerk." She gave him a day-by-day account of their marriage and their divorce. He gained intimate knowledge of her ex's sloppy habits, sexual idiosyncrasies, and spending habits. When Alex dropped her home early, she was mad.

Penny and Karen thought they were going sailing with a guy in their office and some of his male and female friends. It only became clear after they'd left the dock. The women already on board were wearing very short shorts and high heels. The guys were a group of businessmen from Calgary looking for much more than companionship. Penny and Karen sought the protection of the charter's skipper. Fortunately, they got it.

Date from hell.

And here are a few more dates from hell sent in by readers:

Dear Kathy:

I was working for a big law firm downtown. I was without a date for the Christmas Party. I remembered a guy I'd met through a friend the previous week. He dressed nicely, was polite, and good-looking. He had just moved here from a small town back east. He hadn't met many people here, so I thought it was a great opportunity for both of us.

He was to pick me up at 7 p.m. He showed at 7:45 and without a car. We were extremely late.

He really threw back the drinks. At dinner we were seated with one of the senior lawyers. I was worried about how much my date had consumed. But everything was going fine so I started to relax.

Then all of a sudden bread and butter was served. My date said, "Ah, pineapple to clean the palate." The next

thing I knew, he was sticking two cubes of butter in his mouth. Just as fast as they went in, they came out. Everyone was laughing.

Next, lox and capers. My date had capers flying everywhere, including into one of the lawyer's water glasses.

Dinner was finally over and my date disappeared. I found him in the lounge cornering one of the lawyer's wives, trying to kiss her. That lady's husband sent my date home in a taxi.

I've never been so embarrassed. People still tease me about my worst date ever. I heard he moved back to his small town a couple of weeks later. I wonder why.

Embarrassed

Dear Kathy:

In 1991 I had a date with a fellow who owned his own company and was presentable. He arrives at my apartment with a big sports bag. I ask him, "What's that for?"

"It's my overnight bag."

"I'll tell you right now if that's your overnight bag, you'll be leaving with it this evening."

He just chuckles and walks in.

We had reservations at a Mexican restaurant. In keeping with the Mexican theme, out of this bag he pulls a blender, margarita mix, rum, and ice cubes. I think, okay, this must be a fun guy. While he was blending the drinks, he lifts up my skirt and says, "Oh, I just wanted to see what your legs looked like." I couldn't believe it.

We get to the restaurant and the conversation is "How much do you weigh?" "Are those your real fingernails?" etc.

We then drove around the park with his convertible top down. We get back to my place. Of course one of the pins in his convertible top won't clip in. He says, "I'll just have to stay the night. I can't drive home like this. It will ruin my top."

I say, "Put down your top, roll up your windows, turn up the heat, and you'll do just fine."

We go back to my place so he can pick up his blender. He really does have his overnight bag packed. Upon informing him he must leave, all he could say was "I can't believe this. I'm usually so much more persuasive."

The next morning at 6 o'clock. I get a wake up call for him. It's his roommate. He had asked him to call him at my place to make sure he left on time for golf.

Who knows where this guy slept that night. Obviously he was too embarrassed to go home and have his roomy see he was shot down. But there is a good ending. He left his blender. I take it to every office party, we mix a few drinks, and have a good laugh about my date from hell!

Caroline

Date from hell.

Dear Kathy:

I've had a couple of dates from hell in recent weeks. I met both through the telepersonals. Both women were somewhat unbalanced. The first seemed okay until we really got to talking. She said she'd love to spend some time with Charles Manson in his cell, close to him, close to his mind. It was chilling. I could hardly wait to end the conversation and take her home.

The second woman lived with her four-year-old daughter. She told me the child had been molested the night before by her girlfriend's husband. Even so, she gets in the car with me, a total stranger, to go to the beach. She asked me to help the child on with her overalls. I'm thinking, here I'm a stranger and she allows this. And the child is acting weird. And then she tells me she lost the little girl to Social Services some years before. The thought occurred to me that she or the child could turn around and accuse me of child molesting. I got out of there fast too.

Alex

Dear Kathy:

My nightmare date was with a model — a gorgeous vegetarian named Janelle.

I took her to a Chinese restaurant. To my amazement she ate her dishes mostly with her fingers — so much for etiquette. In the restaurant and ice cream parlor she would flirt and flaunt her wares to guys, like a lady of the night looking for action. I was embarrassed. I never called her again. It was a nightmare date.

A Casualty Of Phonies

Dating can definitely have its downside. And it's true — there will be times when you wonder why you bother. But despite dates with the living dead, the egotists, the burned, the bitter, the blind dates, the socially inappropriate, the buffoons, the margarita makers, and the pathological flirts, as long as you keep dating you will eventually find the person who fills your heart and your life.

However, there is just one more date from hell I must tell you about because, sooner or later, you're bound to run into him, or one of the thousands like him.

Herb is 50, divorced for 15 years, and keeps a stack of replies to his most recent companion ad close at hand. At first, Herb seems a fun kind of guy. He loves to play tennis, golf, swim, cycle, jog, party, and take you out on his boat.

Herb has worked his way through perhaps 100 women since his divorce. With all the sincerity he can muster, with his big, wide, innocent blue eyes, Herb will tell you that, during his marriage, he was "as faithful as I could possibly be."

But now, he says, "If they need me, I'm there for them. She doesn't have to beg too long. I think sex is probably the first thing you want when you meet someone, say about ten minutes after meeting. No, change that to eight, but it usually takes about two or three dates. I never force myself. My problem is on the first date they're in love with me, too fast, immediately, because I'm such a nice guy."

At first, it seems that Herb's right. Herb is such a nice guy. He's respectful, open, attentive, complimentary, friendly, and easy going. "I open doors for them. I can adapt to almost everything, except maybe opera. I give them what they want — attention, loving, I say the truth — nice legs, nice bum. If they have a bad point I'll mention that to them. I'm totally for them."

Until you learn more about him, it seems Herb should be giving classes to all those men who don't know how to connect with women. He could show them how it's done. But not how it's continued.

"Before you know it, you're trapped," says Herb, with heartfelt dismay. "They don't give me a chance to phone them. They just come over and take over. I met Jane in the bar. We just talked. There was no sex. We hit it off. The next day I found a note on my windshield: 'I'm totally in love with you Herb.' She'd never been treated so well.

"When they say 'I love and I need you,' it's really scary. I say, why can't you go home and wait until I phone you and if I really want you, I'm going to book ahead. They want to tie me up immediately, hang around, put a cement block around my neck."

But Herb is giving the wrong impression. A lot of his women have allowed him to do the chasing. They have fallen for him and taken his words of love as sincere indications of caring. But as soon as women care, they're toast. He's off to find another, and another, and another.

One former girlfriend calls him a male slut. Another calls him a poor, sad, lonely, little boy. Others just keep calling him. Herb's victims are often women who are very capable or very caring. They are often employed in the helping fields (they like looking after him) or bright businesswomen (who help him with business). Often they're lonely or vulnerable after coming out of a poor marriage and they have low self-esteem. Herb's attentiveness and neediness are very seductive.

Said one woman who three months before meeting Herb had left her abusive husband: "I was down and he was there. I felt so beautiful. I felt reborn. It took off like a wild romance after that. He loved it that he was needed. He likes to help a damsel in distress."

But this woman, who by the way is 15 years younger than Herb and has a fantastic body, is "not looking after herself physically" says Herb. "She's too soft. And besides she has back problems." When a woman gets too close emotionally or when she wants commitment, he criticizes her. And for a woman with poor self-esteem, she's apt to believe these things too.

But Herb maintains his innocence. "I'm not a bad guy. I was the best father. Ask my kids. The way I see it, if you really love somebody you help them out. I help women out all the time. I feel sorry for them. And if they really love me, they let me do what I want."

Asked if he realizes how many women he's hurt, Herb will say, "I feel very sorry about their feelings. Why do they let themselves get involved?" And then he's off again with his defenses: The women are too easy, too domineering, too smothering, too controlling, or too nice. Or she doesn't look after her body well enough or drives too fast or doesn't pay her fair share or isn't totally compatible.

His favorite reason for running away is "I haven't met the perfect girl yet." And if a girl says she hasn't seen him for two weeks, he'll say, "Well it doesn't feel like 14 days, you're here all the time."

If, by chance, he has to spend an evening alone: "It's very lonesome, I don't want to be alone." Herb thinks he's a really nice guy, indeed almost perfect. He says he loves everybody.

A female friend who knows well the trail of broken hearts he leaves behind, says "is that his fault or theirs? I've heard him tell them on the phone that he doesn't want a commitment. They think if they're perfect and they baby him, he'll change his mind. I have no idea why he's like he is. I think he had too many responsibilities too early in life, plus the fact he's over-sexed. He'll jump into bed with anyone who comes along. The ideal for Herb is women who do not want anything more and would not crumble at his feet."

Herb is a predator. He's a man for a good time, but not a long time. He's there as long as he's not bored and as long as a woman doesn't want anything meaningful. Who knows what Herb's unspeakable fears are. Only Herb can deal with them if he ever chooses to. You can't help him. Nor can you help all the others like him who you'll meet in all walks of life and at all income levels.

But you do need to look after yourself. He won't do that for you. He won't let you know he's a predator. Herb admits, "Right at the start, I should be honest and say exactly what I want. I guess I'm not open enough because I'm scared of losing a piece of tail."

Herb's closest male friend says: "He has no conscience. But one day it will all come to a halt."

Whether it ever does, the important thing is to know that men like Herb exist and realize that when you're just out of an important relationship, when your self-esteem is a little battered, it could get worse. Already raw and bleeding, you could be dragged across stumps and rocks and thrown over a cliff, dashed on the boulders below... if you meet a Herb.

Sometimes dates from hell aren't immediately obvious.

19
D*ating for single parents*

It's crucial that single parents do not neglect their children's emotional needs, especially in the first few years when kids are still raw from their parents' breakup. Children should not be confused by a series of parental figures who come and go, adding to their sense of loss. This woman's letter illustrates the dilemma faced by so many single parents.

> *Dear Kathy:*
>
> *I'm 23 and getting a divorce after being married five years. I have a boyfriend. I have two children so I cannot handle relationships the way I did when I was 16.*
>
> *How do I have a boyfriend with my children around without risking their well-being? I don't want to hurt my children, but I really like my boyfriend.*
>
> *Lost In Life*

I advised her to make her boyfriend a plus, but not the focus of her life right now as her children need the caring and stability she can best provide.

I suggested she see this man outside the home. Eventually, he could visit her home as well, but not move in. Things should be kept simple until there is truly a mutual commitment to a lasting relationship.

When her boyfriend visits, I suggested this woman should try to develop a sense of when her children need her undivided attention, when her boyfriend needs her undivided attention, and when she can enjoy a "family type" mixture.

There are no set rules to deal with this. Parents have a right to expect children to be courteous to guests and not constantly try to be the center of attention. Children are apt to be jealous. They need to know there are times to be center stage and other times when this isn't appropriate.

It helps to tell a new boyfriend or girlfriend what's going on, so both adults can work as a team to help the children adjust to his or her presence. Yet the parent, not the new friend, should handle any discipline, at least until the children have developed a good relationship with the new person in their life. Children will only obey adults they've grown to love and respect.

I also asked Lost In Life to look to her local YWCA for a single mothers support group. This is a good way to meet other women going through similar problems.

Sometimes a mother or father and a child have been on their own for years. When the parent starts dating, the child becomes terribly upset. The child has been the parent's best friend and companion. Now the child worries that this new person might take over his or her role. Regardless of age, psychologists say children who have lost one parent may be vulnerable, worrying about losing a parent to a boyfriend or girlfriend. The child needs to be reassured that your love for him or her is special and constant. There is room in your heart for the child and for someone else, and it's healthy for you to have adult companionship, just as it's healthy for your child to have friends.

However, it is a balancing act. Single parents have a legitimate need for adult and romantic companionship as well as a responsibility to protect their children from undue distress.

If your relationship deepens and you plan to marry, realize that having a blended family is one of the most difficult challenges parents and new partners face. Just because you've fallen in love with someone, doesn't mean your children have. To them, this new person is a stranger and often an unwelcome one at that.

I strongly advocate that people attempting to create a partnership under these circumstances get some advice and guidance from a family therapist. You can head off a lot of grief by doing so.

Some single parents fear that having children will prevent them from ever developing a romantic relationship. But I know a lot of parents who have found love. This man, however, hasn't yet been so fortunate.

Dear Kathy:

I get tired of anti-men propaganda in the media. I'm a man but I don't fit any of the stereotypes. I don't shirk my responsibility and I don't oppress women.

In 1980, my wife walked out and left me to raise my three babies. Over the next seven years I had three long-term relationships. They all followed a pattern. These women would say: "You're such a kind, gentle, hard-working man, you shouldn't be alone."

Then we would start going together. They would say they loved me and wanted to marry me. After a couple of years they would suddenly and without warning just disappear. Later I would find out they were living with another man... without kids.

During the past few years I've dated other women, but when they find out I have kids, they turn off.

I don't have a hope of getting out of this situation. I'm 45, with three young children, a very low wage as a sales clerk, and a mortgage that won't be paid off for 20 years. I owe thousands on my credit cards.

Women won't have anything to do with a man who has three kids and doesn't make much money. I'm not complaining about my lot. I'm just fed up with the image of men.

Disappointed

Dear Disappointed:

You're right. Neither sex has cornered the market on good or bad, responsibility, or the lack of it. And blaming each other isn't helpful. Far better to look at what we can do to make things better.

For example, I often hear women say: "There are no good men left; they're all married, gay, or screwed up."

Later you learn that while they've had a few bad experiences, they've also eliminated 90% of good men by long lists of unrealistic expectations.

But I wonder how open you have been to seeing the needs of the women you've known. Is it really the fact you have kids that makes them not want to stay? Perhaps you are not hearing women when they try to tell you they need something you're not giving. In frustration, they simply leave.

Do you expect women to become totally absorbed in your needs and in those of your children? Do you show enough interest in their lives and feelings? Rather than resign yourself to a life without female companionship, explore what happened in these past relationships. Obviously you want a woman who is going to understand fully your love for, and responsibility to, your kids and who will support you in that.

But a woman is also going to want to receive your love and support. I do believe a lot of women would be willing to take on kids and even a very minimal income level — for the love and comfort of a good man. Get counselling and keep looking!

Dealing with your ex

You must make a supreme effort when you become separated or divorced to consider the happiness of your children. No matter how you feel about your ex, how rejected you feel, how jealous you are of his or her new lovers, how wronged you believe you are, you must not let harmful emotions adversely affect your kids.

Children need the love and caring of two parents. Develop a mature attitude with your ex and try to de-escalate conflict over custody, access, and child support. If you can arrange your separation and divorce through a mediator rather than a lawyer, you'd be wise to do so, as some lawyers tend to escalate conflict rather than reduce it.

I believe shared parenting and shared child support is the way to go. Peaceful relations with your ex will make it easier for you when you meet someone and want to date. The other parent's involvement with the children will also allow you to have some time away from your kids in which to initiate and develop a romantic life.

Besides, no loving father should have to be a Mrs. Doubtfire to see his kids!

Yet good relations with the ex are not always possible to develop. Some ex-spouses are simply too unreasonable, as the following letter illustrates.

Dear Kathy:

My girlfriend and I would love to move in together but we are afraid of her husband's irrational behavior and threats to blow us away.

He is acting rather immaturely which, I gather, has always been his problem. I do not know if it is just talk or if he would really do such a thing but I have been warned it is a distinct possibility. Friends say we're wise to continue "under cover."

We are in our early forties and have older children. Assuming he will seek help if offered, is there somebody to help him deal with the loss in a more rational manner? Is there anything legally that can be done to dissuade him? Will the police provide protection or get involved if only threats are made?

I would like to resolve this situation and try to get the husband to accept the fact, as relayed to him by numerous individuals and his wife on a number of occasions, that she is not coming back, ever.

Anonymous

Dear Anonymous:

You are in a very dangerous situation. People have been murdered by angry, violent, jealous, possessive, dependent husbands. Threats are an expression of dependency but still must be taken seriously.

It's unlikely this man is going to take your advice or anyone else's to see a marriage counselor right now. Remember, this man has lost his wife. He's understandably angry and probably believes she has been stolen from him. It will take time for him to see why his wife connected to you — to avoid dealing directly with problems in the marriage.

If your girlfriend is afraid, she may seek safety and counselling at a transition house. She can also ask a lawyer to seek a court restraining order.

And here's another caution: In the first two years after separation, it's not a good idea to make it obvious you're dating. Too many people ask for trouble by flaunting their new relationship, throwing it in the face of the ex. Don't do this. You are rubbing salt in the wounds and it's bound to come back on you and your children. For the first two years, don't take your new partner to your children's school events and risk your ex feeling humiliated. Don't pick up the kids with the new person in the car right away. Give your ex some time to heal first.

Pedophiles

If you've ever read Vladimir Nabokov's literary classic, *Lolita,* you'll know that one of the most frightening aspects of dating when you have kids is the specter of bringing a pedophile into your home. This is a real concern. It's quite common for molesters to access a child by befriending his or her mother. The pedophile's hidden agenda is attraction to your child, not you. But this may not be obvious and it may be too late when you discover what his intentions are.

I have a friend who often took her young daughter to a weekly outdoor community event during the summer. Over the course of a few weeks, a nice-looking and friendly man initiated conversations with both of them. My friend was considering inviting him over to her place for dinner. But then a friend cautioned her that she'd heard the man was a molester.

That, of course, was only rumor. But I have interviewed a number of pedophiles and I've also interviewed several women whose children were sexually abused by men they had dated. Stories appear regularly in the papers. As I write, one man is trying to fight a deportation order. The man had been serving a three-and-a-half year sentence for sexually molesting the two daughters of a woman with whom he was living common law.

And I recall an earlier case in which police issued a warning to residents to be careful of an alleged pedophile who picked his victims by befriending them and their parents. "He builds a relationship with the parents, often single-parent families," a police spokesperson said.

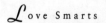

Bill Marshall, an international expert on child sex abusers, says most offenders don't just leap out of the bushes at a school playground. "Most of them strike up a relationship through the parents or are friends of the family or are family members."

Clearly, most men you will meet are not pedophiles. But it's wise to keep this possibility in mind so your children are not at risk.

20
S afety tips

If you're new to today's dating scene, this chapter is important. Don't go out there naively thinking it's like it was in the sixties and seventies.

Today there's AIDS and many other sexually transmitted diseases (STDs). Escalating sexual and other violence is a factor in our society. And it seems there are more people willing to use a relationship to get money (see chapter 17) or whatever else they want.

Increasingly, laws are being enacted to protect women, including sexual harassment laws, but men, too, need to share more of the responsibility for creating a just and safe society.

With dating methods such as telephone personal ads becoming increasingly popular, you need to know how to meet a stranger safely.

AIDS and other STDs

Realize when having sex with one person, you risk disease as though you're having sex with everyone that person has ever slept with. If you don't use a condom, you are open to the enormous variety of easily contracted, sexually transmitted diseases, including AIDS.

So whether you're a man or a woman, make sure you have a good supply of latex condoms at hand — in your purse, in your glove compartment, in your bathroom, in the drawer of your night table, everywhere.

Acquired Immune Deficiency Syndrome (AIDS) is the scariest STD of all. The disease organism that causes AIDS is the Human Immunodeficiency Virus (HIV). The virus is spread through intimate sexual contact, exposure to infected blood or needles, from an infected mother to her baby during pregnancy or delivery, or to a newborn through breast feeding.

So don't allow your semen, blood, or vaginal fluid to enter the bloodstream of another person. The virus can enter a person's body through the vagina, rectum, or opening of the penis, through cuts or sores in the mouth, or through direct entry to the bloodstream. Anal tissues tear especially easily, allowing the virus to enter your bloodstream. And HIV can be transmitted through oral sex. This usually occurs when heavily infected semen comes into contact with a cut or sore in another person's mouth.

Months or years may pass between the time the virus invades the body and the time the person has any symptoms. The average time lapse between infection and AIDS is ten years! So you can be infected by someone who doesn't even know he or she has AIDS. Eventually the immune system and its ability to fight off disease is disabled or destroyed, and the infected person dies.

Dr. Fleur Sack, author of *Romance to Die For,* has watched many people die from AIDS. She understands the human sex drive is strong, sometimes beyond reason, and that love and passion lead women to behave foolishly and dangerously. But, she says, if you don't use a condom, you may be committing sexual suicide.

AIDS is an epidemic and it is certainly not just a gay disease or a disease affecting drug users. It's the fifth leading cause of death for U.S. women between the ages of 15 and 44. In California, it's the leading cause of death for young people — ahead of traffic accidents!

In Vancouver and Toronto, it's the number one cause of "potential years of life lost" — a measure of economic impact on society — for adult males. In Vancouver, a 1994 study of all blood samples found the rate of infection for Vancouver men, 15 to 55 years old, was 93 infections per 10,000 men. It was only slightly lower at 88 infections for men in the surrounding suburbs. The rate for women was 6.8 per 10,000.

Heterosexual contact with an HIV-infected partner is the leading cause of AIDS among women in Canada and the United States, surpassing contaminated blood and tainted drug needles as causes.

A woman is much more likely to be infected by a man than a man is to be infected by a woman. And because women's symptoms of AIDS are mis-diagnosed more than men's, women often die sooner than a man after diagnosis.

If you are HIV-infected, it may be a criminal offense not to inform your sex partners. And you are liable to be sued for damages as well.

Sack says two people about to enter a sexual relationship should be tested for AIDS and should practice safe sex (using a condom) for six months until they can have a second test to be sure. Only then may they choose to stop using condoms — if the relationship is monogamous. And, she says, women should tell their mates that if they cheat, they should wear a condom and be honest enough to say so. If you don't trust your partner that much, insist on a condom when you have sex.

We know AIDS is growing in the heterosexual community and the fastest growing segment of new AIDS victims is women.

Back in 1991, Dr. June Reinisch, director of the famous Kinsey Institute for Sex Research, said that one in 500 U.S. university students surveyed had tested positive for the AIDS virus.

In one survey at a large midwestern U.S. university, those surveyed were all single, heterosexual male and female undergraduates with a mean age was 20. Of those students, 40% were in a serious relationship, 32% were not dating, and the rest were dating, but not seriously. Most were sexually active, many had had many partners, even one-night stands, and only *one-third* used condoms. One in six had tried extremely high-risk anal sex, and 20% of them did not consider anal intercourse as having sex. Of the men, 39% and 37% of the women who said they were in exclusive relationships also admitted to sexual cheating.

Getting a test for AIDS is as simple as visiting your doctor or a clinic for a blood test. The antibodies to the AIDS virus (HIV), which is what the laboratory analyst looks for, generally take at least two to 12 weeks to appear after infection occurs. In rare cases, it takes more than a year for the antibodies to appear. The first test should be taken three months after possible exposure and a second at six months.

In the United States you can call the National AIDS Hotline (1-800-342-AIDS) to find the location nearest you that provides anonymous testing. In Canada, make an appointment with your doctor or call your local provincial health unit (listed in the blue pages of your telephone directory). By law, doctors must keep all test and medical examination results confidential, and that includes the HIV antibody test.

In the United States at confidential AIDS testing sites (called Alternative Test Sites), a person is not required to give a name, social security number, or any other identifying information.

It generally takes two weeks to get test results. Each blood sample undergoes an initial screening test designed to pick up all positive bloods. If the screen is positive, a second, more sophisticated test will be run to confirm the result and eliminate false positives. All this occurs routinely with each sample.

But while AIDS is the ultimately most disastrous STD, there are some 20 others you need to be aware of. Many of these can have a devastating effect on your life. Some reduce your chances of ever having children. One out of every six couples cannot have children and 30% of these cases of infertility are a direct result of damage from an STD.

Some STDs are very painful, some hardly noticeable. Some — if you're a woman — you won't know you've got until serious damage is done. The message isn't to abstain from having sex. The message is to use condoms *every time*.

And it's important to know that a test for one sexually transmitted disease will not reveal the presence of another. Each test is different.

Here is a list of STDs of most concern:

- Chlamydia. The most common STD, 100,000 cases crop up each year in Canada alone. It's caused by a bacteria that infects the urethra in men and the cervix in women. Many people infected with chlamydia do not have any symptoms. If symptoms do occur, they may include burning or increased frequency of urination and discharge from the urethra or vagina. If a woman doesn't know she has it, it can spread and lead to pelvic inflammatory disease (PID — see below). In men, chlamydia can cause sterility. The disease is curable.

- Genital warts. Caused by a virus infecting the genitals, anus, or mouth. The warts can cause pain during intercourse, urination, or defecation, and may increase the risk of developing cervical cancer. It's treatable.

- Gonorrhea. Caused by a bacteria that infects the urethra in men and the cervix in women. It can also infect the anus, the throat, or the inner surface of the eyelids. Untreated, it causes sterility in both men and women. Symptoms are a discharge and pain or burning during urination. It's curable.

- Genital herpes. Caused by a virus. Symptoms begin with a tingling or burning sensation. Two to 12 days after infection, small blisters appear. These break and form shallow, painful ulcers that eventually heal. The infection persists and symptoms can recur from time to time. The drug acyclovir can reduce pain and accelerate healing.

So far there is no cure for herpes or genital warts although researchers are working on vaccines and also on new drugs. A great number of people have these diseases. Through oral sex, one strain of herpes can be transferred from the genitals of one partner to the face of the other and vice versa.

Researchers estimate most people with genital herpes don't realize they have it because they have no visible signs or symptoms. These people either have never had an outbreak or they have perhaps had one reaction which they've passed off as an in-grown hair or jock itch.

While incurable to date, herpes is quite a mild disease compared with other STDs. Many singles who contract herpes initially figure it's the end of their life and their chances of finding a mate. It is not. With proper precautions — using condoms and avoiding oral sex, you can enjoy a good sex life. But, you should always let a prospective intimate partner know you have the disease or you may find yourself in court.

Many major North American cities have herpes support groups. In Canada, ask your doctor or your local sexually transmitted disease clinic for the address or phone number. In the United States call the Herpes Hotline at (919) 361-8488 or write the Herpes Resource Centre, P.O. Box 13827, Research Triangle Park, North Carolina, 27709. Support groups normally meet once a month to share information. (In Vancouver, call the Vancouver Health Support Group — write to Vancouver H.S.G., P.O. Box 3805, Main Postal Station, Vancouver V6B 3Z1 or phone (604) 641-6261 to get more information on this.)

- Hepatitis B. A viral infection of the liver, caused by contact with infected semen, blood, or saliva or by sharing needles, syringes, razors, or toothbrushes. Infected persons may have no symptoms but may experience fatigue, fever, loss of appetite, abdominal pain, nausea, and vomiting. No specific treatment other than rest and diet. Curable, but 10% of infected adults become chronic carriers. Vaccine is available and recommended for the sexually active.

- Syphilis. Bacteria transmitted by contact with lesions or sores during sex. Starts with small, painless sores that go away, followed by rash on the hands and feet, sores in mouth, enlarged lymph nodes and patchy loss of hair. Without treatment, this is followed from two to 40 years later by blindness, paralysis, deafness, and brain or heart disease. Curable.

- Pelvic Inflammatory Disease (PID). A serious condition in young women, often undetected, that can cause sterility and even death. If there are symptoms, they include lower abdominal pain, fever, and deep pain during intercourse. It is an inflammation of the fallopian tubes and/or ovaries caused by an infection, often gonorrhea or chlamydia. The inflamed tube heals by creating scar tissue, which can cause ectopic pregnancy (the egg implants itself in the tube or elsewhere). If this is undetected, the growing egg can rupture the tube, causing possibly fatal internal bleeding.

In the United States, you will be able to get more information on STDs by calling the STD National Hotline, sponsored by the American Social Health Association, at 1-800-227-8922.

I do think the message is starting to get through to people about the use of condoms and about asking a new partner to have an AIDS test before engaging in intercourse without a condom. I certainly hope so. I've interviewed people with AIDS and it's a tragedy I hope you'll never have to face. One person I interviewed was a woman in her mid-twenties who contracted the disease from her boyfriend. She didn't know he was bisexual. That interview took place about seven or eight years ago and I have often wondered if she's still alive.

You cannot afford a partner who refuses to wear a condom. Sure, for a man, making love wearing a condom may be like showering with his socks on. Tough! My view is — no condom, no sex. Why even consider a man who refuses? Right off the bat, he's told you he's selfish and unconcerned about your health. Drop him.

How do you talk about safe sex?

I think you need to be quite blunt before having sex with a new partner. The importance of safe sex now overrides any awkwardness. When you raise the subject, your partner may be surprised, but also relieved.

Your concern shows positive self regard as well as caring for the other person.

You could say something like this: "At some point I suspect our relationship may become more meaningful and we may want to have sex together. I am not willing to risk getting AIDS or any of the other sexually transmitted diseases. When the time comes, will you use a condom?"

Soon, however, there will also be the option of the female condom. This is expected to become widely available in drugstores as distribution is phased in throughout North America in 1994 and 1995. You won't need a prescription. And the female condom allows women to take control without even having to discuss it with their partner. It's a polyurethane sheath which lines the walls of the vagina and can be inserted up to eight hours before a sexual encounter.

Here's an interesting letter from a reader:

Dear Kathy:

After reading all the fuss about wearing condoms, I had to let you know that, after using them for three years, I find them an exciting prelude to sex. Even opening the packet can give me an erection.

Condoms are a necessary fact of life, but they are not nearly as horrible as many people make them out to be. When I first started to use them, I felt like anyone else about them. Condoms were a drag. But I've since learned to enjoy them. Here are some things I learned to increase enjoyment.

Most important, fill the reservoir tip of the condom with KY Jelly or some other water-based lubricant. This greatly increases the sensation and also helps the condom stay on. It's helpful to masturbate with condoms for practice. More important, masturbating with a condom links it to the fantasies surrounding sex and will start the association that will make opening a package sexy.

If you use condoms for every sex act, they'll become inextricably associated with sex and become a turn-on. An advantage of using condoms is precisely the lowered sensation. This helps you last longer to better give pleasure to your partner.

Anonymous

Oh, for a man like that! He knows condoms can assist him in delaying ejaculation and getting more out of the sexual encounter.

Sexual harassment

Men and women were born to flirt and to court (see chapter 9). So in any environment where you find people of the opposite sex together, flirting and courting are bound to happen, including the workplace. That's usually not a problem when the interest is mutual.

But a sexual overture may or may not be welcome. And if it is not, you may get fired or face a sexual harassment suit.

Mariann Burka, director of the British Columbia Council of Human Rights, says an increasing number of complaints filed with the council are about sexual harassment, which has been defined by the Supreme Court of Canada as "unwelcome conduct of a sexual nature that detrimentally affects the work environment or leads to adverse job-related consequences for the victims of harassment." U.S. laws are very similar to those in Canada.

Types of conduct judicially considered to be of a sexual nature include:

- Unwelcome physical contact: touching, fondling, kissing, patting, pinching, grabbing, punching, and sexual assault.

- Unwelcome verbal conduct: examples are crude, sexual, or abusive remarks, sexual propositions, suggestive comments and innuendoes, questions regarding "sex life" and even dinner or other social invitations!

- Conduct that is neither physical nor verbal but clearly of a sexual nature: examples would include an employer fondling himself in front of an employee, appearing naked in front of an employee, gifts of lingerie, or displays of sexually explicit material.

I have just realized while writing this that I might have been open to a charge of sexual harassment in my own newspaper office the other day! A pharmaceutical company had sent me a female condom along with information about it and I was holding the item up to show my colleagues and probably giggling a little. Fortunately they were all interested and the display was welcome.

And that is the point about sexual harassment. The conduct must be unwelcome to be considered sexual harassment. The intention to harass is irrelevant. Lack of intention is no defense. The legal test for "unwelcome" is the reasonable person test. That is, a reasonable person would have known or ought to have known the conduct was unwelcome. And in the United States, some jurisdictions have decided it is the reasonable "woman" test!

However, where a pattern of consent has been established — or where a complainant alternates between consenting and not consenting, an explicit objection may be necessary to decide conduct was unwelcome.

It's important to realize, however, that a complaint will not be rendered invalid just because other employees are not offended by the same behavior. If the complainant is the only person who finds the behavior unwelcome, it can still be sexual harassment. However, some type of objection may be necessary to show that the behavior was unwelcome. Keep in mind the following:

- Consent obtained through fear or coercion, including fear for loss of job, is not considered consent.

- Continuing on the job in spite of the harassment is not proof of consent. Factors such as economic dependence and the need for job experience are considered.

- While conduct must detrimentally affect the work environment, it is generally presumed that unwelcome conduct of a sexual nature will adversely affect the work environment.

- Conduct does not need to be on the work site location. It can occur outside the office on business trips, etc.

- An employer is absolutely responsible for the discriminating conduct of his or her employees. The employer has a responsibility to maintain a harassment-free environment. So a complaint could be brought not only against a co-worker but also against the company.

If you are harassed, the first step may be to warn the offender that the behavior is unwanted. You should also tell a superior about the incident. If the harassment continues, a complaint should be made first to management and then, if there is no resolution, to your human rights council. If you have a union, you may wish to file a grievance.

Laws regarding sexual harassment in the workplace also extend to any situation where there is business/customer or landlord/tenant relationship.

A nationwide U.S. survey by *Men's Health* magazine found publicity about sexual harassment cases has changed the way men treat female co-workers.

Nearly two-thirds of the men surveyed by the magazine said they are more careful about what they say to women in the workplace. Magazine spokesperson Patrick Taylor said the survey showed men are realizing that "even the casual comment you think is totally harmless can be translated into something else."

In 1993, many men in British Columbia were stunned when the B.C. Human Rights Council ruled that a former forest ministry employee, Linda Dupuis, was harassed by her supervisor during a wildlife survey. The council awarded the woman $20,000.

Dale Seip, a wildlife biologist and the woman's supervisor, had accompanied Dupuis to a coastal town where they planned to catch a ferry. They stopped first, however, in another town where Seip rented a motel room with two beds. He was watching TV and invited the woman to sit on his bed with him. He then kissed her and she didn't protest.

Later he took off some of her clothes and she made no objection until he began to remove her underwear or pants. The woman then said she "didn't make love to strangers." Seip stopped. The woman remained on his bed and they fell asleep.

"Some time during the night, he began to caress her again," the report said. "This time, they had sexual intercourse." And they had sex on several later occasions.

The woman's lawyer told the hearing that her client was vulnerable to authority figures because she had a strict Catholic upbringing and had an authoritarian father. That made it difficult for her to say no to Seip, said the lawyer.

The forests ministry argued that sex between the two was consensual. Council member Tom Patch agreed that the fact that the woman remained on Seip's bed "in a state of partial undress" was "naive and foolish," but that it wasn't "sufficient to revoke her refusal of intercourse."

So far there has been no petition for a judicial review of this ruling. The critical issue was that the onus is on an employer or person in authority to ensure that what looks like consent is indeed consent.

Because of the Dupuis case and others, people are becoming increasingly careful. However, they are also becoming more and more cautious, with the result that the mating game is riddled with uncertainty and confusion, as illustrated by this woman's letter to my column:

Dear Kathy:

When I started working at a medical office, I noticed a gentleman — quiet, serious, and very attractive. He was a doctor. When my son needed a specialist, I asked my doctor to refer me to him. By the time I left his office, I was convinced this man was the most intelligent I ever met.

A few months later, my husband and I separated. My son had to go to this doctor frequently and I looked forward to the visits. I felt he was attracted to me, too.

My son only needs to go on a yearly basis now. Last March, I finally got the courage to ask this doctor out for lunch. To my delight, he eagerly accepted.

Two weeks passed but he didn't phone as he said he would. So I sent him a card saying, "How about that lunch?" He immediately phoned me to say that because my son is a minor and I am his guardian, it would be a very thin line he would be walking and he could be slapped with a sexual harassment suit. He said he could not pursue this any further. I was disappointed and got my girlfriend to phone the College of Physicians and Surgeons. She was told exactly the same thing.

I can't get this man out of my mind. I considered changing doctors but decided against it as it would make me feel cheap.

I no longer work at the same office. My son's appointment is approaching soon and I need to know how to deal with the situation. His treatment may be over or may go on for a few more years.

This doctor is bound to feel uncomfortable. I have been separated for two years and am not even interested in anyone else. My social life is non-existent. If I had to pick my dream man, he is it. Your opinion?

Somewhere Over The Rainbow

Dear Somewhere:

This doctor may well be attracted to you, but he has made his position clear and you need to respect that. Attend your son's appointment and keep your mind focused on the medical issue.

It is probably time to develop a new social life, expanding your network of same-sex and opposite-sex friends. To get started, join some singles clubs and get involved in sports, cultural, and perhaps even political activities.

If you're a man reading about sexual harassment, you may wonder how to defend yourself against being falsely accused. Experts say you should never ignore or shrug off any allegations made against you. As soon as you learn you have been unfairly accused, you should inform your superior and marshal support. Explain possible motives for the charge. If necessary, hire a lawyer.

When you see your boss, take a detailed written log and other evidence of your case. Try to reconstruct relevant meetings and prior disagreements with your accuser. Document everything.

Once someone formally accuses you, discuss the charges frankly with all co-workers who can vouch for your character.

Meeting a stranger safely

If you are using companion ads or telepersonals to meet new people, take some commonsense precautions:

- Don't give out your last name, home address, or phone number until you have met the person — if necessary, several times — and feel very confident he or she is a reasonable and honest person.
- If you don't want your phone number to be read on his or her call display phone line, contact your telephone company to activate the "call blocking" feature.
- Meet during the day, in a public place.
- Use your own transportation to and from the appointment.
- Don't invite someone you don't know into your home.
- Use the buddy system of letting a friend know where you are going, who you are meeting, and when you expect to return.

- Report any concerns to the police as well as to the service you are using. Your efforts may save someone else from an unpleasant, if not dangerous, situation.

Stalking

Laws exist in Canada and the United States that permit police to charge anyone who without legal authority harasses a person to the point where that person reasonably fears for his or her own safety or that of others. Harassment may involve following someone from place to place, repeated and unwanted communications, watching a person's home or business, and engaging in threatening conduct.

When to hire a private investigator

Faced with the threat of AIDS, increasing violence, and a desire to protect their increasing financial worth, some women are turning to private investigators to check out a new man.

And there are even more serious reasons to know who you are dating. Pedophiles often start dating a woman who has a child they want to molest, as discussed in chapter 19.

All you need to give a P.I. to start the search is the person's full name, including middle initial, and postal or ZIP code, or just a license plate number. Basic information might include verification of where a person lives, where he or she works, and whether he really got that university degree. A little more digging can tell you his old addresses, a ballpark figure on his salary (this will probably be based on credit information that he may have likely filled out himself, so it might be exaggerated), and whether his driver's record has any convictions.

You can find if he has any criminal convictions, local or federal civil suits; if he's using more than one social insurance or security number; whether he owns property, and if there is a lien on that property; and whether he had an honorable discharge from military service.

One of the first questions often asked — is he married? — can be time-consuming to answer unless you know the county and approximate date of the marriage. However, a spouse's name often appears on joint property records. An investigator can also talk to neighbors to find out if he's married.

And on garbage day you may have someone pick up his or her trash and haul it away to rummage through it. The contents can be very revealing. Be careful, if you're caught you may face a civil suit.

But before you hire a P.I., there are certain things you can check out yourself. Talk to his landlord. Phone the university where he got his degree.

Divorce records are public information. Go to the courthouse, ask for the name, and sit down and read the divorce judgment.

There's even a kit to test for drugs but it isn't available on the market yet. All you have to do, apparently, is pretend your toilet doesn't flush. After your date urinates, dip some urine samples onto the plastic in the kit and within 20 minutes some test results will appear. You'll know whether your date has traces of cocaine, heroin, opiates, marijuana, PCP, or amphetamines in his or her body.

So goes the technology of dating in the 1990s.

21

Getting to know you

Getting to know the man or woman you're dating can be one of the most exciting experiences of your life. Here's a column I wrote about five or six years ago, early on in my relationship with my sweetie.

My guy has just sold his house. I'm going to miss it, particularly the fridge and main bathroom. Opening a bachelor's fridge is always such an adventure. When I first started dating him, the fridge was like an archaeological dig. There were bits of food left over from previous girlfriends who likely felt sorry for him and cooked.

Eight jars of mayonnaise, with expiry dates going back four years. Six jars of mustard. Kraft singles slices, dating back to the hula hoop.

Chilled by the thought he might surprise me and actually try to cook something, I decided to decontaminate. I threw out the mayonnaise, the limp brown carrots, the Baggie of green slime (possibly a former green pepper or broccoli), and oranges the size of peas.

Now, of course, I realize he never cooks and never will. The fridge is merely used for storage.

This man is frugal. He never throws anything out.

To make sure I don't go the way of my predecessors, I rarely cook at his house and I certainly don't bring in anything I won't use. If I need Oxo, I bring one cube, not like the others who figured they'd be around for awhile — 20 pounds of flour, kilos of macaroni, rice to feed an army. I tried to imagine the woman who bought the sack of potatoes whose sprouting tentacles had opened a cupboard door all by themselves.

What he lacks in culinary expertise, he makes up for in housekeeping. The very first time I entered his house, he told me to take my shoes off at the utility room. Too shocked to protest, I acquiesced.

Good thing I did. A previous date had asserted herself, refused to take off her shoes, and was promptly driven home.

The point is, he likes to keep his carpets clean. How clean? So clean he's never had to use his vacuum once in six years.

The living room is always neat. It contains one sofa, two chairs, and a TV that rarely works properly. Not the kind of place you're going to spend much time...or make a mess in. (By contrast, his bedroom is very comfy. This man is not stupid.)

Fortunately, the house has three bathrooms. When his kids come over, their mess, by decree, is confined to the basement bathroom. He has the main bathroom. And I adopted the en suite. Apparently previous women had done the same thing. I found hair spray (a cheap brand) and a teensy, weensy bikini in the medicine cabinet.

When I confronted him with these items, he grinned and suggested I might be able to use them. I had to take it as a compliment. Not many men have suggested I could get a size 12 into an 8.

"My" bathroom is spotless; his is something else. It features toothpaste without cap, drawers full of 20-year-old prescriptions (it's amazing what you can learn about a guy this way), razor stubble confetti in the sink, and a toilet bowl you do not want to know about.

Then there's the towels. Red ones, orange ones, and yellow ones. No shampoo. No face cloth. I gather real men don't use them.

To be fair, this man changes the sheets regularly, cleans his bathtub each time he uses it, and is always up to date on laundry. His kitchen floor is spotless, the counters are *pretty good, and I choose to ignore Miss October on the wall.*

And I can learn from him...maybe. Things like how to change a tire, replace tap washers, level the fridge, replace a frayed electrical plug, clean gutters, and where to shut off my gas after an earthquake.

Yes, I'm going to miss that house. After this column, I hope I won't have to miss him, too.

Actually, sweetie's move from that house was his first step in making a commitment to me. Later he used some of the money from the sale of his house to buy a lot. A few years later I sold my house and we built a house together on that lot.

But commitment is something that mystifies many men.

Fear of commitment

Here's a joke that's been around for awhile.

Q: How does a single woman get a roach out of her apartment?

A: She asks for a commitment.

That issue is explored by Drs. Sonya Rhodes and Marlin Potash in their book *Cold Feet — Why Men Don't Commit*. These two New York City psychotherapists contend that more than ever before women are seeking emotional involvement from partners.

But to men, emotional involvement often translates as loss of freedom and, to some, even loss of identity. Many men may know how to make the mortgage and utility payments but are scared by all the yummy cuddling and conversation that women thrive on.

"Men are overwhelmed by women's demands at the same time that they are thoroughly attracted to women who are strong, sexy, and outspoken about their needs and expectations," say the authors.

"At this emotional crossroads — where he is torn between dread and desire — a man experiences cold feet."

Rhodes and Potash have identified the following types of men when it comes to fear of commitment:

- Good Enough Guys. (I prefer to call them great guys.) These men are basically sympathetic to women and do not feel threatened or engulfed by them. While these men may feel uncomfortable about opening up and showing their feelings, they can do it.

Still, they fear losing freedom and, having opened up, they'll likely get scared and say they need more space. Gradually they learn they can have space and be intimate, too.

While at first the idea of monogamy may send some men into a cold sweat, eventually a series of conquests and ended relationships loses its allure. Such men may find monogamy provides a deeper and more satisfying relationship.

Love this man. Back off a bit if something you say or do sends him into convulsions. Accept him as he is with all his fears. Gradually, he will find them unfounded.

- The Good Guy Today/Gone Guy Tomorrow is a risk. He not only fears loss of freedom but also loss of identity.

When he gets close to a woman, he feels as if he's losing pieces of himself. When he has to give up some of his activities in exchange for the relationship, he feels robbed.

He constantly needs to lock a woman out to reassert his identity as a man and as a person. He can get close but can't sustain the closeness.

In the past, social conventions concealed the conflicts many men had. Society frowned on relationships that didn't end in marriage. And being a husband then didn't require emotional closeness. A man simply had to go through the motions — provide the money, protect the family, and turn up for Sunday dinner.

Today, this kind of guy doesn't have to get married and for him dating or a series of live-in relationships is all he ever wants. As soon as a woman starts discussing commitment, he packs his bags, or hers.

It's hard to tell whether he can ever become a Good Enough Guy. Perhaps he is a guy who's simply not ready. Give him a little time — but not a lot. Don't assume living together is a step towards marriage.

- The Good for Nothing Guy is full of fear. He literally feels he's being swallowed up or eaten alive by a woman when he gets close. How do you spot him? He's immediately charming and attentive and easily able to charm the pants off a woman.

He's tender, understanding, and in hot pursuit — at first. But after sex, you may not hear from him for days, if ever. During sex, personal boundaries dissolve. While most men can handle this because they know it's temporary, the Good for Nothing Guys are terrified.

This man is truly sad. His problems stem from early childhood. But don't try to be his therapist. Drop him before you get hurt.

Remember, while many decades ago sexual intimacy usually indicated a relationship was serious, today it does not. And although some women still equate sex with love, men rarely do. And don't be naive and think that a man who says he loves you in the heat of passion is going to necessarily be around tomorrow or ever again. "I love you" in the sack means "I'm enjoying this" — nothing more for many people.

So to assess the seriousness of your relationship, Rhodes and Potash have what they call The Five Levels of Commitment. The levels recognize that men and women are emotionally very different. Women tend to progress faster and more evenly through these levels to commitment.

Men, on the other hand, may backtrack to a previous level when they fear loss of freedom. They tend to set up defenses when they think they're getting in too deep.

All sorts of theories and entire books have been written about why men do this. The most widely accepted explanation goes something like this:

Images of closeness and intimacy are based in infancy when babies are held, cuddled, and are one with their mothers. Because fathers are not as involved as psychologists would like, intimacy and closeness are associated with women, not with parents. For a boy to become a separate individual, at some point he must pull himself away from closeness and from his mother's femaleness. He must reject her and the intimacy that goes with her.

It's not so difficult for girls because they can develop as individuals without rejecting the closeness as much.

If this separation process was difficult in childhood, as an adult the man must do one of two things to maintain his manhood and his individuality: He must control and dominate the woman in his life, so she doesn't control him, or he must flee from intimacy.

On the other hand, if the process in infancy was fairly easy, as an adult the man does not need to control his partner nor flee intimacy. He feels strong enough within himself and has a clear sense of his own identity and masculinity. He will move through the levels to commitment more steadily, evenly, and reliably.

So here then is the Rhodes and Potash guide to help women determine how serious the relationship is:

- Casual Dating: If after one to four months there is still no regular pattern to the times you see each other, scale down your expectations. Don't sleep together if you think you'll become emotionally involved.

- Steady Dating: You are more comfortable with each other. You are seeing each other with more regularity. You know you like each other, but there's still no commitment. You both may be dating others. Avoid the urge to tell him you think you're falling in love. That'll scare him. Don't close your mind to dating others. Don't suggest taking a vacation together.

- Monogamy: You are building a real relationship and you both have made a decision to sleep only with each other. This is the first level that signals the beginning of a commitment. Notice how often he includes you in activities with family and friends. But don't panic if he doesn't call once or twice when he's supposed to or occasionally shows up late.

- Monogamy Plus: You've been going together for six months to two years. You are including each other in your lives on a regular basis. You are a twosome. You vacation together. People ask you when you're getting married. This can be a turning point for men with cold feet. If he begins to distance himself, suddenly needs space for long periods, or if you notice a great change in the way he treats you, take it as a warning. He's having some trouble with commitment and may want to step back to a lower level. Recognize he needs space and you probably do too. Do less talking and more playing. If he gets stuck at this stage, you may have to give him up.

- Living Together: This can involve an enormous range of commitment from none at all (just convenience) to a fully committed relationship (if you both don't believe in marriage). Living together is not necessarily a prelude to marriage. Don't move in together as an experiment. If you want marriage, have a clear, agreed-upon time frame.

- I would add a sixth level of commitment: Marriage, for those who believe legal (and sometimes religious) action formalizes their commitment. You both have decided you want to go through life together come what may, through hell or high water. You each have decided you will do everything you can to overcome difficulties. You have assessed your own and your partner's ability to work things out and you believe you're ready to exchange lifetime vows.

The "L" word

I'm often asked by women in the getting-to-know-you stage, why some men avoid the "L" word — love. If he loves me, why doesn't he say it?

For secure and confident women, unspoken feelings are often enough. Loving actions are there and that's all they need. But I'd guess many women, and maybe to a lesser extent many men, occasionally want to hear the words — *I love you.*

Some women, so needy, must hear the words constantly, and if they don't, they end up asking desperately, "Do you love me?" The man may cringe, knowing no matter how often he says it, it's never enough.

No one ought to have to ask it. Those who love should say it — volunteer willingly, joyously in fact. Those who are loved should trust it's there.

Yet some men, for reasons of their inner self, cannot volunteer these words. Robert Masello explains some of the reasons in his book, *Of Course I Love You.*

(a) Unmanliness. Any betrayal of deep or profound emotion is extremely suspect because of the way many men in our culture are brought up. The strong, silent type is silent about everything.

(b) Control. "I love you" to some men is not an in-charge remark.

(c) Some men are unable to allow themselves to feel vulnerable, even in intimate relationships where they're safe.

(d) Public humiliation and scorn. Says Masello: "Every man has memories of crossing a gym floor to ask a girl to dance and she said no. 'Do you want to dance?' becomes the terrifying subtext of 'I love you.'"

(e) Fear of commitment. The "L" word is about as close to the dreaded "C" and "M" word as this man ever wants to get.

(f) Obviousness. This is the most popular explanation for silence. "He will tell you actions speak louder than words," says Masello. And that's so true. Still, for women, words mean a lot. And Masello says many relationships would be better if men were more able to express themselves. For women, not hearing "I love you" may also mean,

(g) I don't.

And for some men, the answer depends on what is meant by love. Does it mean, I need you, or I want you, or your happiness is important, or your happiness is more important than mine, or I will stay with you forever, or I will stay with you as long as I can?

It's not always men who have trouble with commitment. Here's a letter from a woman.

Dear Kathy:

When I like a guy, I basically only see his good qualities and his bad ones aren't as noticeable. But as soon as I find out he's interested in me, or that I might even have a chance with him, I start to pick him apart.

I'm very critical and unsure of how I feel about him. It usually then ends up with me not liking him any more romantically.

I can't help this, even though I know it's wrong to focus on people's weaknesses. Why is this and how can I change my attitude toward my boyfriends?

Fickle

Dear Fickle:

This tendency is common. We may want attachment to another person, but we're afraid of it too. We have difficulty trusting and making ourselves vulnerable in an intimate relationship. We can tolerate a lot more in friends than in intimate relationships. So, unconsciously, we may sabotage the intimate relationship.

Develop a friendship first before you become intimately involved. This will allow you to see the whole person first.

The fact is, everybody has good and bad qualities. And most qualities can be seen in either a positive light or a negative one. For example, you can see someone as strong or rigid. You can see someone as vulnerable or wimpy.

Seeing only the good qualities in someone usually happens in the early stages of a relationship. So pace yourself. As well, take a realistic look at what you are looking for in another person. People often try to find in a mate what's missing in themselves. Instead, develop those qualities in yourself.

Marriage contracts and cohabitation agreements

Finally, it's a good idea to know something about marriage and cohabitation agreements.

If you're young and have little money or assets, a marriage or cohabitation contract probably isn't necessary. But if you're older and have a fair bit of money and some assets, a marriage contract makes sense, especially for people who've been married before and fear being "sub-divided" again. Such a contract may also ensure your existing children's inheritance if that's what you wish in the event of your death or of marriage breakdown.

As well, a woman with a well-paid job may marry a man but have to give up her job in the process, perhaps because they will live in another province or state. She should have financial protection provided in a marriage contract, stating just what her job sacrifice would be worth in the event of divorce. Giving up a good job for marriage is probably foolish anyway. How able would a woman, or a man, in the 40-plus age bracket be to snag another equally lucrative position?

Marriage and cohab agreements are becoming increasingly common among ordinary folk, not just among the Sylvester Stallones, the Joan Collinses, and the Donald Trumps of the world. People often ask if they're worth the paper they're written on. Yes, they are. These contracts are usually only overturned when they're clearly unfair. To be as sure as possible your contract will stand up in court, you each should have independent legal advice, even if you want to draft the document yourselves. And it's important you each see different lawyers.

Make sure the contract is in place well before you finalize everything else. Drawing up the contract a mere week or so before the wedding may spell trouble later. It might be impossible under those terms to negotiate an agreement that would be considered legally binding.

The contract should also be fair. If a couple splits up after a 25-year marriage and four children, a judge may choose to ignore a marriage contract that cuts her out of his business assets. She may be able to persuade the court that she sat alone nights because of his work, that she entertained his business associates, that she supported him emotionally, and that it's not fair she gets nothing.

As well, there should be full disclosure of assets. If one of you tries to hide the true extent of wealth, the contract may later be successfully challenged on this basis.

There are certain things not to include in marriage contracts. For example, children. The courts will ignore any provisions you make regarding children as you cannot bind their rights. And there's no point in trying to spell out household duties! Who does the dishes and who dusts is legally unenforceable. There's no point either in stipulating a "fat clause" where each partner must stay healthy and in good shape. Even an agreement that the couple will see a marriage counselor if either partner wants it, is unenforceable!

You can decide, however, how property is to be disposed of should you break up and whether you could claim maintenance.

When one partner expects to inherit from his side of the family, the contract may include a provision that a gift or inheritance will not be considered joint property.

Here are a couple of other pieces of important legal information:

- In most jurisdictions, if you have a will, it is automatically void when you marry, unless it states you are contemplating marriage to a particular person.

- If you don't make a will after you marry, in most states and provinces your spouse will automatically receive a certain portion of your estate after you die. The balance will then be divided between your spouse and children.

For more information on the rights of married or common law couples in different regions, you may want to refer to popular books written for the lay audience, including *Marriage, Separation, Divorce, and Your Rights,* also published by Self-Counsel Press (not available for all jurisdictions).

22

M aking love stay

Okay. You've finally found the man or woman of your dreams and you've been seeing each other for more than a year. You're in love and planning to marry. But in quiet moments you wonder, will this relationship last? Will we be part of the 60% in Canada or the 50% in the United States who stay married, or will the marriage end in divorce?

The prospect of divorce is so ugly you likely shudder and think quickly about something else. After all, true love conquers all, right?

Wrong. As a daily newspaper love columnist I get dozens of letters each week from people who were deeply in love when they married but now have relationship problems they don't know how to solve.

You have to know a few things to keep love alive through marriage. One of the first is to get rid of some of your unrealistic expectations. Marriage is not always going to be lovey-dovey. There will be times when it will be boring, routine, filled with problems, lonely, and unfulfilling.

You may have heard the saying, "women marry, hoping he'll change; men marry, hoping she'll never change." There's a lot of truth in that. Trying to change him is one of the biggest mistakes women make. If you believe you can change a man with your love, you may go for someone who is far from a suitable partner, then hang in there still hoping he'll change, even if it's an abusive relationship.

Realize, instead, that what you see now, is what you get. You can't change him. If you try, you will be frustrated and angry. And he will resent your criticism and lack of acceptance. An ongoing effort to change him will destroy the relationship. Criticism, no matter how valid, gradually builds a wall between people. When change does happen, it's because the individual wanted to change himself or herself, not for someone else. Positive regard is the way to go.

On the other hand, men who expect women to stay the same as the day they married are also enormously unrealistic. Women are great changers. That's what makes them so interesting. If a man rolls with the punches and sees his wife through her many stages, he may actually find the marriage more interesting, less boring.

Marriage partners also need to realize that, while love is a special, intense connection, it is not the answer to all or even most of life's problems. Don't try to make your mate responsible for your happiness or expect him or her to rescue you from your problems or your fears. Two halves do not make a whole. If you're looking to him or her to supply what's missing in you, you may be disappointed. Far better to find it for yourself and be the whole person you want to be.

People often have the fantasy that once they get married, they will no longer be lonely. Then, when they find themselves still missing something, they think the marriage must be bad, that it must not be working. People need to be able to be happy on their own and develop their own resources. Too often, a husband or wife blames the marriage partner when things aren't working the way they want.

For example, it's quite common to expect your partner to make your life interesting and exciting by taking you out and doing things. Certainly, sharing interests and activities is an important way to keep the marriage alive and fun. But sometimes we have to solve our needs for excitement ourselves — by changing careers, by getting our own interests, sports, or hobbies, by becoming more independent, by taking responsibility for our own happiness, and by looking to our friends, not just our husbands or wives, for some of the things we need. I doubt many husbands, for example, can come close to providing the type of communication women have with close female friends. And why should women expect that?

Also, I often wonder why women drag their husbands shopping for clothes, when the husbands are clearly frustrated and irritated by this activity. How many husbands really expect their wives to get off on carburetors, chain saws, or football power plays? Don't expect constant togetherness from marriage. Give yourself freedom to be apart and enjoy different things.

I think men and women also need to learn how to be assertive in a relationship. That doesn't mean aggressive. A big mistake many still make is being passive, stuffing down their feelings, manipulating others, nagging, ignoring one's own needs, and taking on the job of making everyone else happy. Then they explode or become chronically depressed. Either way, they're impossible to live with.

Being assertive involves knowing what we value and who we are. It means being clear about what we want and need. Then it means being able to express it calmly, matter-of-factly, as we go along. Don't expect your husband or wife to be a mind reader. Of course, asserting your needs doesn't mean you'll always get what you want. But there is something empowering in stating one's case.

Now I think there are some underlying tensions between men and women in relationships that can undermine the relationship if they're not understood.

Dr. Herb Goldberg, a professor of psychology at the University of California at Los Angeles and author of a number of books on relationships, focuses on these. He says the very differences that initially attract men and women to each other can spell trouble later on. Being able to embrace these differences, rather than criticize them, is the path to marital happiness.

According to Goldberg, in his book *The Inner Male,* men and women are emotionally different and so all the communicating in the world sometimes doesn't work.

As the couple grows familiar, says Goldberg, she may eventually overreact to the real him, which is more autonomous and emotionally independent than she is. And he may eventually overreact to what he sees as her dependency and emotionalism. She wants to talk about emotional things. He doesn't.

That's because men generally feel more secure and competent in the external world, and very incompetent and vulnerable in the inner, emotional world, says Goldberg. He gets overloaded when he enters her world, tries to listen, communicate, and be emotionally involved. He finds her endlessly demanding.

She, with a greater capacity for connection, gets frustrated with his short attention span and feels rejected. Sometimes she feels too vulnerable after sex, even though she enjoyed it. He can't understand that because it doesn't make him feel vulnerable. Commitment and closeness make him feel vulnerable. She can't understand that because, to her, commitment is comforting and necessary.

Goldberg writes that men and women have different definitions of a good relationship. To the man, it means freedom to be left alone while they're together, without feeling guilty. To the woman, "it means achieving a fantasy of deep, intertwined closeness, a melting together that he couldn't possibly be capable of." The result, says Goldberg, is she's in great pain over being distanced by him and he's tense and raw over feeling pursued and pressured for closeness he can't give. "In his psyche, she is everywhere (even when she isn't there) and threatening to engulf him. In hers, he is never really there."

In arguments, he's trying to be rational but she feels he's cold and rejecting. When she's expressing feelings, he sees her as irrational and manipulating.

Goldberg's way around this "agony" is not in trying to get our mates to be more like us emotionally. That never works. Rather, we need to change ourselves. We need to see our partner's emotional responses as a result of being male or being female, and not something they are doing to us.

Goldberg says for women, this means:

- Stop expecting him to give you all that yummy closeness and connecting all the time.

- Stop your compulsive focusing on emotions.

- Stop saying, "You're always pushing me away."

- If you choose a man who is ambitious, productive, aggressive, decisive, logical, and autonomous, understand that all of this comes with a price. The more he's like that, the less he's able to relate personally, intimately, and sensitively.

- Stop resenting his autonomy. Get some autonomy yourself. Find your own abilities to succeed in the external world.

- Recognize his distancing comes from a fear of being taken over.

- Stop looking to him to "make things happen."

- Develop your capacity for sustained, goal-focused, and impersonal productivity.

- Stop demanding to be treated "sensitively" all the time.

- Stop longing for fulfillment of your romantic fantasies.

- Stop expecting everything to be "nice" and without problems.

- Develop a clear sense of yourself.

- Enjoy sex as sex without it always having to be an expression of love.

- Stop doing things for him that he doesn't really want. For example, he may simply want to be left alone when he's troubled rather than being pestered by your need to nurture.

As for men, says Goldberg:

- Loosen up.

- Balance your aggressive, competitive nature with playfulness.

- Develop a capacity to freely attach and need.

- Learn to tolerate challenges and threats without feeling compelled to respond.

- Stop trying to control everything. Recognize there doesn't have to be a controller. (Or, as I tell my sweetie sometimes, retire as general manager of the universe.)

- Become motivated less by ego and self-protection.

- Stop working so hard and so long "for her" when she would rather you be with her more. At the very least, be honest that you're really doing it for yourself.

- Stop fearing you will be engulfed, taken over, and controlled if you get close to her. The fact is, this fear is exaggerated. It isn't a fear of something that will actually happen. It comes from your childhood.

- Recognize your distancing as a defensive reaction to her yearning for closeness.

- Balance your intellectual side by developing your feeling and intuitive side.

- Stop using logic as a weapon to disconnect from the personal and emotional.

Essentially, Goldberg is saying whether you're a man or a woman, you need to move towards a middle zone.

Finally, to the most important aspect of making love stay: develop a style for handling fights or differences that won't destroy the marriage. We have to be able to share negative as well as positive feelings in a way that doesn't eat away the love and respect. It's easy to love and feel close when things are going well. But mutual respect and goodwill will be tested in times when you really don't see eye to eye and the issue is important to each of you.

You need to realize that conflict is inevitable in a long-term relationship and you needn't fear it and figure all is lost because you disagree. Conflict is actually healthy. Now that doesn't mean you look for it and make it happen. Happily married couples don't make an issue over everything. Unless they're like the Bickersons described below, they don't sweat the small stuff. They ask themselves, "Is this something I can live with? Are there enough other good things in my marriage to balance this off?"

But important differences usually do need to be addressed. That's unless both partners know the problem is unsolvable and basically agree to disagree and avoid the issue.

Arguments themselves don't kill marriages, but fighting patterns do. I've seen people divorce who actually still love each other, but they just can't get along.

Long before their love is eroded, they do something they just can't seem to help doing. It doesn't matter how stupid or intelligent they are, or even how few or many things are wrong with their relationship. What they do is let their different fighting styles get out of hand. Most of us learn how to fight from the families we're brought up in. Some of us learn to be blamers. Others learn to be avoiders. Some are bullies. Some fly off the handle. Some are chronic accommodators. The list goes on.

Dr. John Gottman, a professor of psychology at the University of Washington at Seattle and author of *Why Marriages Succeed or Fail,* is one of North America's top marital researchers. He says he can predict with 94% accuracy which couples will stay married and which ones will divorce, simply by watching them interact. Couples headed for divorce often have a mismatch of relating styles: "A hothead may be married to a cold, distant, unemotional withdrawer, for example," says Gottman.

He says four things propel couples to divorce: criticism, defensiveness, contempt, and stonewalling. In stonewalling, one partner withdraws from the issue either by leaving the room or putting on a poker face or a stony silence of disapproval, icy distance, and smugness.

In long-lasting marriages, on the other hand, there's little criticism or contempt. The positive communication outweighs the negative by five to one. There is five times the amount of agreement as disagreement. And there's more laughter and affection.

I think these couples sometimes make a choice to see the partner positively instead of negatively. For example, you can see your husband as either strong or rigid, for exactly the same behavior. It's how you look at the behavior.

Dr. Gottman says it's not just the couples who resolve conflict by the book (using good communication and listening skills as well as validating one another's point of view) who have happy marriages. He found that conflict avoidance — which conventional psychological wisdom says is divorce in the making — is a "completely good style of having a marriage."

"These couples take the view that it can be very healthy not to solve the problem," Gottman told me. "They have a common base of values for minimizing the conflict. There's no change of the problem. But what matters is that they have a lot of things they love about each other, despite the problem or problems, a lot of things in common."

Another surprise from his research is that the Bickersons-style marriage is okay too. "These people will argue about the tiniest things, like how to load the glasses in the dishwasher. They're terrible listeners. It's constant combat and they love it. There's also a lot of affection, confrontation, teasing, and humor. They're kind of like lawyers. They enjoy the process of evidence and dispute. These are the only couples who stay romantic — still courting after 30 years of marriage. It's a union of strong individuals who stay fairly separate. They may even have separate offices or areas in the house."

Gottman's advice for making love stay: Calm down — take a 20-minute break from a fight. Use non-defensive listening and speaking. And use validation — show genuine empathy for the other person's feelings. And practice the first three over and over again until you get it right.

Gottman also gives this piece of advice to men: If you're not getting enough sex, trying doing more housework! He says these two conflicts — how frequently the couple has sex and who does more housework — are the two biggest marital hot spots. And he says, men who do more housework and child care have better sex lives and happier marriages than others.

He says people need to realize that boys and girls are socialized in such different way throughout childhood. Each gender receives an almost opposite message about lovemaking. "Boys learn to see sex either as pure pleasure disconnected from emotional commitment, or as a vehicle for getting close to a girl. Closeness is the goal, not the cause.

"In contrast, most women need to feel physical and emotional closeness and tenderness before wanting to have sex. Making love confirms intimacy rather than creates it for most women. I can't count how often I've heard women complain, 'He never touches me or says sweet things unless he wants sex, and I need affection on a daily basis in order to feel sexy.'"

Gottman says men must learn to empathize with their wives' prerequisites for sexual intimacy. Generally these are to be physically affectionate, considerate, attentive, and respectful toward her at other times, not just when he wants sex.

As for conflicts over housework, Gottman says this is a major issue for women and it affects their sex life. "Almost every man overestimates the amount of housework and child care he does. Treating your wife as a servant will almost inevitably affect the more intimate, fragile parts of a relationship. Being the sole person in a marriage to clean the toilet is definitely not an aphrodisiac. The message you send your wife when you do so little around the house is a lack of respect for her."

My feeling is that if fighting styles or the way people handle disagreements is so crucial to the survival of the relationship, it's a very good idea to take a conflict resolution course before you start living together.

And back to what Dr. Gottman says about the happy couples — their positive communication outnumbers negative communication by five to one. Elizabeth Douvan, a professor of psychology and a research scientist at the Institute for Social Research (University of Michigan in Ann Arbor) says that the communication of loving attitudes is by far the strongest predictor of marital quality. Happily married couples seem to have the ability to see each other realistically, yet positively. A wife may know, for example, that her husband needs to go on a diet, but she doesn't nag him about it.

Unconditional approval from one's mate through non-verbal exchange is so powerful in marriages, says Douvan, it brings about a remarkable transformation. Each person winds up moving toward the spouse's innermost ideal of a partner. "If he is accepted for the way he is, he winds up doing things her way," says Douvan. "And she moves toward his way."

Along the lines of developing more positives in your relationship than negatives, here are some little things to do on a daily basis to keep those loving feelings alive:

- Touch your partner affectionately. Give him a hug. Give her a kiss, a touch. You'd be surprised how effective this physical contact is in keeping you emotionally connected and even, in some cases, dissolving little resentments. Smile when he or she comes into the room.

- Acknowledge the nice things she or he does by saying thanks. Do nice things for him or her.

- Give a compliment. If, for example, his choice of a movie was a good one, say so.

- Be his or her best friend.

- Be there for the tough times.

- Address issues assertively. Avoid nagging, put-downs, criticism, and sarcasm.

- Never withhold sex to punish. Instead, resolve the problem directly.

- Spend some time together on a regular basis without kids and relatives.

- Plan some romantic times — going out for dinner, taking a walk on the beach, enjoying a nice fire, listening to music, bathing together, planning a small trip. Don't let the business of life take over.

- Make sexual intimacy an important part of your relationship. Realize that men and women are different when it comes to sex. Most women need to feel loved and safe to have sex. Most men need to have sex to feel loved.

So there, you have reached the objective. Finding love and making love stay.

I sincerely hope this book has been helpful to you in all of the areas discussed. I would be delighted if, in any way, it assists you in finding the companionship of a suitable partner and the happiness to be found in sharing life.

I wish you a healthy relationship, filled with what my column has been about for these past eight years... love.

$\mathcal{A}$ppendix

Connections throughout North America

This is a guide for those of you who may wish to contact any of the organizations that cater to singles. The list is by no means complete. It doesn't even scratch the surface of what's out there for singles, but the list may pique your imagination.

I've included a lot of organizations in my area, British Columbia, and you may want to look for similar groups where you live.

If what you're looking for is not listed here, use your Yellow Pages under the listings "Clubs, Associations, or Dating Services" to find similar organizations. But be wary. In the occasional Yellow Pages listings, such as those for Anchorage, Alaska, dating services seem confused with escort agencies and are lumped together!

Also look under "Coming Events" in the classified ads section of your local newspaper.

Before you try a singles club or business, phone the organization first and ask questions — what age group attends, how much does it cost, what kinds of activities are offered, what is the ratio of men and women, etc.

When you attend an event, find out what else is available by talking to people. Do research and write down your findings. Keep a list of phone numbers. Share information with other singles. The more singles who know about these clubs and events, the more will turn out and you'll have a wider variety of men and women from which to choose!

It is not possible for me to vouch for the legitimacy of all of the organizations and businesses listed here, or whether they all are in business at publication time. So I ask you to check each one carefully yourself. Also, if you have information about singles organizations in your home town or have feedback on what's listed here, please write me — Kathy Tait, Love Smarts, The Province, 2250 Granville Street, Vancouver, B.C., Canada V6H 3G2. I'd like to update this Appendix at each reprinting.

International organizations

Toastmasters International is a great way to meet people and learn public speaking at the same time. It has 8,000 non-profit clubs in 60 countries. To find out about the club nearest you, check the phone book, or write to Toastmasters International, P.O. Box 9052, Mission Viejo, CA 92690. Toastmasters helps people overcome their fear of speaking in public, build self-esteem, and advance their careers through improved leadership and communication skills. It will help you increase self-confidence and build better relationships.

Parents Without Partners is a non-profit social organization for single parents with or without custody of their children. It puts on events for parents and for their children. For a group in your community write to Parents without Partners: In Canada, at Box 1219, Station B, Oshawa, Ontario, V1J 5Z1 or phone (905) 433-2255. In the United States, the head office is at 401 North Michigan Avenue, Chicago, IL 60611-4267. Phone (312) 644-6610.

The Single Gourmet Club. An international social, dining, and travel club for singles. It has offices in 12 U.S. cities, four Canadian cities, and one in London, England. World headquarters is at 30 Park Road, Toronto, Ontario, Canada M4W 2N4. Call (416) 944-9221. Membership is $200 a year. In the United States, write to The Single Gourmet, 133 East 58th Street, New York, NY, 10022, or call (212) 980-8788.

Science Connection is a singles network based in Ontario to help unattached science professionals, amateur science enthusiasts, and naturalists meet. It recruits members throughout Canada and the United States by placing ads in science publications. Company president Anne Lambert says the network circulates information about members and allows them to contact each other. Cost for membership is $70 a year. Members currently range in age from 21 to 74. Write to Science Connection Inc., P.O. Box 389, Port Dover, Ontario, N0A 1N0 or phone (519) 583-2858.

Mensa. If you're among the 2% of the population with an I.Q. of 132 or above, Mensa is an opportunity to meet someone of similar intellect. Two-thirds of the members are male and 52% of all members are single. Mensa Singles Special Interest Groups publish newsletters. The Mensa Bulletin accepts personal ads. For information on Canadian Mensa call 1-800-2MENSA2 or write to Box 1025, Station O, Toronto, Ontario, M4A 2V4. For American Mensa write to Box V-92, 2626 East 14th Street, Brooklyn, NY, 11235.

The Single Booklovers' Club, Box 117, Gradyville, PA, 19039, U.S.A. Phone (215) 358-5049. This is an international club for book lovers who would like to meet someone of the opposite sex. You will be sent an application form.

Classical Music Lovers Exchange. Box 31, Pelham, NY, 10803-0031, U.S.A. Call (800) 233-2657.

The **National Association of Christian Singles,** 1933 W. Wisconsin Avenue, Milwaukee, WI 53233, U.S.A. or call (414) 344-7300. Christian Dating Service can introduce you to Christian singles throughout North America. Call 1-(800)-829-3283.

Seminars Unlimited presents its singles workshop "How to Create the Relationship You Want" in Alberta, British Columbia, Saskatchewan, Manitoba, Ontario, Washington State, Oregon, California, Colorado, and Texas. These workshops are a good way to meet other singles. Cost is around $50. Call them toll free from the United States or Canada at 1-(800)-461-9581.

The Learning Annex is another seminar company that presents courses in many major U.S. and Canadian cities. Check the white pages or look in the Yellow Pages under Seminars or pick up their course publication at a bookstore or newspaper vending box. Many Learning Annex courses provide good opportunities to meet other singles. For example, one Learning Annex publication I picked up in San Francisco offered courses on How to be a Sex Goddess in 101 Easy Steps, Relationships and the Path to Love, Small Talk: Make the Most of Mingling, It's Never too Late to have a Happy Childhood, Body Talk with Voice Dialogue, Finding Love and Romance, How to Attract Women, Wine Tasting — Meet new friends, Getting to Meet You Party, Learn to Flirt, Ballroom Dancing, and Golf.

Your local **Young Men's Christian Association YMCA** or **Young Women's Christian Association YWCA.**

Wine appreciation clubs. Most cities have wine appreciation clubs, which are nice ways to meet new people. For example, Canada's largest national wine club and cooperative is The Opimian Society. It has 14,000 members across Canada. Write to the national headquarters at Ste. 410, 5165 Sherbrooke Street W., Montreal, H4A 1T6 or call them at (514) 483-5551 for the contact in your province. The society holds a variety of events including wine tastings, winery tours, dinners, cruises, and banquets. Couples and singles are members.

Handicap Introduction Service is a non-profit introduction service for handicapped people in the United States and Canada. It was started in 1982 by psychologist Dr. Don Gibbons. It has 1,200 active members in Canada and the United States and so far has created 200 marriages among members. Write to P.O. Box 1215, Manahawkin, NJ 08050. Membership is $75 (U.S.) for six months or $125 for one year.

Loners on Wheels is an association of singles in the United States and Canada who enjoy camping together, travel, caravaning, and social activities such as pot lucks and dancing. The club has been operating for 23 years and has more than 55 chapters throughout North America. For singles only. Members who marry must leave. Annual membership is $36 for Americans and $45 (U.S.) for Canadians. Includes monthly newsletter. Has two winter-long rallies in the desert southwest. Annual directory of members costs $4.50 ($7.50 for Canadians). For information write to Loners on Wheels, P.O. Box 1355, Poplar Bluff, MO 63902 or fax (314) 686-9342.

Great Expectations claims to be the world's largest video dating service and has offices in many major U.S. cities. Check your Yellow Pages under Dating Services.

Also check the same listing for **Matchmaker International** and **Together** introduction services.

CANADA

British Columbia (Lower Mainland)

The Province Singles Show is a major event for singles in Vancouver, attracting more than 3,000 men and women mainly in their twenties, thirties, forties, and fifties. *The Province* and myself, and producer Marilyn Taylor, put on the show at a major downtown hotel twice a year — usually in September or October and again near Valentine's Day in February. The show is two or three days of talks on relationship issues given by qualified therapists and other experts, topped off each night with dances. For information call 980-4203.

TGIF caters to singles aged 30 to 60. Call Len Macht at 980-2901 to receive the monthly newsletter of events. The club offers dinners, dances, bike trips, camping trips, ski trips, dance lessons, weekend trips, card parties. Members number 250. Fee is $80 a year.

Flying Solo, a part of Toastmasters International, is especially for singles, mostly aged 35 to 45. Learn public speaking and meet new people. Initiation fee is $35, plus annual fee of $80. Call 872-2472.

Simply Lunch! is a new service arranging lunch meetings for singles. The company interviews clients and confidentially selects a compatible lunch date. Very convenient for busy Vancouver business people. Call 681-6122.

Dinner for Six puts together groups of three men and three women for dinner. Membership is $110 for six months and $150 for a year. The organization has members in the 28 to 58 age range and averages 100 people each evening. Membership fee does not include the price of your dinner. Call 687-7334 or 988-1011.

Eight at Eight is a service to create dinner parties for eight people, ages 25 to 45, at a table. You may organize your own eight people or be matched with seven others. One night a month, it is for singles; one night a month for couples, and one night a month for single parents. Membership is $150 per year, not including cost of meals. Call 682-7848.

Parents without Partners. Orientation meetings for new members are held on the second and fourth Thursday of every month at 7 p.m., Coquitlam Recreation Centre. Has 80 members in B.C. Two-thirds are mothers. Call 944-1075.

Single with Kids is a new group for single moms and dads with kids of all ages. It meets once a month so parents can meet other parents and share a pot luck dinner and social activity with their children. To register call the Marpole Oakridge Community Centre at 327-8371.

Singles Sailing Sundays offers Sunday sailing trips for singles. Cost is $30 per person for the day. For information call 876-2749.

Barnet Sailing Co-Operative provides affordable sailing to both novice and experienced sailors. Costs $300 for a single (300 hours of sailing) and $385 for a family (400 hours of sailing), plus a one-time initiation fee of $100. Access to four sailboats. Also offers sailing picnics, weekend cruises in the Gulf Islands, casino nights, speakers, overseas trips. Call 936-1218, 526-0638, or 526-4066.

The **North Shore Group**, for singles 40 and up, offers hiking, cycling, and social activities, including four dances a year. Has 80 members. Membership is $40 a year. Includes monthly newsletter. Phone 925-2644.

The **WISE Club** is a private neighborhood pub-type club for singles and couples, open Tuesday to Saturday evenings. Yearly membership fee is $15. Call 254-5858.

West Coast Activities Club is for singles and couples interested in a range of summer and winter sports, parties, arts, and special events. Call 737-3105.

The **Vancouver Art Gallery's Young Associates Program** sponsors dances, fashion shows, and parties to raise money for the gallery. It's not limited to singles. Up to 400 people in their twenties and thirties attend each event. Annual membership is $49 and each event costs $20. Call 682-4668.

The **Opimian Society** is not a singles club but a national wine cooperative which holds special wine tastings, winery tours, dinners, and banquets. Call 732-1517 or write to 2433 West 1st Avenue, Vancouver, V6K 1G5, or call 658-0186 in Victoria. For information on other wine clubs, contact the Editor of the BCL Guide, c/o Communications, B.C. Liquor Distribution Branch, 2625 Rupert Street, Vancouver, V5M 3T5.

Connecting is a publication for the single traveler, filled with information on tours, cruises, and other travel especially for singles. A year's subscription is $20. Call 737-7791 or write to P.O. Box 29088, Delamont Postal Outlet, 1996 West Broadway, Vancouver, V6J 5C2.

TravelMates is good if you're looking for someone with whom to travel. It has 400 members who attend monthly meetings to discuss travel destinations. Matches can be two females, two males or members of the opposite sex. Married people whose spouses don't like travel are also members. Membership is $45 a year. Call 739-9615.

Hostelling International. B.C. region. Inexpensive lodging and social functions. Call 684-7111.

Pacific Ski Club offers social, dinner, and sports events and trips, not just skiing. It is not a singles club but is a good way for singles to meet. Members are mostly in their thirties. It costs $50 a year, which includes a monthly newsletter and members' rates on trips and events. Call 877-1422 or 985-6952.

The **Vancouver Group**, for singles 45-plus, offers dances, potluck suppers, curling, golf, etc. Cost is $40 a year, including a monthly newsletter. Call 599-4693 or 939-2694.

New Leaf (hotline at 290-9640) is a friendship club for the 50-plus singles. Membership is $35 per year. Quarterly newsletter. Offers parties, dinners, brunches, golf, nature trips, etc.

No Kidding! is a social network for non-parents. Age range is 20 to 70 with most in their thirties and forties. Members host three to six social activities a month. Most are smoke-free. They talk about careers, studies, travels, interests, sex, politics and religion, but not about kids. Membership costs $35 per year for singles and $60 for couples. Call 538-7736.

New Concepts Singles Club puts on dances and cruises for singles, aged 20 to 40. Call 299-7093.

West Coast Activities Club is for singles and couples interested in a wide range of summer and winter sports, fund raising, arts, and special interest groups. Membership is $30 a year for singles and $45 for couples. It offers parties, trips, and special events. There's a monthly newsletter. Average age of members is 30s. For info, call 737-3105.

Willingdon Church in Burnaby has a number of singles groups, for various age groups, open to people throughout the Lower Mainland. It also holds a singles conference once a year. For info call 435-5544.

Discovery is a singles group that meets every first and third Friday evening every month at the Unitarian Church, 49th and Oak. (For information call 261-7204 or 733-9927.) The format is discussion groups and then dancing. The group also has picnics, potluck dinners, hiking, and theater events.

The Living Through Loss Counselling Society of B.C. at 873-5013 has divorce and separation therapy groups for people who aren't quite ready to look for love but would enjoy the friendship of others going through the same experience.

Several singles clubs for Jewish people: **Singles 35 Plus Club** has social, recreational, educational, cultural, and getaway opportunities. Call the Jewish Community Centre at 257-5111. Also call the centre for the **Vancouver Westcoast Social Group** for those aged 20 to 40. The **Teva Club** offers hiking, cycling, and kayaking. Call 275-1012. Also the **Young Associates of Canadian Friends of Hebrew University** has activities for singles. Call 263-0413.

White Rock Singles — a social club for those 35 plus. Offers monthly dances, potluck dinners, restaurant nights, and bowling. Membership is $12 per year. Call 538-1910 or 535-6341.

Delta Sunshine Singles. For single parents with or without custody. Social events, including dances every month, plus activities for children. Membership is $15 a year. Call 572-4650 or 588-0018.

Executive Singles is new to B.C. It is not a club or dating agency and it has no membership fee. It holds a get-together every two weeks in Vancouver for single business and professional people age 25 to 55. It puts out a newsletter every three months, no charge. Events (cocktails and dancing) cost $12 per person. Dress code: suit and tie, cocktail dress. To receive a newsletter, write P.O. Box 37069, Gorden Park, Vancouver, V6P 4W7 or call 435-7389.

Single Again Society is based in Surrey and caters to the 25-plus age group. It has social and sports activities for adults and for children. $10 a year. Call 574-5271.

P.M. Dining, Social and Travel Club puts on Saturday dinners and Sunday brunches. Call cellular 889-9258.

Every summer the **Vancouver Board of Parks and Recreation** puts on free dances in Stanley Park at the Beach Avenue entrance (Ceperley Park). These dances run each Monday through Thursday evenings. The dances start at 7:30 p.m. and go till 9:30. Instruction is given at the beginning.

After Five Singles Club (224-4000), dances for those 20 to 39.

VIP Singles Club (734-1000), dances for singles 40 and up.

Vancouver Dance Connection. Learn the cha cha, street hustle, west coast swing, tango, or triple jive with dance instructor Barry Hall every Tuesday night at the Mardi Gras at the Century Plaza Hotel from 7 p.m. to 9 p.m. Lessons cost $5, and afterwards a party for only $3. For information call 688-2646.

The Association for the Preservation of Swing and Big-Band Music. Memberships available to singles and couples. Dances held in the Regency Ballroom of the Hyatt Regency Hotel. Call 732-1922 for info.

Square dancing (and its New England version, Contra dancing) is popular with single people from 20 to 60. You don't need to go with a partner or know how to do it. For information phone dance caller Marian Rose at 254-5678 or Nelson Bevington at 531-6066.

The Swinging Singles Square Dance Club. Call Joan Carlson at 857-0455 or Mel Austin, 591-2841. All ages from 20s to 70s, most in 30s to 50s.

Introduction services (B.C. Lower Mainland)

Personal Choice International Singles Video Network is new. The introductory offer is membership for one year for $800. Phone 681-1199.

M.S. Oriental Dating Service introduces Oriental women living here or in Asia to local men. Service is free to women. Men pay $349 per year for unlimited introductions. Photo magazine available with 500 women seeking friendship and marriage. For copy send $7 to #900 - 525 Seymour Street, Vancouver, V6B 3H7. Call 687-1759. Holds singles dances every Saturday.

Venus Oriental Introduction Service. 688-7973. Also holds dances.

Candlelight Matchmaking Agency Inc. provides five qualified introductions over one year for $299, 15 over two years for $599 and long-term membership for $1,500. Call 436-1869.

Connections Introductions Service, located in Langley. Call 534-4492. Owner Marni Jefferies says to date she has signed up 265 members and has brought together 35 couples. Cost is $149 for six introductions. Male clients range in age from 20 to 78 and women from 21 to 67.

Christian Connection Friendship and Dating Service. Fees range from $19 for one month to $99 for lifetime membership. Write to Box 8525, Victoria, V8W 3S1 or call 388-0869 in Victoria or 1-(800)-661-2206.

In the B.C. Interior

The Kelowna Gourmet Club for Singles. Dine every second week. Membership is $50 a year. Write to Box 2, Comp 2, 356 Yates Road, Kelowna, V1V 1R5. Call 762-9861.

The West Kootenays Singles Club serves Cranbrook, Nelson, Castlegar, and Trail. It has a variety of social events, potluck dinners, skiing, dancing, hiking, and camping. Average age is 40. Call Diane at 368-8322 or Brian at 352-6649 or Colleen at 365-0063.

On Vancouver Island

Flo and Friends is a Victoria social club for singles and couples age 30 plus. It meets three times a month for dinners, golf, etc. Fee is $49 a year. Call 384-4280.

Dinner for Eight is for Victoria area singles and couples. You are matched at dinner with people of similar interests. $25 per year. Call 386-6368.

Friday dances are held at the **Princess Mary Restaurant** in Victoria every Friday night at 8:00 p.m. $8 admission. Phone 477-0384 or 652-6467.

Art Gallery of Greater Victoria, through its Young Associates Program, organizes monthly get-togethers and an annual bike tour. Although not restricted to singles, most people who attend are single and the average age is 35. Call 384-4101.

Singles Happening Dances. Call 383-1961.

Single Parent Resource Centre provides a variety of support services for single parents, including short-term counselling and groups for single mothers and single fathers. The centre also offers workshops. Call 385-1114.

The **Victoria Family Institute** sponsors an Opportunities evening for singles to meet and expand their network of friends. Usually held every two or threee months. Call 388-5004.

Vancouver Island Personal Best Training. Meet people through these personal development courses. Call 652-2391.

Victoria Chamber of Commerce holds a business mixer once a month which welcomes non-members. Not just for singles but a good way to meet people if you're a good mingler. Call 383-7191.

The **Nanaimo Singles Association** holds dances on the first and third Saturdays of the month. Age range is 20 to 80 with most people in their forties. Admission is $6. Held at the Departure Bay Activity Centre, Wingrove Street. Box 1015, Nanaimo, V9R 5Z2.

On the B.C. Coast

The **Cameo Singles Club** in Gibsons. For singles 19 and up. Has potluck dinners, lunches, dancing, hikes, camping, and crib. $15 per year. Call 886-0954 or 885-5384.

Alberta

In Calgary

The **Calgary Singles Council** is a non-profit volunteer support group for singles formed in 1978. It provides educational and emotional support for those experiencing adjustment following divorce, separation, or widowhood and an opportunity for singles to meet new people. It has workshops, seminars, weekly drop-ins, dances, pub nights, breakfasts, hiking, tennis, bingo, etc. Annual membership is $60. Box 2208, Station M, Calgary, T2P 2M4. Activities line: call (403) 270-0837 or call the office: 270-8838.

Seminars Unlimited. See description above under International Organizations.

Adult Singles Ministry, sponsored by the United Church, has a monthly singles group with potluck suppers and monthly discussion nights. Call 276-2551.

Business After Hours is a monthly reception sponsored by the Chamber of Commerce. Not just for singles but a good way to meet people. Call 263-7435.

Singles Night at the Symphony. After a symphony performance singles only are invited to meet and mingle in the upper level of the Jack Singer Concert Hall lobby. Call 294-7420.

Bow Valley Golf and Curling Club also offers barbecues and dances. Annual membership is $25. Call 298-8310.

Calgary Ski Club also offers hiking, cycling, tennis, golf, bridge, theater, dinners, and dances. Singles and couples. Call 245-9496.

Dance Partners Unlimited. Join other singles for dancing every Sunday and Monday night in a non-smoking, non-drinking environment. Dance lessons available. Call 284-4706.

Going Solo is a singles club offering a wide variety of activities including international travel, monthly dinners, day hikes, camping, trail rides, white water rafting, dances, and theater. Annual fee is $50. Call 256-7871.

Glenbow Museum offers singles nights one Wednesday a month. Most feature a one-hour lecture followed by wine and food. Call 268-4100.

Gourmet Adventures sponsors dinners at various restaurants. Call 262-2965.

InterChurch Christian Singles is for 40-plus singles who meet for potluck dinners, barbecues, and other social events. Call 244-6310 or 228-7726 or 259-4285.

Only You holds social events attracting hundreds of singles. Cost to attend a dinner dance is about $20 for members and $23 for others.

Personal Best Seminars is an opportunity to meet people through personal and professional development courses. Seminar prices start at $39. Call 269-2378.

Rendezvous Club offers trips to Las Vegas, free dance lessons, hiking, golf, camping, and card games. Call 640-1890.

Professional Singles Association offers dining and dancing, dinner theater, Sunday brunches, outdoor recreational activities, and travel. Membership is $200 a year. Call 640-9196.

Singles Dinner Parties holds progressive dinner parties (tables of six, three men and three women, the men move to a new table after each course of the meal). Dinners are followed by dancing. Each meal costs $40. No membership fees. Call 640-1890.

Women on the Move. Homestay travel network for women. Box 82, Site 22, RR 12, Calgary, T3E 6W3.

In Red Deer

One Parent Encouragement Network. Support services and activities for single parents and their children. Call 342-1684.

Personal Dimensions introduction services and social club. Call 346-1525.

Red Dears introduction service and social club. Call 347-0203.

Country Introductions for rural singles. Call 662-4267.

Steppin' to Country is a computer service to help singles find dance partners. Call 342-STEP.

In Edmonton

Singles Resource Centre of Edmonton is a non-profit society offering information about organizations and services of interest to singles. Drop in evenings with cards, board games, and conversation take place every Friday and Saturday from 7:00 p.m. to 10:30 p.m., 10009 101 A Avenue, Edmonton. Call (403) 482-1293.

Seminars Unlimited. See listing under International Organizations. Call 1-(800)-461-9581.

Club Du Soleil sponsors dances, camp-outs, golf, and other events for singles. Call 425-8545.

Country Club is for single fans of country and western music. It offers concerts, dances, potluck dinners, and parties. Call 988-3864.

Edmonton Art Gallery holds singles nights from time to time. Call 422-6223.

Edmonton Bicycle and Touring Club offers ski trips in winter and bike tours in summer, along with year-round sports and social activities. Singles and couples. Call 424-2453.

Fifty Plus Singles Society has regular meetings and social events. Call 457-3152, 424-6836, or 454-4166.

Loners on Wheels. See description above under International Organizations. Write to Pearl Jones, B1107, 15411 - 87 Avenue, Edmonton, T5R 4K3 or phone (403) 483-0728.

One to Another Christian Companion magazine. 200 - 10806 107th Avenue, Edmonton, T5H 0X2.

Introduction by Design. Write to 006A Le Marchand Mansion, 11523 - 100 Avenue, Edmonton, T5K 0J8 or call 403-482-1293. After you complete a questionnaire and pay $50 for a three year registration, the matching process selects individuals who meet your profile.

Gourmet Adventures Ltd., 4 - 9912 109 Street, Edmonton. Call (403) 424-5958. Offers singles a chance to meet and go to the theater, symphony, and out for dinner without the pressure of a date.

One Parent Families Association holds dances and other events. Call 459-4094.

New Beginnings Singles Club offers dances, barbecues, slo-pitch ball, and other social events. Call 461-8528.

Personal Best Seminars. See listing under Calgary. Call 448-2378.

Professional Singles Association offers golf tournaments, volleyball, baseball, skiing, brunches, dinners, theater, white water rafting, car rallies, and more. Call 433-0685 or 432-1540.

Semi-Adventurers is a club for singles who love adventure. Activities include an annual trip to Mexico, skiing, house boating, and a helicopter trip. Call 463-7108.

Strathcona Singles Network Association offers Friday night drop-in, singles dances, golf tournaments, curling, hayrides, barbecues, and dinner parties. Call 464-0452 or 467-2029.

Country Introductions is a dating agency for the rural community. Call 662-4267.

Video Introductions. Call 421-1000.

Saskatchewan

Parents without Partners, 34 - 320 Sangster Boulevard, Regina. Phone 545-8137.

Toastmasters International. 736 Horace Street, Regina. Call 949-4849.

National Computer Date. Personal introductions. 115 3rd Avenue South, Saskatoon. Call 931-6647. In Regina, at 1717 13th Avenue Call 525-2795 or 525-2806.

Manitoba

Adventure for Successful Singles offers discussions, dinners and dances, socials, sports, travel connections, "picking up the pieces" seminars, complimentary newsletter. Box 3065, Winnipeg, R3C 4E5. 775-3484.

Loners on Wheels. See description above under International Organizations. Write to Evelyn Downey, 95 Campbell's Tr. Crt., Brandon. R7A 5Y5 or call (204) 728-2304.

Kane Dating Club has been operating 35 years. 308 - 283 Portage, Winnipeg. 942-2997.

Personal Encounters video introduction service. 209 - 309 Hargrave Street, Winnipeg. Call 943-4389. Serves singles in Saskatchewan, Manitoba, and Ontario.

One-to-One Dating Club. B-1125 Rosser Avenue, Brandon. 725-1087.

Hart Introduction. 231-1614.

Singles Club, 392 Wardlaw, Winnipeg. 453-8775.

Singles Today, 3 - 222 Osborne, Winnipeg. 452-8092. Introduction and matchmaking service. Offices across Canada.

Singles Travel Club, 2nd Floor, 5 Donald, Winnipeg. 477-0277.

Winnipeg Travel Club. Social club meets to discuss travel. 23 Kennington Bay, Winnipeg, R2N 2L5. Call 256-6767.

Ontario

As mentioned in chapter 12, Peter Crocker, a doctoral student in clinical psychology, has prepared *A Consumer's Guide to Dating and Introduction Services in Ontario*. This is available by writing to his company, Consumer Satisfaction Research Associates at 2424 Danforth Avenue, Suite 201, Toronto, Ontario, M4C 1K9. He is also researching consumer satisfaction with agencies in other provinces and in the United States. Phone (416) 690-3100 or fax him at (416) 690-6402.

The Single Gourmet. See description above under International organizations. In Toronto, 30 Park Road, Toronto, M4W 2N4. Call (416) 944-9221. In Ottawa, call (613) 737-7528. In London, (519) 657-4086.

In Toronto

The Graduate Club of Toronto. A private, non-profit social club for university graduates. Founded in 1964. Has dances every two weeks in local country clubs, bridge every Saturday night, a dinner theater, and other activities. For information call (416) 626-5520 or write to president Alex Macnaughton, 246 Cortleigh Boulevard, Toronto, M5N 1P7. Membership costs $50 per year, which includes a regular newsletter.

The Society of Single Fathers. 70 Clipper Street, Toronto. Call (416) 491-9936.

Simply Sociable. Not a dating club, not specifically a singles club, simply a member-supported club of sociable people. Wine and cheese bridge, gourmet/ethnic dining, antique junkets, jazz/classical evenings, tennis, golf, sailing, skiing, exotic travel. Fee $55/year, regular newsletter. Call (416) 445-3951.

Loners on Wheels. International association for single RVers. Write to Marjorie LeDrew, 76 Damsel Circle, Sutton West, Ontario, L0E 1R0 or call (905) 722-6605.

The Allied Network, an introduction service in Toronto. Call (416) 596-2319.

In Hamilton

The Graduate Club of Hamilton. Similar to the above club. Write to P.O. Box 68011, Blakely Postal Outlet, 773 Main Street E., Hamilton, L8M 1L0. Annual fee is $35 which includes a regular newsletter. Phone (416) 544-0492 or (416) 528-1060.

The Simply Social Club of Hamilton. Provides non-dance social activities. Call (905) 842-2135.

In Ottawa

Single Friends. 1540 - C Beaverpond Drive, Gloucester, Ottawa. Call 741-4476.

Personal Choice Introductions. Introducing people for long-term relationships for 26 years. Write P.O Box 64224, 1620 Scott Street, Ottawa, Ontario, K1Y 4V2 or phone 819-684-3798.

In Mississauga

Selective Singles Travel Registry. Group travel for singles. 2245 Dunwin Drive, Mississauga, L5L 1A3. Call (416) 820-1442.

In Kitchener-Waterloo

Thompson Adult Social Club for single professionals. Members pay a one-time $100 fee. They include teachers, nurses, professors, social workers, police officers, business owners, accountants, electricians, carpenters, and engineers, with about 80% in the 35 to 45 age range. The club has weekly get-togethers, horseback riding, white water rafting, corn roasts, day trips, picnics, fine dining and dancing. Call (519) 741-5890.

Love Lines, a video introduction service in Kitchener. Costs $280 for six months or $400 for a year. Call (519) 570-4650.

In London

Single Professionals Association is for singles 30 and up. Members meet at different restaurants for Sunday brunch, Wednesday night dinner, and other social activities. Call 438-5973.

Single Gourmet is a social network for singles 25 and over offering dinners, dances, and sporting activities. Call 657-4086.

Sapphire Club is for single professional or business persons, 35 or more. It offers a weekly mix and mingle and dinner, plus weekend dinner dances, golf, theater, and concert events. Call 679-9940 (Thursdays only).

Adventure in Friendship Inc. offers dining, dancing, theatre, and golf. Call 434-4061.

Club Oasis holds dances and other recreational activities for those 21 and over. Call 453-4259.

Happy Gang offers dining, crafts, speakers, and demonstrations for widows only. Call 455-6627 or 685-7168.

Jewish Singles Social Club for those singles over 30 offers social activities including dinner, golf, and dancing. Call 673-3310.

Met Set offers cards, movies, bowling, dinners. Call 432-9552.

Notre Rendezvous Singles Social Club Inc. is for singles over 21 and offers Friday night dances, Wednesday evening roller skating, Saturday night supper club, and an annual golf tournament and picnic. Call 434-1588.

PM Club Inc. is a social and friendship club for singles 40 and over. Call 673-6203.

Sunday Night Dances are held at the Dutch Canadian Club. Call 455-7170.

Widowed Persons Club offers social and recreational activities. Call 471-7738 or 438-5780.

Phoenix Club offers dinners, dances, and travel to widows and widowers. Call 657-1383.

Parents Without Partners. See listing under International Organizations. Call 268-8934.

London Beginning Experience offers weekend retreats for separated, divorced, or widowed persons. Call 649-2961.

Time of Transition offers support for the newly divorced or those separated for at least three months. Call 433-0183.

Quebec

Dozens of listings are found in the Yellow Pages under Dating and Introduction Services. These also include numbers for the voice personals.

Loners on Wheels. See description above under International Organizations. Write to Ann Gregory, 100 Churchill Road, Baie D'Urfe, Quebec, H9X 2Y6 or call (514) 457-3137.

The Single Gourmet, Montreal. Call (514) 595-3333.

The 60 Plus Golden Age Association, 5800 Cavendish, Montreal. Phone 489-7651.

The Loners Club, 3694 Wellington, Montreal. Call 761-6442.

New Brunswick

Selective Singles. Saint John. Call 672-6085.

Matchmakers Inc. Moncton. 858-8640.

Singles Choice. Moncton. 372-4068.

Nova Scotia

Executive Singles is not a club or dating agency and it has no membership fee. It holds a get-together every two weeks in Halifax for single business and professional people age 25 to 55. It puts out a newsletter every three months, no charge. Events (cocktails and dancing) cost $12 if you book in advance or $15 at the door. Dress code, suit and tie, strictly enforced, cocktail dress. To receive a newsletter write to 7051 Bayers Road, Box 22101, Halifax, B3L 4T7. Phone (902) 443-4966. Also attracts singles from New Brunswick and Newfoundland.

The Star Club holds dances and other social events in Halifax. Caters to 40-plus singles and puts out a newsletter. Call 902-455-3836.

The Brunch Club holds brunches every Sunday morning, as well as ski bashes, famous movies night, dinners, and softball, in Halifax. Call (902) 457-0962 or (902) 462-0056.

Maritime Introduction Bureau, Halifax. Call 429-2303.

Prince Edward Island

A. and M. Dance Studio. Ballroom and social dancing. Country and western. In Charlottetown call 628-2211. In Summerside, call 436-1718.

U.S.A.

National Association of Single Persons. Write to 1656 - 33rd Street N.W., Washington, D.C., 20007.

America's Society of Separated and Divorced Men. 575 Keep Street, Elgin, IL 60120. Call (313) 695-2200.

Committee for Mother and Child Rights. 8 Seneca Drive, Chappaque, NY 10514. Call (914) 238-8672.

Alabama

The **Connections Flyer** has personal ads and other items of interest to singles. Box 16104, Huntsville, AL 35802. Call (205) 880-5804.

Great Expectations video dating service. One Perimeter Path S., Birmingham. Call (205) 970-0028.

Dating Your Choice. Birmingham. Call (205) 879-DATE.

Southeast Singles Assn. Inc. Call (601) 872-1717.

Alaska

Parents without Partners. Anchorage. Call (907) 345-4502.

Farthest North Bridge Club. Couples and singles. 810 Barnette, Fairbanks. Call (907) 452-3000.

Arizona

In Phoenix

The Spirit of the Senses is a forum of evening salons for creative expression in the arts and sciences. The concept of salons is traced to Louis XIV who liked to have his favorite writers and artists gather in the palace reception halls. The idea spread to the living rooms — salons — of high society ladies. The forum is usually located in a Phoenix private home or mansion, even a car dealership. It includes a talk, refreshments, and an open discussion. Individual membership is $150; married couples pay $250. It has 230 members, the majority in their 40s to 60s. Comprised of 88% single members and more than half are women. Call (602) 955-0117.

All Singles Dance is held on Fridays, sponsored by Single Scene newspaper. Call 946-4086.

Arizona Country Dancers Association hosts monthly dances with free lessons, plus non-dancing activities. Mostly singles. Call the hotline at 846-1425.

Arizona Outdoor and Travel Club offers hiking, backpacking, camping, bicycling, skiing, etc. Mostly singles. Write to Box 24025, Tempe, 85285 or call 224-9094.

Arizona Swing and Latin Dance Club Workshop. Mostly singles. Call 266-3611.

Baby Boomers/Sports Plus is a social group for Jewish singles ages 35 and up. Call 968-1000 or 926-4670.

Bachelors 'n' Bachelorettes is a square dance club. Call 843-4613 or 924-3280.

Catholic Alumni Club is for single Catholics 21 and up. Call 235-2588.

Central Arizona Tall Society offers dances, house parties, volleyball, happy hours, camping, etc. for tall men and women, mostly single. Call 252-0013.

Christian Singles. Non-denominational. Call 249-1936.

Citywide Jewish Singles for ages 25 to 40. Write to the Jewish Community Centre, 1718 W. Maryland Avenue, Phoenix, 85015.

Desert Sailing Club. Boat not required. Call 248-9261 or write to Box 40053, Phoenix, 85067.

East Valley Singles Golfers. Ages 45 to 65. Call 898-8248 or 396-3924.

Euchre Card Club. Call 278- 1734.

500 for Singles (500 is a bidding card game) Call 849-4956.

Ironmen is a men's support group which meets weekly. Call 978-6048.

Jewish Association of Singles Services for ages 21 plus. Call 249-1832.

Lite and Lean is a weight loss support group for singles of all ages which meets weekly. Call 942-3724.

The Lone Rangers is a club for single horse enthusiasts. Has monthly trail rides and camp outs for experienced riders. Call 821-6840.

Merrymakers. For 30 plus. Dance to big band music. Call 972-7900 or 947-4421.

North Phoenix Social Singles offers speakers, house parties, potlucks, cards, picnics etc. Call 992-4220 or 971-2527.

Parents without Partners. Call 938-8105.

Phoenix Ski Club offers singles ski trips, water skiing, camping, hiking, river rafting, house boating, evening socials, and community service projects. Meets first and third Wednesday at Quality Hotel on N. Second Avenue.

Pinochle Group for 40-plus pinochle and cards players. Call 934-5651.

In Scottsdale

Scottsdale Sea and Ski Club. Call 222-5999.

Scottsdale Singles Fellowship. Baptist Church. Call 946-2182.

Herpes Support Group meets weekly. Write to 172, P.O. Box C-900, Scottsdale, 85252.

Single Desert Toastmasters. Call 265-4642, 222-8815, or 997-6569.

Single Golf Association. Call 994-0371.

Single Graduates. Membership restricted to college or university graduates or equivalent qualifications. Offers social and intellectual activities. Dancing, house parties, biking, hiking, golf, and bridge. Call 279-1959.

Single Non-Smokers. House parties, happy hours, picnics, etc. Call 954-6442 or 973-5424.

Single Sailors. For singles 21 and over. Call 254-4971.

Singles Tennis Clinic. Call 945-6321.

Singles Together. Social group with about 200 members from Mesa, Chandler, Tempe, Scottsdale, and surrounding area. Ages 35 to 55. Offers brunches, happy hours, hikes, house parties, game nights, day trips, etc. Call 831-2291.

Society for the Arts. Professional men and women who support the arts. Call 230-8990.

Solitaires Singles offers dancing, travel, and socializing for Sun Cities and West Side. Call 972-0980.

Speakeasy Toastmasters serves North Valley singles. Call 930-7706.

Squaw Peak Hiking Club offers hiking, social activities, trail preservation. Call 438-2021.

Unstrung Racquets offers singles and mixed doubles tennis every Friday and Sunday. Call 945-8464.

Valley Singles Camping Club. All ages. Children welcome. Call 867-9136.

Valley Wide Singles. Call 846-0205.

Widowed Men and Women of America. Call 967-5852.

In Prescott

The Singles Connections Club offers live music and dancing. Call 445-5045.

In Tucson

Parents Without Partners. Call 622-8120.

The Network is a social group for singles over 30. Call 886-8383 on weekdays.

Tucson Happy Hour. Call 721-8544.

Tucson Singles Bridge Party. Call 885-8660.

Tucson Swingin' Singles. Call 795-4674 or 297-9753.

Arkansas

Together dating service. Little Rock. Call (501) 221-0779.

California

In San Francisco

Dinner for Eight. Arranges dinners for four women and four men at a table. Call (415) 387-2964.

How about Lunch? Call (415) 951-1099.

Trellis Singles Parties and Magazine. Call (415) 941-2900.

The Jewish Community Centre of San Francisco has a program called New Partners. Write to them at 3200 California Street, San Francisco. Or phone (415) 346-6040.

The Singles Supper Club puts on cruises, tennis tournaments, barbecues. In San Francisco call (415) 327-4645.

Professionals Guild. Singles social group. Call (510) 937-4744.

In the Los Angeles area

The Single Gourmet. (813) 349-0006, (310) 271-7088 in Los Angeles.

Long Beach Single Sailors Association, 2301 East First, Long Beach, California, 90803, or call (213) 434-3552.

Pasadena Ballroom Dance Association, 997 East Walnut, Pasadena, California, 91109. Phone (818) 799-5689.

Younger Men-Older Women Matrimonial Agency finds younger men for older women and older women for young men who sign up and pay for the service. Cost is from hundreds to thousands of dollars, depending on the effort involved in making the match. Call (800) 848-9669 or (510) 934-7779.

The Working Vacation. Recruits potential gentlemen hosts for cruise lines. 4277 Lake Santa Clara Drive, Santa Clara, 95954-1330. Call (408) 727-9665.

In Orange City

The Single Gourmet. (714) 854-6552.

In San Diego

Athletic Singles is for sports-minded singles. Includes private parties, tennis, sailing, bicycling, volleyball, excursions. Call 530-2114.

Singles Club Association of San Diego, P.O. Box 5682, San Diego, CA 92105 or call (619) 296-6948.

The Single Gourmet. (619) 238-4300.

Backgammon. Call 295-3526.

Ballroom Dancing for Singles is every Wednesday evening. Call 284-9505.

Bogies and Birdies is a new golf and traveling club for singles, 40 plus. Call 483-6565.

Singles Breakfast group every Saturday morning at 9:00 a.m. at Denny's, Clairemont Mesa Boulevard and 163. Ask hostess for group.

Bridge — Smoke free. Sundays at 7:00 p.m. Call 433-7818.

Classical Music Society. Call 276-3965.

Computer Group Meeting. Call 525-3899

Dances for Singles 30-plus. Call 571-5054 or 259-6166.

Divorce Anonymous is a free support group that meets every Friday at the adult center, 7050 Parkway Drive. Sponsored by the Alvarado Parkway Institute. Call 465-4411.

Dolphins offers single adult fellowship for those 40 plus. Dances, parties, dinner club, theater, potlucks, cultural activities. Call 287-1943.

El Camino Singles Club. Ages 40 plus, meets 9:00 a.m. every Saturday for breakfast and a beach walk starting at the Oceanside Pier. Call 940-9648.

Expressions Discussion Group meets the second and fourth Friday of each month at 7:00 p.m., Vineyard, Shopping Center, East Valley Parkway and Rose Street.

Go golfing with the **Mission Bay Singles** every Saturday morning. Call 277-9725.

Hiking or jogging in the mountains or on the Pacific Crest trail. Call 296-8217, ext. 2.

Horseback riding for singles 50 plus. Call 588-8972.

The **Lunch Bunch** is a group of senior singles who get together every Wednesday at noon to eat lunch at different restaurants. Look in the Single Magazine and Entertainment Guide for listings.

Matchless Speakers is a singles Toastmasters group. Learn to do public speaking and make new friends. Call 571-5012.

Oceanside Sailing Club sails every Sunday at the Harbor Lighthouse in Oceanside at 10:00 a.m. Also classes, parties and other social events. Call 1-800-289-3661.

O'Hum Ski Club is for all age singles. Downhill and cross-country. Call 581-1517.

Party bridge. Intermediate. Call 296-9028.

Parents Without Partners. Call 294-4555.

Polaris Sailing Society. Call 491-1400.

P Singles. A social group for single mental health professionals for networking, referrals, and socializing. Call 438-4358.

Russian Singles. Organized singles trips. Call 632-2247.

Scrabble. Single players welcome. Call 441-8826.

Single Skiers. 40 plus. Call 530-2274.

Single Spinners offers square dancing and classes too. All ages. Call 226-4487 or 465-9205.

Singles Adventure Club offers motorcycling, paragliding, whitewater rafting, skiing, and other physically demanding sports. Call 450-1868.

Singles Art Walk meets every Sunday at noon at the San Diego Museum of Contemporary Art. Call 452-2787.

Singles Only Travel Club is for those 20 to 70. Call 434-1171.

Singles Writers Group. Call 489-8421.

Solitaire Sams RV Club is for all who are legally unmarried and own a self-contained recreational vehicle. Call 466-2034 or 273-2462.

Suddenly Alone is a 12-step recovery program for those who are, or have been, separated, divorced, or widowed. Call 484-0381.

Tall Singles. Call 693-TALL.

Tennis Exchange. Tennis socials, clinics, tournaments, parties, and trips. Call 276-2309.

Theater-Goers. Meets regularly for dinner and theater. Call 592-8848.

The Group. Cocktail parties and social events held twice a month in private homes. For business and professional singles over 40. Call 286-7072.

Seebreeze Singles Co-Ed Grass Volleyball. Call 465-6619 between 6:00 p.m. and 8:00 p.m.

Widows or Widowers of San Diego. Call 560-6420.

Young Executive Singles. Business and social networking group for single professionals ages 25 to 49. Call 272-1600.

Colorado

Get-Two-Gether Magazine offers personal ads and singles news. Call (303) 221-4544.

Rocky Mountain Singles Club Inc. Denver. Call (303) 695-9501.

Video Connections Inc. 3570 East 12th Avenue, Denver. Call 303-388-6383.

Connecticut

Great Expectations video dating. 40 York Road, Hartford. Call (203) 938-8989.

Date Book Magazine offers personal ads and singles news. Call (203) 866-6617.

Delaware

Dance Partners Exchange Club. Wilmington. Call (302) 798-5115.

Let's Go Dutch. Greenville. Call (302) 658-3283.

Sunday Brunch for Two. Greenville. Call (302) 477-1548.

District of Columbia

Georgetown Connections Inc. (202) 333-6460.

Compatible Interests Dating Service. (703) 212-8600.

Florida

The Knights of Columbus, a Catholic service organization, sponsors dances for singles in Marian Council in North Dade.

American Singles Association is new and based in Broward County, Florida. Sponsors business-card exchanges for singles and plans to start a business-oriented singles newsletter this summer. Phone number and address not available at publication time. Check advertising locally.

Camping Singles. Write to Peggy Cook, 4858 Lake Charles Drive North, Kenneth City, 33709.

First Tampa Singles Civitan Club, 17539 Willow Pond Drive, Lutz, FL 33549. (813) 949-7354.

Georgia

Heart to Hearts Social Club. 2539 Bankhead Hwy. N.W., Atlanta. Call 799-8996.

Atlanta Singles Club. Singles trips. Matchmaking. 300 W. Wienca Road N.E., Atlanta. Call 255-3283.

Singles Choice Inc. Atlanta. Call 455-1115.

Atlanta Singles Magazine. 1780 Century Circle. N.E. Call 636-2260.

Hawaii
Parents Without Partners Inc., 664 Ulumalu, Honolulu. Call 262-6442.

Compudate. Hawaii's only computerized video dating service. Ste. 611, 1188 Bishop Street, Honolulu. Call (808) 926-3283.

Idaho
Let's Do Coffee. Boise. 331-1926.

Single's Register. 1610 Vista Avenue, Boise. Call 345-3353.

Illinois
The Single Gourmet, 2920 W. Grand Avenue, Chicago. Call (312) 772-3535.

Singles Cuisine Club of America, 500 N. Michigan Avenue, Chicago. Call 440-1888.

Great Expectations Video Dating Service, 350 West Ontario Street, Chicago. Call (312) 943-1760.

Matchmakers Jewish Dating Service. Chicago. Call 674-4022.

Together dating service. Chicago. 413-0400 or 954-3600.

Personal Interactions. In the Joliet region. Call (708) 963-8833.

Indiana
Christian Singles of Indianapolis. 4701 N. Keystone Avenue. Call 257-3339.

Matchmaker International. Indianapolis. Call 844-3283.

Iowa
Single's Again Inc. 1226 72nd Street, Windsor Heights, Des Moines. Call 277-9986.

Dating Service and Roommate Service. Des Moines. 288-4032.

Kansas
Executive Companions. Kansas City. Call 931-8720.

Friendship Exchange Dating Service, 1103 Westport Road, Kansas City. Call 531-5683.

Kentucky
Singles Unlimited of Louisville. Call 239-4022.

Singles Choice. Louisville. Call 896-2105.

Louisana
Lunch Partners Inc., New Orleans. Call 866-1712.

Matchmakers International. New Orleans. Call 455-5600.

Southeast Singles Association Inc. New Orleans. Call (601) 872-1717.

Maine

Maine Dating Club. Bangor. 1-800-564-3283.

Creating Couples. Brunswick. 1-800-870-3318.

Sparks Dating Service. Scarborough. Call 883-1003.

Maryland

Jewish Singles Social Network. 7310 Park Heights Avenue, Baltimore. Call 358-5776.

Matchmakers. Baltimore. 760-1616.

Dateline Voice Personals. 976-DATE. Baltimore.

Massachusetts

LunchDates is a Boston-based dating service in business for 11 years. Call 254-3000.

Together. Call 1-800-348-DATE (3283). In operation 19 years. Has over 100 offices worldwide. Serving Boston, Chestnut Hill, Woburn, N. Andover, Hingham, Framingham, and Cranston, Rhode Island.

Michigan

Great Expectations. 25925 Telegraph, Southfield, Detroit. Call 354-3210.

Interactions Inc. dating service. Call (810) 559-8500.

Matchmaker International in Birmingham.

Minnesota

The Single Gourmet, Minneapolis. Call (612) 731-8722.

Metro Singles Christian Dance Club. Minneapolis. Call 935-3347.

Lunch Dates. 4912 Lincoln Drive, Minneapolis. Call 933-3868.

Mississippi

Mississippi Bridge Association. In Jackson. Call (536) 978-3130.

Southeast Singles Association Inc. Introductions and magazine personal ads. P.O. Box 267, Biloxi, 39533. Call 872-1717.

Missouri

Loners on Wheels. International association for single campers. P.O. Box 1355, Poplar Bluff, 63901. Fax (314) 686-9342.

Heart to Heart Introductions. 16 N. Central Avenue, St. Louis, 63105. Call (314) 863-4000.

Together. Ste. 203, 711 Old Ballas Road, St. Louis, 63141. Call (314) 878-9966.

Montana

Billings Dance Club. Weekly party mixers. 2646 Grand Avenue, Billings. Call 656-6676.

Nebraska

New Beginnings Video. 13937 Gold Circle, Omaha. Call 333-0300.

Together Dating Service. 11930 Arbor Street, Omaha. Call 697-9797.

Nevada

Partners Unlimited. 1705 South Eastern Avenue, Las Vegas. Call 457-7772.

Toastmasters International. 5775 W. Sahara Avenue, Las Vegas. Phone 367-1973.

New Hampshire

Appalachian Mountain Club. Outdoor adventures. P.O. Box 298, Gorham, 03581. Call (603) 466-2721.

Dream 'n' Diners, 44 W. Broadway, Derry. Phone 434-0552.

Together, 721 Chestnut, Manchester. Call 624-4552.

New Jersey

Singles Almanac. 725 Route 440, Jersey City. Call (201) 433-8644.

The Single Gourmet, Monmouth. Call (908) 290-7447.

New Mexico

Let's Dance (Albuquerque) Inc. Call (505) 275-8447.

Albuquerque Singles Network. 10601 Lomas Boulevard N.E. Call (505) 299-6060.

New York

Everything for Singles. 381 Park Avenue South, New York City, NY. Phone 779-2382 or 213-5515.

Singles Guidance and Counselling Service. 205 East 78, New York City, NY. Call (212) 249-9034.

Single Parent Resource Center Inc. 141 West 28, New York City, NY. Call (212) 947-0221.

Mensa Greater New York. 205 West End Avenue, New York City, NY. 595-3726.

Singles for Sailing and Skiing. 15-96208 Pl Bayside. Brooklyn, NY. Call (718) 279-2680.

Together Introduction Service. 879-6974.

The Single Gourmet. 133 East 58th, New York City, N.Y. Call (212) 980-8788 in Manhattan or (516) 674-6186 in Nassau.

Travel Companion Exchange, Inc. Companion registry, hospitality exchange. The company claims to the largest and most successful match up service for travel-minded singles in North America. For all ages. Newsletter. For free brochure write to P.O. Box 833, Amityville, New York, 11701-0833. Call (516) 454-0880.

Tedel Inc. of Yonkers is a firm that conducts communication workshops for singles. Call toll-free 800-735-2832.

North Carolina

Metrolina Singles magazine offers personal ads and singles information. Call (704) 542-4747.

Single Professionals Inc. Charlotte. Call 543-6911.

Single's Forum magazine. Call 542-4747.

North Dakota

Friendship Connection. Fargo. 233-7019.

Ohio

Ohio's Finest Singles News and Views magazine offers personal ads and singles news. Call (216) 521-1111.

Great Expectations, Ste. 151, 8044 Montgomery Road, Cincinnati, 45236. Call (513) 793-7733.

Together, 760 — 655 Eden Park Drive, Cincinnati, 45202. Call (513) 792-2248.

Companions Dating and Referral Service. Cleveland. Call 292-1080.

Cupid's Connection Inc. video dating. 4701 Great Northern, Cleveland. Call 777-7017.

Oklahoma

International Marriage Bureau. 9125 S. Sheridan Road, Tulsa, 74133. Call (918) 492-1812.

Single Station Network, Ste. 100, 2501 E. 51st Street, Tulsa, 74105. Call (918) 745-0003.

Matchmaker International. Oklahoma City. 722-7500.

Singles Christian Outreach U.S.A. 843-4403.

Oregon

Active Single Friends offers hikes, dances, potluck, and other social events in Eastern Oregon. Write to P.O. Box 7763, Bend, OR 97708.

Dinner For Eight in Beaverton. Call 524-5934.

Introductions Northwest dating and activity service. Suite 115, 10250 S.W. Greenburg Road, Portland. Call 452-5887.

Mensa. P.O. Box 4502, Portland. 223-4503.

Pennsylvania

The Philadelphia Canoe Club, 4900 Ridge Avenue Phone 487-9674.

The Big and Beautiful Dating Club for larger and taller men and women. Pittsburgh. Call 247-1977.

Jewish Association Serving Singles. 5738 Forbes Avenue, Pittsburgh. Call 422-5277.

The Professional and Business Singles Network, Philadelphia. Call (610) 353-5544.

Let's Go Dutch, 1710 Locust, Philadelphia. Call (215) 545-3433. They set up a lunch in a restaurant for single professional clients. You have to sign up for ten dates over a year and pay $450 up front.

The Single Gourmet, Philadelphia. Call (215) 238-1448.

Singles Connections Magazine. Pittsburgh. Call 561-2277.

Greater Pittsburgh Matchmaking Associates. 2007 Noble Street, Pittsburgh, 15218. Call (412) 271-2900.

Rhode Island

Two of Hearts. 1445 Wampanoag Trail, East Providence. Call 433-6880.

Introductions. 203 S. Main, Providence. Call 331-9855.

South Carolina

Together dating service, 27 Gamecock Avenue, Charleston. Call (803) 571-2600.

South Dakota

Solo RFD magazine offers personal ads and singles news. Call (605) 335-0900. For a free past issue call 1-800-UALONE2. Also serves North Dakota, Iowa, Nebraska, and Minnesota.

New Beginning Introductions. 5909 W. 12th Street, Sioux Falls. Call 336-1224.

Tennessee

Delta Sailing Association. Memphis. 680-0380.

Singles Register Introduction Service and Social Club. 5830 Mt. Moriah Road, Memphis. Call 365-3988.

Great Expectations video dating service. 5552 Franklin, Nashville. Call 370-0222.

Texas

Singles Social and Travel Club. 11202-A Waxwing, Houston. Call 721-1680.

First Kiss Introductions. Houston. 355-KISS.

Great Expectations. Ste. 100, 50 Briarhollow, W. Houston, 77027. Call 623-6495.

Club Dallas. In Dallas, call 373-1133. In Irving, call 659-1944.

Texas Association of Single Adults, P.O. Box 2090, Harker Heights, TX 76543. (817) 699-7506.

Visiting Friends. See listing below under International Travel.

The Single Gourmet. Houston. Call (713) 558-8627.

Utah

Let's Do Lunch. 262 E. 3900 South, Salt Lake City. Call 266-5600.

Virginia

Armed Forces Cycling Association. International cycling club. #205 — 120 Cameron Street, Alexandria, 22314. Call (703) 836-4904.

National Senior Sport Association. Golf, tennis, bowling trips for seniors. 10560 Main Street, Fairfax, 22030. Call (703) 758-8297.

The Single Gourmet, Norfolk. Call (804) 623-0687.

Together. 10120 W. Broad Street, Richmond. Call 273-9500.

Together, 780 Lynn Haven Parkway, Virginia Beach. Call 468-0832.

Washington

Bremerton Business/Professional Singles for singles 21 and over. Has weekly socials and dances, as well as many sports and recreational activities including biking and skiing. Call (206) 674-2618.

New Beginnings is a social support group and offers pot lucks, workshops, dining out and dances. Call 659-2340 or 743-7982.

Singles Dine Out Club for those over 30 offers restaurant dining in Snohomish county. Call 743-7982.

Longview/Kelso Secular Singles have monthly birthday parties at local restaurants plus hiking, potluck, and other parties. Smoke free. Call 578-1326.

O Solo Mio is a singles travel group. Trips all over the world. All ages. Call 1-800-959-8568.

Single Buddies. P.O. Box 97303, Tacoma, WA 98497 or call 588-7599.

Parents Without Partners, Seattle chapter. P.O. Box 15279, Wedgewood Station, Seattle, 98115-0279 or call 523-7112.

Tacoma Singles Civitan Club. Civitan is an international corps of community service volunteers. Call 565-0204.

Discovery South. Meets every Friday evening. Call 661-1590, 242-8122 or 735-7381.

Singles Dine Out Club. A no-fee club for singles over 35 who enjoy dining out together in Snohomish County restaurants. Call 743-7982.

Scuba Singles is scuba diving for singles, what else! Call 946-5668.

Singletonians is a non-profit club for singles 40 and over in the Seattle area. Activities include brunches, bowling, cards, dining out, dancing, trips, theater, and potluck dinners. Call 483-8287.

United Singles offers dances and other activities. Call 438-3969 in Olympia or 531-7232 in Tacoma.

Secular Singles of Seattle is for non-religious singles. Call 285-7642.

South Sound Singles. Learn to square dance. Call 531-2140 or 536-8104.

Tall Friends is for 40-plus tall people. Write to 1425 South Puget Drive, Suite 211, Renton, WA, 98055.

Divorce Lifeline. For Seattle, Bellevue, Federal Way information call 624-2959. For Everett call 337-6433. In Tacoma, call 383-4005.

Single Style is a interdenominational group providing friendship, social activities, camping, out of town trips, and speakers for singles. Call (509) 248-7789 or (509) 965-5988.

Christian Singles Fellowship is for singles around the greater Seattle-Tacoma area. Call the hotline at 528-2525.

Golden Companions. A companion registry for mature travelers. P.O. Box 754, Pullman, 99163-0754. Call (208) 858-2183.

The Wihski Club in Seattle is a social and sports club for singles and couples. It has 300 members mainly in the 35 to 50 age range. Membership is 50/50 men and women. Meets the first Tuesday of each month at 6:30 p.m. at the Seattle University Plaza Hotel, 400 N.E. 45th, Seattle. For info call (206) 782-4529.

A New Beginning — the Christian Singles Network, the largest Christian Singles Introduction Service in the northwest. Names and phone numbers are exchanged by mutual consent only. Does compatibility testing. 241-0815 in Seattle.

Northwest Singles Club is a Bellingham-based social club. Most members are in their 40s, 50s, and 60s. Activities include dinners out, dances, bridge, potlucks, camping trips, theater. Write to P.O. Box 914, Bellingham, WA 98227, or call (206) 384-6448.

Seattle Singles Yacht Club (233-8511) meets each Monday night at 7:00 p.m. at the Hunan Harbor restaurant on Westlake in Seattle. It has 250 members, mostly in the 25 to 55 age range.

Single Sailors is for singles who own a boat or not. Activities include day sails, weekend sails, monthly potlucks, and weekly social events. Call 523-2717 or 624-2251.

Chancellor Club of Seattle is a social, cultural, and spiritual Christian club for singles, ages 21 to 40. Call 632-4162.

Sound Singles serves singles in Lakewood, Lacey, and Olympia areas. Call 754-0835 or 456-2343.

Mix 'n Mingle is a single group coving the Everett/North Seattle area. Call 347-3749.

Single Travelers. A new group for singles over 40 to share travel experiences and find travel companions. Write to P.O. Box 97303, Tacoma, WA 98497.

Herpes Singles Group offers support, plus parties and other social events. Call 727-2640 MWF from 6:30 p.m. to 9:00 p.m.

Single Jewish Information. Call 232-7115 or write to 3801 E. Mercer Way, Mercer Island, WA 98040 for information about the variety of groups for Jewish singles.

Singles Resource Club. For professional singles over 30. Meets every Friday at 6:00 p.m. at the Goodtimes Restaurant and Lounge in Tacoma. Call the hotline at 591-9273.

Selective Singles introductions. Call 633-2348 in Seattle and 347-5133 in North End.

Single Helpers is for singles who want to do volunteer and community service work. Call 784-8170.

The Mountaineers, 300 3rd W., Seattle. Offers hiking and dances. For membership call 284-6310. To sign up for activities call 284-8484.

Cascade Bicycle Club offers bicycle and social events. 444 N.E. Ravenna, Seattle. Call 522-3222 or 522-2453.

Automobile Dating. 624-5130.

Class Act Dating Services. 227-9385.

The Club. Call toll free 1-800-538-2467.

Events and Adventures. 885-0291.

Great Expectations Services for Singles is a video introductory service. Call 454-1974.

Intro's — Tacoma. 474-4240.

Matchmaker in the Market 621-9101.

Matchmaker International 646-8700.

Pacific Singles matchmakers. Call 972-4857.

Seattle Singles. 285-3354.

Together personal introduction service. 450-0082.

West Virginia

The National Singles Directory. Huntington. 1-800-447-4645.

Wisconsin
Single Attractions Dating Service. 933 N. Mayfair Road, Milwaukee. Call 774-7764.
Singlelife Magazine. 271-9700.

Wyoming
Flirt Alert Dating Club. Cheyenne. Call 637-8917.

Singles publications
In the United States there are more than 100 singles publications, most of them geared to local and regional markets, and most containing personal ads and articles of interest to singles. In the Chicago area, for example, there is *Singles Choice* magazine. For a $12 subscription, contact the magazine at 113 McHenry Road, Buffalo Grove, IL 60089.

For a list including addresses of other singles magazines covering the United States, write to Cote Publications, P.O. Box 1898, Mt. Pleasant, SC 29465-1898. Cost $12 U.S.

In Canada, In Enterprise Publications Ltd. puts out a bi-monthly magazine *Singles Lifestyle Connections* with companion ads and articles aimed at singles. It is distributed in B.C. and Alberta. To subscribe write to their head office at 304-1324 11th Avenue S.W., Calgary, Alberta, T3C 0M6.

International travel contacts
Visiting Friends Inc. An exchange network of visiting friends gives singles the opportunity to add more locations for trips. Membership includes singles and couples. Nationwide in the United States, plus Canada and England. Visits are arranged through headquarters in Texas. Lifetime membership is $25 (U.S.). Write to P.O. Box 231, Lake Jackson, TX 77566, U.S.A.

Gallivanting. Program worldwide caters to singles. 515 East 79 Street, Suite 20F, New York, NY 10021, U.S.A. Call 1-800-933-9699.

Singles Bicycle Tours. 150-2 Saint Paul, Collingwood, Ontario, L9Y 3P2. Call (705) 444-2813.

Backroads in California. Cycling, walking, cross-country ski trips for singles only. 1516 Fifth Street, Berkeley, CA 94710-1740. Call 1-800-462-2848.

Singleworld Cruises and Tours. Cruises and tours year round for singles. 401 Theodore Fremd Avenue, Rye, NY 10580. Call (800) 223-6490.

Windjammer Barefoot Cruises. Selected number of cruises each year just for singles. P.O. Box 120, 1759 Bay Road, Miami Beach, FL 33119-0120, U.S.A. 1-800-327-2601.

Loners on Wheels is a club for singles who enjoy traveling and camping. Many of its 3,000 members (65 in Canada) are seniors and life-long campers who choose to continue their motor home lifestyle after the death of their spouses. Activities include camp outs, cook outs, potluck meals, tours, restaurant dinners, and just hanging out together. For singles only. Couples not welcome. For more information, write P.O. Box 1355, Poplar Bluff, MO 63901.

Friendly Roamers. A club for RVers. Write to 112 Whittier Avenue, Ben Lomond, CA 95005.

RVing Women. A support network for women RVers. $29 U.S. per year, includes bi-monthly newsletter. Write P.O. Box, 8206, Kenmore, WA 98028.

Elderhostel organizes learning vacations for people over 60. Elderhostel Canada, 308 Wellington Street, Kingston, Ontario K7K 7A7. Call (613) 530-2222. Elderhostel USA, 75 Federal Street, Boston, MA 02110. Call (617) 426-8056.

Rainbow Adventures. Adventure world travel vacations for women over 30. Most trips are geared for beginners and are rated from easy to challenging. 1308 Sherman Avenue, Evanston, IL 60201.